LCRAR

East Asia's Monetary Future

NEW HORIZONS IN MONEY AND FINANCE

Series Editor: Mervyn K. Lewis, *University of South Australia*

This important series is designed to make a signifiant contribution to the shaping and development of thinking in finance. The series will provide an invaluable forum for the publication of high quality works of scholarship on a breadth of topics ranging from financial markets and financial systems to monetary policy and banking reform, and will show the diversity of theory, issues and practices.

   The focus of the series is on the development and application of new original ideas in finance. Rigorous and often path-breaking in its approach, it will pay particular attention to the international and comparative dimension of finance and will include innovative theoretical and empirical work from both well-established authors and the new generation of scholars.

   Titles in the series include:

Banking Reforms in South-East Europe
Edited by Zeljko Sevic

Russian Banking
Evolution, Problems and Prospects
Edited by David Lane

Currency Crises
A Theoretical and Empirical Perspective
André Fourçans and Raphaël Franck

East Asia's Monetary Future
Integration in the Global Economy
Suthiphand Chirathivat, Emil-Maria Claassen and Jürgen Schroeder

East Asia's Monetary Future

Integration in the Global Economy

Edited by

Suthiphand Chirathivat

Chulalongkorn University, Thailand

Emil-Maria Claassen

Université de Paris-Dauphine, France

Jürgen Schroeder

Mannheim University, Germany

With the support of the Bank of Thailand, The Asian Development Bank, The Volkswagen-Stiftung and the Kenan Institute Asia

NEW HORIZONS IN MONEY AND FINANCE

Edward Elgar

Cheltenham, UK • Northampton, MA, USA

Published by
Edward Elgar Publishing Limited
Glensanda House
Montpellier Parade
Cheltenham
Glos GL50 1UA
UK

Edward Elgar Publishing, Inc.
136 West Street
Suite 202
Northampton
Massachusetts 01060
USA

A catalogue record for this book
is available from the British Library

Library of Congress Cataloging in Publication Data

International Conference on 'Monetary Outlook on East Asia in an Integrating World
    Economy' (2001: Bangkok, Thailand)
    East Asia's monetary future: integration in the global economy/edited by Suthiphand
Chirathivat, Emil-Maria Claassen, Jürgen Schroeder.
        p. cm. — (New horizons in money and finance)
    Revised papers presented at the International Conference on 'Monetary Outlook on East
Asia in an Integrating World Economy' held in Bangkok, 5–6 September 2001.
    Includes bibliographical references and index.
    1. Monetary policy—East Asia—Congresses. 2. East Asia—Economic
integration—Congresses. I. Suthiphand Chirathivat. II. Claassen, Emil Maria, 1934–
III. Schroeder, Jürgen, 1940– IV. Title. V. Series.
HG1270.5.I58   2001
332.4'95—dc22
                                                                2004043492

ISBN 1 84376 462 8

Printed and bound in Great Britain by MPG Books Ltd, Bodmin, Cornwall

Contents

Figures

Tables

Contributors

June Charoenseang, Chulalongkorn University, Thailand
Suthiphand Chirathivat, Dean, Faculty of Economics, Chulalongkorn University, Thailand
Emil-Maria Claassen, University of Paris-Dauphine, France
Ricardo Hausmann, Kennedy School of Government, Harvard University, USA
Takatoshi Ito, Hitotsubashi University, Japan
Ngiam Kee Jin, Research Fellow at the Institute of Southeast Asian Studies, Singapore
Masahiro Kawai, Ministry of Finance, Japan
Srinivasa Madhur, Asian Development Bank, the Philippines
Pornkamol Manakit, Chulalongkorn University, Thailand
Ronald I. McKinnon, Stanford University, USA
Robert Mundell, Columbia University, USA
Chayodom Sabhasri, Chulalongkorn University, Thailand
Jürgen Schroeder, Mannheim University, Germany
Shinji Takagi, Adviser, Independent Valuation Office, International Monetary Fund, Washington DC, USA
Shu-ki Tsang, Hong Kong Baptist University, Hong Kong
Peter Warr, Australian National University, Australia

Preface

In recent years, we have often asked what lies ahead for East Asia in the new century. East Asia, for its part, had discovered, before the recent crisis, growth and huge potential for development and progress. The region had been quite successful in trade and production within its own economies.

Much had been said about the Asian crisis of 1997–98. We, economists, from various academic origins, have spent much time and energy explaining and analyzing the causes and implications of this crisis. One thing for sure is that we cannot ignore relevant economic principles. In order to fix the problems we face and move ahead with future challenges, we must also attempt innovative thinking, while showing some leeway for what we are willing to improve and to do next. The latest crisis has helped to remind us how relevant economic principles are.

This volume has grown from the revised versions of papers presented at the international conference on 'Monetary Outlook on East Asia in an Integrating World Economy', jointly organized by the Faculty of Economics, Chulalongkorn University; the Faculty of Economics, University of Paris-Dauphine; and the Department of Economics, Mannheim University, on 5–6 September 2001, in Bangkok. It addressed several critical issues and questions we all need to explore, as we did in that gathering. It was also an important exercise for East Asia, in general, and Thailand, in particular.

We deliberately avoided the term 'globalization' since this worldwide used slogan may shift the responsibility of domestic economic policies to external ('globalized') events on which the concerned country has no impact at all. Thus, an economic crisis (decline in output), a financial crisis (breakdown of the banking sector) and a monetary crisis (collapse of a fixed exchange rate) may be ascribed to foreign countries or external ('globalized') events, even though they are caused by the misconduct of internal policies, and in particular, by an inappropriate monetary policy (including an inappropriate exchange rate policy).

The conference participants also had a chance to show their respect to Her Royal Highness Princess Maha Chakri Sirindhorn during the event, which included among others Professors Robert Mundell and Ronald McKinnon, two distinguished contributors in this volume, and many other scholars. The conference could not have been organized without the great efforts and energy of Professors Thienchay Kiranandana and Sriwongse Sumitra, who were assisted by other key Chulalongkorn University colleagues led by Professors Sothitorn Mallikamas, Chuta Manaspaibool, Salinee Worabantoon, Buddhagarn Rutchatorn and Narong Petprasert, all of whom had played his/her special role to make this conference a true venue for academic exchange. We would like to thank conference chairs and discussants as follows: Juanjai Ajanant, Mohamed Ariff, Alian Bienayme, Soedradjad Djiwandono, Michael Hutchison, Sailesh K. Jha, Thienchay Kiranandana, Oh Jong Nam, Hubert Neiss, Yoko Wake, Peter Welfens, Paitoon Wiboonchutikula and Jeromin Zettelmeyer. Rudolf Shelley, our language editor, and Bulanchai Udomariyasap, Lawan Thanasawangkul and Thanatchaporn Thananaken, our publication assistants, merit a special mention here for finalizing all manuscripts into book form. We are also indebted to the tremendous help and assistance and correspondence with Alexandra Minton and Suzanne Mursell from Edward Elgar Publishing. Without them, we could not have produced this publication. All other thanks must also go to authors, advisors, conference participants, students and conference staff who are too many to list. Finally, we are grateful to our sponsors who financed this important event up to the publication of this volume.

Suthiphand Chirathivat,
Emil-Maria Claassen
and Jürgen Schroeder

1. East Asia's monetary future: an introduction

Suthiphand Chirathivat, Emil-Maria Claassen and Jürgen Schroeder

1.1 THE CONFERENCE

Chulalongkorn University is Thailand's oldest university, and it is among the highest ranked in Southeast Asia. King Rama VI founded the university in 1917. He dedicated the campus – lying in the heart of Bangkok and nearly as big and green as Stanford – to his father, Chulalongkorn, who had been King Rama V from 1868 to 1910.

On 5–6 September 2001, 'Chula' – as it is known by insiders – celebrated the 30th anniversary of its Faculty of Economics with an international conference on the prospects for East Asian monetary integration. Organized in co-operation with the universities of Paris-Dauphine and Mannheim, the conference assembled a group of approximately 30 authors and fellow colleagues. It drew approximately 100 participants from the academic, business and policy-making communities as well as a large number of Chulalongkorn students, and was sponsored by the Central Bank of Thailand, the Asian Development Bank, Volkswagen-Stiftung, Thai Airways International and the Kenan Institute Asia.

Over the past decade, applied economic research on East Asia had been concentrating on issues such as the 'Asian-value' controversy and the 'growth miracle' phenomenon. Monetary issues had been rather insignificant – even among Asian economists. One reason for this lack of interest could have been the previously astonishing performance in price stability within the Asian region (including China) over the foregoing 20 years – in contrast to Latin America and Africa.

With the arrival of the East Asian monetary and financial crisis in 1997, the interest of Asian and Western economists shifted from the 'real sector' (including international trade considerations) to the 'monetary sector' and, in particular, to exchange rate mechanisms. As a matter of fact, under pressure of the 'external' crisis event, the 'crisis' countries abandoned fixed exchange rates and switched to the mechanism of floating exchange rates.

The immediate scientific output on the causality of the Thai crisis had been concerned with country-specific causes of the turmoil, stressing common causes like ailing banking sectors ('bad loans'), public sector budget deficits and the lack of fine monetary tuning under fixed exchange rates. Restructuring of banking, fiscal discipline and implementation of (free or managed) floating exchange rates vis-à-vis the US dollar had been among the usual major recommendations, until recently.

However, global views and analyses on the long-term monetary prospects of the East Asian region (including China and Japan) are still somewhat lacking. The global view concerns the intermediate monetary solution and establishment of 'currency areas' within East Asia, or only within Southeast Asia, as a 'compromise' between past fixed exchange rate mechanisms pegged to the US dollar and present floating exchange rate systems – still related to the US dollar as the international anchor currency.

The conference volume contains 11 contributions that are outlined below.

1.2   CURRENCY AREA FORMATION AND THE EAST ASIAN REGION (ROBERT MUNDELL)

At the very outset, one should be reminded of the traditional conference codex that explains the delay between the conference year and the publication year. Each author has to produce, after the conference, a second version of his or her paper where he or she has to take into account, if necessary, critical comments of his or her discussant and of other members of the conference. In principle, the second version should be better than the first. However, in the case of Robert Mundell, the procedure is usually different: there is no paper at the very beginning of the conference, he immediately improvises his introductory oral remarks to the rather unfamiliar audience, and his paperwork begins several months afterwards.

Furthermore, besides the various 'press conferences' he likes to give, he has talked to Thailand's Central Bank (which, by the way, is consistent with his preferred central bank relationships during the last 15 years) and to 500 alumni of Chula's Faculty of Economics during a dinner debate that raised the funds for the Faculty's library, while the other participants of the conference had an excellent supper on Bangkok's beautiful Chao Phraya River.

His written contribution to the conference is one of his most excellent papers on applied international monetary economics delivered over the last 10 years. It is a masterpiece in the field of fixed versus floating exchange rates, and it is for that reason that we have divided the summary into 'early Mundell' and 'later Mundell'. Indeed, his present paper is a combination of 'history of economic thought' and 'applied economics'.

1.2.1 Fixed Versus Floating: Once Again (*early* Robert Mundell)

If one compares, over recent time, East Asia with Europe, one could not have imagined a more spectacular contrast in the evolution of their monetary systems. After Southeast Asia's currency crises, the dogma for fixed exchange rates became an anathema to Asia, while Europe converged to irrevocably fixed exchange rates and a common, single currency. This divergence is unexpectedly revolutionary.

According to Mundell, the emergence of a 'non-system' of managed, flexible exchange rates had become a source of global financial instability – and that phenomenon had taken place not only in Southeast Asia. The shift towards flexible exchange rates had started among the industrialized countries in the early 1970s. After the US relinquished its gold standard, the US dollar became the anchor currency of the world economy (the pure dollar standard).

The case for flexible exchange rates had been put forward by James Meade and Milton Friedman during the 1950s. Meade considered that flexible exchange rates would be a better means for the British socialist government to manage its economy. Friedman argued for flexible exchange rates as a preferable alternative to foreign exchange controls, but he rejected flexible exchange rates for developing countries.

In the recent 'Nobel Monetary Duel' between Milton Friedman and Robert Mundell,[1] both 'adversaries' arrived at the common conclusion that the real debate is not about fixed versus flexible exchange rates, but should rather deal with the more fundamental issue of 'currency targeting' (i.e., exchange rate targeting) versus 'inflation targeting' (i.e., monetary targeting). In other words, the debate should be reformulated with respect to the 'old and new' question of which monetary system – or which exchange rate system – would be the most adequate to achieve price stability.

However, as one could easily imagine, there are still opposing views. The concerns still voiced mainly deal with the issue of whether the targeting of price stability should be taken from a single country point of view or from a worldwide perspective. Furthermore, price stability targeting, or more precisely, inflation targeting should perhaps be reformulated in a more sophisticated format of 'inflation forecast targeting'.

According to Mundell – as one might expect – successful implementation of inflation forecast targeting could be achieved with a fixed exchange rate as advocated by him for several decades. The fixed exchange rate has the advantage of being installed rather easily and unambiguously. However, it implies the existence of a suitable stable anchor currency within the world economy. Furthermore, the anchor currency (e.g., the US dollar) has to follow a successful inflation forecast targeting policy. For that reason, the US dollar cannot be a candidate for proper exchange rate stabilization. Consequently, the US monetary policy has to pursue a rule of benign neglect with respect to its exchange rates; its only aim is to achieve internal price stability.

1.2.2   The Hong Kong Dollar as a Common Currency for East Asia (*later* Robert Mundell)

The present currency regimes within the East Asian region look divergent, even though all countries share a common international monetary anchor, or reference currency – whether fixed or floating – which is represented by the US dollar (see also McKinnon). Looking at the larger countries, China and Japan, the former strictly follows the regime of a fixed exchange rate (even though accompanied by exchange controls), while the latter belongs to the traditional industrial group of floating currencies. The other side of the scale in terms of size can be illustrated by Hong Kong with its Currency Board and Singapore as a traditional 'floater' (to which Brunei also belongs as part of the currency union with Singapore, in existence for several decades).

Each country within East Asia still has its proper national currency. Several authors deal with the question, whether East Asian countries (or a group among them) should follow the European example of a single currency (euro) by abolishing national currencies and replacing them with a single, common currency. As a matter of course, the answer by Mundell is fully in favor of the common currency, even though its implementation may be realized only over the very long term. Ignoring the fact that there has not been even the slightest beginning of a customs union within any part of East Asia, Mundell traces the stages of how to implement the 'Asian Monetary Union'.

His gradual approach consists of the co-existence of two currencies within each country of East Asia, or in a more moderate way, within each country of the smaller Southeast Asian region. His proposal consists of the maintenance of the national currency accompanied by the introduction of an additional money that circulates as a parallel currency with the national currency. This second currency should be simultaneously used, in a later stage, as 'common' currency in all other member countries of the future Asian Monetary Union.

According to Mundell, this long-run process could be induced by replacing the Hong Kong dollar with the US dollar, which has a history of stability stretching over the last century second to none. The Hong Kong would fall to New York levels. Hong Kong would become the focal point for an Asian Monetary Fund and 'Asian dollar'. China would have the advantage of having on its doorstep a region using the most important currency in the world and it would have access to a world-class capital market and financial center. Mundell's interesting idea is that in the long run this dollar-based currency area, starting from Hong Kong, including China and – most probably – other Asian countries, could be used as a platform for an independent Asian currency that could become the standard unit of account of an Asian Monetary Fund.

1.3 ONE COUNTRY, TWO MONETARY SYSTEMS: HONG KONG AND CHINA (SHU-KI TSANG)

Hong Kong, under the framework of 'one country, two systems', enjoys full autonomy from China (including monetary autonomy) except in two areas: defense and diplomacy. After all, it is one of China's Special Administrative Regions (SARs). Both currencies circulate as parallel currencies in Mainland China as well as Hong Kong: the Hong Kong dollar in China and the renminbi (RMB) in Hong Kong. While the renminbi is not yet a fully convertible currency (exchange controls), the Hong Kong dollar has achieved the status of a respectable currency. In Mainland China, the Hong Kong dollar is exchanged with the renminbi close to parity (one Hong Kong dollar being equal to one renminbi), even though the Hong Kong dollar is pegged to the US dollar at the rate of 7.80, while the renminbi's exchange rate against the US dollar has been 'floating' around 8.20–8.30 since 1995.[2]

In fact, Hong Kong is not eager to form a monetary union with Mainland China – at least for the moment – through official currency unification between the Hong Kong dollar and the renminbi; nor is the latter. The phenomenon of a Hong Kong dollarization could be conceived through the mechanism of spontaneous competition. Furthermore, as Tsang emphasizes, the Hong Kong dollar as a parallel currency is already used widely in the Pearl River Delta, but it declines rapidly when one moves further north. A spontaneous and gradual implementation might be a signal for Mundell's proposal as the means to bring about a Hong Kong dollarization within East Asia or, more modestly, within Southeast Asia plus China and probably without Singapore.[3]

1.4 THE ROLE OF THE YEN IN EAST ASIA (TAKATOSHI ITO)

Did the yen become an important international currency over the last 10 years within the world economy and, in particular, within East Asia? Ito's empirical answer is no. By presenting elementary statistics until the arrival of the euro in January 1999, he shows that the share of the yen within total foreign exchange reserves held by other central banks amounted only to 5 percent, while the

US dollar attained the top level of 57 percent. By looking at the international bond market, bond issues from Japan and other countries denominated in the yen, amounted equally to 5 percent. Thus Japan, as an 'economic giant', which, in addition, has an impeccable history of price stability, seems to be a dwarf among key international currencies.

A particular talisman of Japanese economists – but also shared by other East Asian economists – seems to be the notion of a 'basket currency', indicating their belief in the need to regard or even influence the 'effective' exchange rate. This concept describes the weighted average, in the case of Japan, of the yen with respect to the dollar, the euro, British pound, China's renminbi, and to the Hong Kong and Singapore dollars, etc.; this 'multilateral exchange rate' is necessarily expressed by an index. The index therefore indicates the average volatility of the yen with respect to Japan's most important trading partners.

In a generalized world of floating exchange rates, the effective exchange rate fluctuates less 'wildly' than bilateral rates. Consequently, the concern of monetary policy, if it addresses exchange rates, could be to manage this multilateral exchange rate indicator. However, from a one-country point of view, the effective exchange rate can only be influenced by *one* bilateral exchange rate, which – in the case of Japan – is the yen-dollar rate.

As a matter of course, Takatoshi Ito knows this simple rule of arithmetic for exchange rate policy. Nevertheless, what he has in mind is co-operation between central banks to intervene *collectively* in foreign exchange markets in order to avoid 'competitive' depreciations. If one considers the triangular yen–euro–dollar relationship, and if one assumes that Japan's central bank wants only a depreciation of the yen–dollar rate, Japan would have to persuade the European Central Bank to intervene equally in the euro–dollar market to bring about a similar depreciation of the euro–dollar exchange rate, such that the yen–euro relation would not be affected.

1.5   THE DOLLARIZATION DEBATE: IS IT OVER? (RICARDO HAUSMANN)

An apparently opposing view to Mundell's proposal could be derived from Hausmann's chapter, which classifies countries by virtue and vice. Virtuous countries do not need fixed exchange rates for realizing price stability because they would also have price stability under floating exchange rates. In opposition to them are vicious countries that are so hopelessly inflationary that they need fixed exchange rates as a credible institution for import price stability; the most often quoted country of this type had been Argentina, which installed a Currency Board in 1991 in order to seek an end to its inflationary nightmare. However, Argentina of the 1970s and 1980s cannot be compared with contemporary Southeast Asian countries that have introduced floating rates (since the crisis of 1997), because they realized over the last decade reasonable price stability.

Hausmann pleads neither for floating nor for fixed exchange rates, but for dollarization. He starts with the observation that economic history has shown very little floating, particularly among emerging countries. What explains their 'fear of floating',[4] and what makes some countries even want to dollarize their economy?

To the various prerequisites for a credible fixed exchange rate belongs fiscal solvency. In Argentina's winter of 2002, its exchange-rate system broke down not because of its proper Currency Board system, but because the former (historically) richest country (in terms of natural resources) among Latin American nations allowed itself to become fiscally insolvent. Fiscal insolvency, or even the slightest doubt about a possible future fiscal misalignment, aggravates the consequences of the 'original sin' to which developing and transition countries are exposed, namely, the 'default risk premium' on international credit markets. The phenomenon of the original sin implies exorbitant interest rates (comparable to 'usurious' levels) on their treasury bonds, even if they are denominated in dollars, yen or euros. Consequently, the public debt burden could become rapidly unsustainable: under fixed exchange rates, a currency crisis could emerge; and under floating exchange rates, the exchange rate could overshoot.

There is no redemption from the original sin. Nevertheless, Hausmann proposes the following 'holy' solution. The concerned 'sinner' country should adopt the currency of those neighbor countries with highest credibility, not by fixing but by 'dollarizing'. For Latin America, it is the US dollar, and for East Asia, it may be the yen, the Singapore dollar or the Hong Kong dollar. At any rate, the default risk on credit markets cannot be eliminated. There is no absolute redemption. But the default risk premium can be minimized by dollarization, which at least avoids exchange rate risk.

1.6 THE EAST ASIAN EXCHANGE RATE DILEMMA AND THE WORLD DOLLAR STANDARD (RONALD MCKINNON)

By proposing an alternative pragmatic option to Ricardo Hausmann's dollarization, McKinnon chooses a less dramatic solution for East Asia's exchange rate dilemma by simply proposing a traditional fixed dollar peg.

A common currency for East Asia like the euro is not foreseeable in the near future for two reasons. First, East Asia still does not have the degree of economic integration that the countries in the European Union had, where the Single

European Market – with free movement of goods, services, capital and labor – had existed since 1993. Secondly, East Asia is far away from having the necessary political cohesion for introducing an independent regional currency similar to the euro.

The other extreme of monetary integration, namely dollarization (as discussed by Hausmann) is also not an adequate solution for East Asia. Unlike most countries in Latin America and Africa, countries in East Asia – with the possible exception of Indonesia – have collectively exhibited sufficient fiscal discipline to secure regional monetary stability, i.e., they do not need to use the inflation tax for fiscal reasons, or to 'suffer' from the subsequent currency depreciations.

McKinnon favors an East Asian monetary standard. The objectives of such a regional monetary standard, far from the euro model, should promote: (1) greater long-run exchange rate stability among East Asian economies; (2) a common and highly credible monetary anchor against inflation risk and default-risk fear in the East Asian debtor countries, as well as against Japan's deflation risk and fear; and (3) mutual understanding toward more appropriate policies for regulating banks and international capital flows. To reach these objectives, McKinnon proposes an East Asian Dollar Standard. The East Asian countries, including Japan, should fix their currencies to the US dollar, that is, they should use the US dollar as their monetary anchor.

However, there are two important question marks related to his proposal. First, why should smaller East Asian countries fix their currencies to the dollar and not to the yen, given the fact that Japan is by far the largest economy in East Asia? McKinnon gives a twofold answer. The dollar, and not the yen, had been used before the 1997 crisis; at that time, smaller East Asian countries had a *de jure* dollar peg, and after the crisis, most of the smaller East Asian countries implemented a *de facto* dollar peg. Therefore, fixing to the dollar (and not to the yen) makes these operations work more effectively. Furthermore, the problem with fixing East Asia's currencies to the yen is that the yen is not an international currency (see the chapter by Ito). For a decade, Japan has been unable to get rid of its ongoing price deflation and economic slump. Thus, other East Asian countries, by pegging to the yen, would not be well advised to import deflation, implying near zero interest rates as Japan experiences them for the moment.

Another important question concerns Japan's proper exchange rate policy. Why should it be in the interest of Japan to take part in the East Asian Dollar Standard? McKinnon argues that fixing the yen to the dollar (instead of the present float) and using the dollar as a monetary anchor by Japanese monetary authorities would end the threat of an ever higher yen (appreciation) and of an ongoing internal deflation that would not help to overcome Japan's prolonged economic slump. Fixing the yen to the dollar would be a huge economic advantage, not only to Japan, but also to all other East Asian countries, because of their strong economic links with Japan.[5]

It should be emphasized that McKinnon's East Asian Dollar Standard would only be successful under two assumptions. First, the anchor currency, namely the US dollar, would have to be stable and expected to remain stable in the future (in full harmony with one of Mundell's preconditions of a worldwide dollar standard). Second, East Asian countries must be willing and able to conduct a free market-orientated economic policy. If these conditions are fulfilled, and if East Asia, especially Japan, is ready and willing to accept the US dollar as the monetary anchor, then the implementation of McKinnon's East Asian Dollar Standard would undoubtedly contribute to the needed monetary integration in East Asia and would be compatible with Mundell's Asian dollar proposal since his proposed Hong Kong dollar as parallel currency is fixed with respect to the US dollar, as well.

1.7 CAUSES OF THE CURRENCY CRISIS: INDONESIA, KOREA, MALAYSIA, THE PHILIPPINES AND THAILAND (CHAYODOM SABHASRI, JUNE CHAROENSEANG AND PORNKAMOL MANAKIT)

There could be some doubt whether there had been an 'Asian' crisis since it was limited to five countries – namely Thailand, Indonesia, South Korea, Malaysia and the Philippines. Countries like Singapore, Hong Kong, China, Taiwan and Japan had been bystanders, and had not been affected, fundamentally. The latter five 'happy few' had three stability factors in common: large foreign exchange reserves, low external debt and a successful anti-inflationary monetary policy, even though Japan over-reacted by gliding towards the deflationary syndrome.

The Southeast Asian crisis started on 2 July 1997, when Thailand left its fixed currency exchange rate, which signaled a different future for Asian economies. Already, during December 1996 to July 1997, the baht had come under speculative attacks.

The reader should notice that the three Thai authors analyze, in an extensive and fascinating survey, the crisis scenarios not only for Thailand, Indonesia and Korea (as in the following chapter by Peter Warr), but they address, in addition, the same issue for Malaysia and the Philippines.

After the float, Thailand's monetary policy shifted to the 'modern road' of an inflation targeting framework by letting the currency float from its pre-crisis level of 25 baht to 40 baht per dollar over recent time (2003). Thailand's success story has been based on a rather constant price level for non-tradable goods, whereas prices for tradable goods adjusted smoothly to the depreciation of the baht.

However, as one could have expected, Thailand's 'conservative' monetary policy under floating exchange rates had been challenged continuously by 'excessive' budgets deficits. The fiscal package had been considered as a necessary stimulus to recover the economy from its poor economic stance, even though the risk of large budget deficits could also enhance devastating long-lasting outcomes. On the other hand, there had been doubts about the ultimate independence of Thailand's central bank despite the new 'Bank of Thailand Act', whose successful implementation still remains to be seen, since credibility has to be built *inter alia* on past performance.

1.8   EXCHANGE RATE POLICY AND THE ASIAN CRISIS: THAILAND, INDONESIA AND KOREA (PETER WARR)

Thailand, Indonesia and Korea had been outstanding economic performers prior to the financial crisis of 1997. Each considered the fixed exchange rate as the cornerstone of its macroeconomic stability. The currency crisis (rapid outflow of financial capital in anticipation of devaluation) occurred first, and financial crisis (collapse of domestic banks) resulted from the float. The economic crisis (loss of output) arose from the combined effects of both. This scenario of the three types of crises took place in all three countries. Thailand was the first to be hit by the loss of confidence, and the other two followed with similar breakdowns, which could be explained by the 'contagion' phenomenon of currency crises.

The contagion theory is a panic theory that is well known in the literature on self-fulfilling bank runs. An alternative term for contagion would be 'vulnerability', as Peter Warr suggests. According to this less dramatic concept, economies are vulnerable without the necessity of crisis – meaning currency crisis – occurring; they are only susceptible to currency crisis. There are three indicators that assess a country's vulnerability to a currency crisis: adequacy of international reserves compared to the volume of volatile capital, financial sector fragility and real exchange rate misalignment.

The unorthodox message of Peter Warr's paper is that all three IMF bailout countries showed the same three vulnerabilities, and that the contagion hypothesis is misleading, since the currency crisis in Thailand, Indonesia and Korea could be explained sufficiently as if each country had been isolated from the other two. In each of the three countries, the financial crisis (breakdown of the domestic banking system) and the economic crisis (absolute decline in output) would not have taken place without the currency crisis.

1.9 INFLATION TARGETING AFTER THE CURRENCY CRISIS: THE CASE OF THAILAND (CHAYODOM SABHASRI, JUNE CHAROENSEANG AND PORNKAMOL MANAKIT)

Several East Asian countries that have suffered from the crisis have turned to new macroeconomic policy management aimed at economic recovery and prevention of further economic and financial crisis in the future. Some countries like Thailand have altered their monetary policy framework from nominal exchange rate anchors or monetary aggregate targeting to inflation targeting. Inflation means the anchoring of the domestic (internal) value of money. Furthermore, one should learn from the experience, industrialized countries and some Latin American countries have had already in the adoption of inflation targeting. The case of Thailand – which is among the newest countries to employ inflation targeting – is analyzed in this chapter to see whether the new framework will be able to accommodate recovery from the economic decline. In particular, the policy mix (monetary fiscal policy) is reviewed in the context of whether a sharp turnaround in the economy had been possible with an excessive budget deficit without facing that parts of the deficit are financed by money creation leading to an inflation level that lies above its proper target.

1.10 RETHINKING CAPITAL CONTROLS: THE CASE OF MALAYSIA (MASAHIRO KAWAI AND SHINJI TAKAGI)

During colonial times, and until June 1967, Malaysia and Singapore shared a common monetary history in terms of their Currency Board, established in 1897. The Straits dollar circulated in the Straits Settlements (Singapore, Pulan Penang and Melaka) and in all Malay States, and was renamed the Malayan dollar in 1938. By 1950, new members had joined the Malaysian currency area: the Borneo territories of Sarawak, British North Borneo (now Sabah) and Brunei.

On 12 June 1967, a currency split took place between Malaysia and Singapore. Malaysia replaced its Currency Board with the Bank Negara Malaysia, while Singapore issued its own currency with the Currency Board of Singapore. The outcome was three new currencies, namely the Malaysian ringgit, the Singapore dollar and the Brunei dollar. However, during the next six years each country's currency circulated as a parallel currency in the other's economies at a strict par of 1:1.

That currency interchangeability arrangement between Singapore and Malaysia was officially terminated in May 1973, together with the split in their common stock market.[6] One month later, in June 1973, Singapore decided to let its dollar float. The next day, Malaysia followed the same policy.

Even though the exchange rate of the Malaysian dollar with respect to the Singapore dollar was maintained roughly within the range of 1:1 throughout the remainder of the 1970s, Malaysia's monetary 'independence' or 'sovereignty' became obvious in the 1980s, when its external currency value depreciated progressively with respect to the Singaporean dollar. During the first half of the 1980s, there was still the dogma in the Bank Negara Malaysia to stay within a 10 percent-margin of the Singaporean dollar. From 1985 onward, the Singaporean dollar was completely abolished as a nominal anchor.

When the Thai baht began to float, Malaysia followed the same floating exchange rate policy as Thailand did. Between July 1997 and early January 1998, the Malaysian ringgit depreciated 80 percent with respect to the US dollar – as did the baht. Furthermore, both floating currencies appreciated 20 percent in the period January to August 1998. On 2 September 1998, Kuala Lumpur decided to fix the exchange rate at 3.8 ringgit to one dollar (while the Bank of Thailand continued to float) and implemented a 'moratorium' for financial capital outflows. As Kawai and Takagi formulate it, Malaysia wanted to recover 'under a capital account umbrella', where the country attempted another 'salutary' safeguard, replacing the financial bailout by the IMF.

The capital controls consisted mainly of a complex bureaucratic system to prescribe which capital outflows were permitted to leave the country and which potential capital outflows had to stay within the country. As one could imagine, the general scheme had been guided by the 'principle' of not discouraging new future capital inflows (including mainly trade credit and foreign direct investment). Consequently, profits on former investments (realized before September 1998) were allowed to be transferred to foreign countries, while their principal had to remain, accompanied by a gradual differentiation to limit short-term capital outflows and to liberalize long-term capital outflows.

As the authors correctly emphasized, once a country has introduced capital controls for a while, even for a very short period, foreigners will remember the experience of the possibility of 'currency inconvertibility'. Or in other words, capital controls are remembered by future generations.

1.11 SINGAPORE AND BRUNEI: LESSONS FOR MONETARY CLUSTERS WITHIN EAST ASIA (NGIAM KEE JIN)

Within East Asia, there are two special geographical entities belonging to the group of 'industrialized nations', namely Hong Kong and Singapore. Both are the birthplace of Currency Boards, where, in addition, two national currencies circulate as parallel currencies at a fixed parity.

Hong Kong–Mainland China is the first example. As we already mentioned in the paper on Hong Kong, since the establishment of Hong Kong's Currency Board in 1982, the renminbi had been used increasingly as a means of payment and a store of value within Hong Kong and, in a similar way, the Hong Kong dollar within South China. In addition, both currencies are linked to the US dollar by fixed pegs.

In contrast to the Hong Kong–Mainland China area, the Singapore dollar has been floating since 1973, as did the currencies of many other industrialized countries. As mentioned in the context of Malaysia, the official currency area of Singapore–Malaysia broke down in 1973, but the monetary 'cluster' of Singapore–Brunei remained intact, despite all subsequent worldwide crises. The use of Brunei's banknotes in Singapore and the circulation of Singaporean banknotes within Brunei (where one Singapore dollar is equal to one Brunei dollar) has been such a common tradition that the two currencies have grown up 'as if' they were a single currency. However, from a monetary policy point of view, only the 'Monetary Authorities of Singapore' are responsible for 'managing' the floating exchange rate with respect to the US dollar.

Ngiam's contribution uses the traditional method of cost–benefit analysis of optimum currency areas, even though this specific currency area is called a monetary 'cluster' within the region of Southeast Asia.[7] The disadvantage of any currency area (which is a specific case of a regional exchange rate peg) is the emergence of adverse shocks, namely asymmetrical ones, hitting – in our present case – either the Singaporean or Brunei economy. The likelihood of such an event is rather high within the Singapore–Brunei area since the dissimilarity of their production structure is a 'masterpiece' of extremes. Ninety percent of Brunei's exports are concentrated in oil and gas, while Singapore's trade consists mainly of industrial goods and financial services.

Nevertheless, Brunei did not glide into the trap of the 'Dutch disease', which had been the case for so many other countries producing primary commodities. Singapore's most important feature of monetary policy had been the maintenance of the regime of floating rates with respect to the US dollar. Consequently, it could strictly follow the target of higher price stability in a better shape than its US counterpart, with the result that the Singapore–Brunei dollar has experienced a long history of a steady and smooth appreciation with respect to the US dollar.

The main advantage of the 'Monetary Union between Brunei and Singapore' as the author calls it, lies on the side of Brunei having chosen the Singapore dollar as its monetary anchor (one Brunei dollar is identical with one Singapore dollar). Between 1967 and 1997, Brunei's mean inflation rate had been 3.07 percent and Singapore's rate had been at the higher level of 3.81 percent; meanwhile, Malaysia's mean inflation rate stayed at 3.93 percent, which had also been an excellent score. However, Thailand having never been a member of any currency area, realized an average inflation rate of 5.30 percent, despite its fixed peg to the US dollar. Its inflation rate 'overshot' the permissible limit and provoked, over the long run, the breakdown of its fixed exchange rate system.

1.12 COSTS AND BENEFITS OF A COMMON CURRENCY FOR THE ASEAN (SRINIVASA MADHUR)

Madhur compares the suitability of the ASEAN countries (Association of Southeast Asian Nations) for a common currency to the suitability of the EU countries. The integration process in Europe – from its beginning with the Treaty of Rome in 1957 until the introduction of the euro in 1999 – took a long and stony path. According to Madhur, this tedious long-run process over 40 years should not be an argument for being pessimistic about a faster monetary integration process within the ASEAN.

First, the East Asian capacity for time compression should not be underestimated. During the last few decades, these countries have produced economic achievements at an unprecedented speed. Secondly, the ASEAN can use the European experience to great advantage. Thirdly, politicians in the ASEAN countries will come to realize that a stable common monetary framework is a precondition for higher economic growth within Southeast Asia.

There are nevertheless serious constraints to introducing a common currency in the ASEAN. Madhur discusses four of these constraints: (1) the diversity in the level of economic development; (2) the weakness of the financial sectors in the various countries; (3) the lack of a regional-level resource pooling mechanism, plus the absence of institutions required for forming and managing a currency union; and (4) the lack of political preconditions for monetary co-operation and, in particular, for a common currency.

1.13 SUMMARY

By summarizing the 11 contributions to this volume, East Asia's monetary future may be described as a bundle of 'futurist' scenarios. An enlarged Singapore–Brunei currency area could be a possible avenue for monetary integration. Another alternative, going beyond Southeast Asia, could be the Hong Kong–China area increased by Taiwan, named a 'Greater China Monetary Bloc'. As the participants of the Bangkok conference suggested, monetary imagination is endless: even a 'Northeast Asian Bloc' (Japan–Korea) is conceivable. Finally, by referring to the guest country of the conference, a monetary 'cluster' of

Cambodia and Laos around the Thai baht could be a realistic option, since the baht circulates in these two neighbor countries already for many years as a parallel currency, and the Thai currency is accepted as readily as the US dollar, despite the latter's worldwide use as the nearest currency substitute.

Among the possible future monetary outlines, one should not forget the initial Japanese proposal suggested at the outbreak of the Southeast Asian currency crisis in late 1997. Japan had been prepared to contribute 50 billion US dollars (out of its present reserves of 300 billion US dollars, held by the Central Bank of Japan) to a new institution to be called the Asian Monetary Fund as a parallel and competent competitor to the IMF.

NOTES

1. Milton Friedman and Robert A. Mundell, 'The Nobel Monetary Duel', *National Post of Canada*, December 2000.
2. 'Foreign exchange certificates' (FECs), expressed in US dollars, used by China. They were abolished in 1995. It is interesting to note that an 'outsider' within Southeast Asia, namely Myanmar (former Burma, with 45 million inhabitants, and since 1997, a member of the Association of Southeast Asian Countries, ASEAN) has recently increased the use of this instrument as a third currency beside the US dollar and the domestic kyat. Like in China previously, the parity between FECs and the US dollar is 1:1. As a matter of course, the heavy foreign exchange controls, together with a high inflation tax rate on domestic currency, brought about a black market exchange rate on the kyat to the US dollar of about 1,000:1 where 1 is the official exchange rate. The obvious reason for the existence of FECs is the seignorage gain to be absorbed by Myanmar or by its military authorities.
3. Singapore can be compared with another industrialized country, namely Switzerland, having a stable (floating) currency and not being a member of the euro currency area.
4. G. Calvo and C. Reinhart, 'Fear of Floating', *Quarterly Journal of Economics*, vol. 117, 2002, pp. 379–408.
5. McKinnon's proposed East Asian Dollar Standard has still another advantage. A credible long-term exchange rate peg keeps the purchasing power of domestic bonds fairly constant so that the risk premium between bonds at the center of the system (USA) and at the periphery (small East Asian countries) should become smaller (in analogy to Ricardo Hausmann's 'original sin' hypothesis). This reduction in the monetary asymmetry between the center and periphery is extremely important for the development of a long-term bond market in the small East Asian countries.
6. However, the currency union continued to exist until present time for Singapore and Brunei (see Chapter 11 by Ngiam Kee Jin).
7. The econometric technique of cluster analysis examines the similarities and dissimilarities of the economic structure and groups of countries according to various sets of criteria. Its aim is to obtain membership co-efficients indicating the degree of 'belongingness'. The highest coefficient would indicate the group (or 'cluster') to which this country is most likely to belong.

PART ONE

East Asia's Monetary Future

2. Currency area formation and the East Asian region

Robert Mundell

2.1 INTRODUCTION

This chapter explores currency areas in general, and Asian currency areas and economic developments in particular. The subject has become much more moot since the so-called Asian currency crises and the advent of the euro.

Perhaps the contrast between these two areas – Asia and Europe – is a good place to begin the discussion. It is hard to think of developments more different than the currency crises in Asia and the movement toward fixed exchange rates and a single currency in Europe. Throughout the Asian crisis, Asian countries were bombarded with sage advice from the international monetary authorities to destabilize their exchange rates. This was at the very time that 11 (now 12) European countries were moving in the opposite direction to fixing irrevocably their exchange rates with the ultimate intention of doing away with their national currencies.

The contrast could not be starker. What was thought to be good for Asia – flexible exchange rates – was completely rejected by Europe; and what was thought to be good for Europe – fixed exchange rates – was anathema for Asia. Why would policies fit for 12 of the most advanced countries in the world be castigated for the fast-growing tigers of Asia?

This chapter will present a discussion of this issue. It will argue that a great mistake was made in the 1970s when the international monetary authorities rejected the foundation of the postwar international monetary order based on fixed exchange rates anchored to the gold-convertible dollar, and adopted in 1976 a Second Amendment to the Articles of Agreement of the IMF a non-system of managed flexible exchange rates. It will argue that this mistake – the crime of 1976 – has been a source of global financial instability and inhibited much needed reform of the international monetary system.

2.2   POSTWAR INTERNATIONAL MONETARY SYSTEM

The international monetary system that was agreed at Bretton Woods, New Hampshire, in 1944 was not a new system. Its roots lay earlier in the 20th century, when the dollar had achieved a dominant position in the international monetary system. As Keynes put it in 1923 in his *Tract on Monetary Reform*, the 'gold standard had already become a barbarous relic', dominated by the policies of a few central banks. In this comment, he included the Bank of England and the Bank of France along with the Federal Reserve System, but in reality, only the United States had the power to determine the way the gold standard worked. During World War I, the United States was the only country that stayed on the gold standard and it was from this date that currencies started to be reckoned in dollars. To be sure, a version of the gold standard had been restored in the 1920s, but its operation depended primarily on policies of the Federal Reserve System. In any case, it broke down in successive steps in 1931, when Britain and the sterling area left it, when the United States left it in 1933, and when France left it in 1936. The system ratified at Bretton Woods dated from 1934, when the United States ended its policy of floating and raised the official price of gold from $20.67 per ounce to $35 per ounce. Then, in 1936, after France had left gold, and Britain, France and the United States had accepted the idea, they codified in the Tripartite Agreement of that year to notify each other of changes in currency policy.

By 1934, most other countries had given up on the use of gold and linked their currencies to the anchored dollar. When the Bretton Woods conference was held, the dollar was pre-eminent as the global unit of account and the only currency linked to gold. The 1944 gold dollar was accepted as the unit of account for the postwar system and all the major countries linked their currencies to the dollar. For this reason, the postwar international monetary system, and the one endorsed at the Bretton Woods conference, can be referred to as an anchored dollar standard.

The postwar system, however, broke down in three steps in 1968, 1971 and 1973 when, respectively, the free market price of gold was de-coupled from the official price, the United States renounced gold convertibility, and all the major countries moved to flexible exchange rates. The root cause of the breakdown was the fact that the 1934 price of gold at $35 an ounce had, after three important wars, become obsolete and gold under-priced. The price levels expressed in dollars and other major currencies had tripled, while the price of gold had been maintained at its official parity. There was a provision in the IMF charter for a universal change in par value that could have raised the price of gold without altering exchange rates, but political tensions between the United States and Europe, as well as reluctance to improve the terms of trade for South Africa and the Soviet Union ruled that out. When faced with requests for large conversions of dollars into gold in August 1971, the United States took the dollar off gold and the other major currencies took their currencies off the dollar.

None of the major countries (with the possible exception of the United States) were content with the new arrangements of flexible exchange rates. A fixed exchange rate system was restored in December 1971, along with a minor devaluation of the dollar (a rise in the inoperative official price of gold to $38 an ounce). The new system was again based on the dollar – though one that was no longer convertible into gold – even for foreign central banks. It was a pure dollar standard. But this system, too, broke down over disagreement between the United States and Europe on the US balance of payments deficit and the common inflation rate. After another rather useless devaluation of the dollar, the Committee of Twenty – newly created to reform the international monetary system – disbanded it, and the global economy moved on to flexible exchange rates.

2.3   THE SECOND AMENDMENT

The demise of Bretton Woods and flexible exchange rates brought pressure to bear on international monetary authorities to announce that a new 'system' had come into being to replace the one that had just been disbanded. This pressure led, in 1976, to the Second Amendment in the IMF Articles of Agreement endorsing managed flexible exchange rates – 'dirty floating'. Ever since that date, the International Monetary Fund has been waging a battle to destabilize the external values of the currencies of member countries.[1]

The IMF was not always so enthusiastic about flexible exchange rates. Before 1971, staff members were instructed to support fixed exchange rate systems. Fixed exchange rates were defended and flexible rates ridiculed in the IMF *Annual Reports* of 1950 and 1962.[2]

The shift to flexible exchange rates did not occur as a result of any fundamental new idea or IMF study. Of course, the idea of stabilizing some price level index instead of exchange rates or gold has an old history, harking back to ancient times. In the modern era, it started perhaps in Swedish history during and after the wars with Russia in the 18th century and to British history after the Napoleonic Wars.[3] In the early decades of the 20th century, both Irving Fisher and John Maynard Keynes had supported price stabilization as a preferable target to gold or exchange rate stabilization, and Keynes had constructed, in the pit of the Great Depression, an index of commodity prices that he thought could be used as a target for stabilization in an international monetary system. The emphases in these cases, however, were in finding an antidote to a potential or actual instability of gold.

Frank Graham, Charles Whittlesey, James Meade and Milton Friedman, writing independently in the 1940s and 1950s, brought the case for flexible exchange rates into the modern literature, but for very different reasons; Graham and Whittlesey wanted to de-couple the dollar from gold in order to prevent what they called the 'Golden Avalanche' – the influx of gold to the United States in the late 1930s. In the postwar world, Friedman argued for flexible exchange rates as a preferable alternative to exchange controls, and Meade argued for flexible exchange rates as a means by which a socialist government could better manage Britain's economy. None of these arguments were very relevant to the world economy and the international monetary system in the 1970s. Moreover, Milton Friedman rejected flexible exchange rates as unsuitable for developing countries, and Meade came to accept a European currency as a good idea.[4]

Moreover, support for flexible exchange rates has dropped even among those most responsible for putting them into effect. The agreement to move to flexible exchange rates was a decision made in 1973 largely by three men: George Schultz, US Secretary of the Treasury, Giscard d'Estaing, Minister of Finance in France and Helmut Schmidt, Minister of Finance in Germany. George Schultz was a distinguished labor economist and had been a colleague of Milton Friedman (and the author) at the University of Chicago in the 1960s, and went on to become Secretary of State in both the Nixon and Reagan cabinets. Giscard d'Estaing and Schmidt went on to become, respectively, President of France and Chancellor of West Germany. Subsequently, both Giscard and Schmidt have realized that the move to flexible exchange rates was a mistake.

A distinction here has to be made between the position of the United States and the countries in the rest of the world. It can be argued that a move to flexible exchange rates could benefit the United States and enhance the role of the dollar. This was not so for Europe or the rest of the world. Already Europe had embarked on its project for monetary union, set to be achieved by the year 1980. The European economies in the 1950s, 1960s and early 1970s, with currencies fixed to the dollar, had achieved a high degree of economic convergence of inflation rates and interest rates. The abandonment of the dollar anchor for their currencies undermined progress toward monetary union. Monetary union in Europe, which was set to be a ten-year project, completed in 1980, took an additional two decades because of the breakup of the international monetary system.[5]

The movement to flexible exchange rates in the 1970s was completely different from earlier episodes. In the past, countries have been forced off existing exchange rate parities because of external shocks, hyperinflation or fiscal instability. Some elements of flexible exchange rates are likely to be inherent in every pluralistic international monetary system. Neither the bimetallic nor gold standard systems of earlier centuries, nor even the postwar economic system is an exception. But the 1970s inaugurated a new era. For the first time in world history, the absence of an international monetary system and exchange rate fluctuation came to be regarded as the norm of correct behavior and the International Monetary Fund persists to this day in applauding countries that destabilize. This new norm of behavior was developed without any coherent prior analysis or comprehensive economic theory.

2.4 WHICH MONETARY RULE?

Economic discussion has been rife with debate over the 'merits of fixed and flexible exchange rates'. But the choice is an oxymoron. A fixed exchange rate is a monetary rule; a flexible rate is the absence of a fixed exchange rate monetary rule. Flexible rates are consistent with hyperinflation, hyper-deflation or price stability. All the great hyperinflations in history have involved flexible exchange rates; none have or could have taken place with fixed exchange rates.

Comparing fixed and flexible exchange rates is like comparing the merits of a particular government with its absence! It would be another oxymoron. The relevant choice is between a particular government and a feasible alternative, not anarchy.

The monetary rule of fixed exchange rates should be compared with alternative monetary rules, thereby contrasting whether any system is capable of producing (in principle) monetary stability. The alternative to fixed exchange rates is not flexible rates, which by themselves cannot deliver monetary stability, but are inflation, monetary or gold targeting.

In the 'Nobel Monetary Duel' referred to above, Milton Friedman and the author agreed early on that they were not debating fixed versus flexible exchange rates, but rather currency targeting versus inflation or monetary targeting. In other words, the debate was constrained to policies that could achieve monetary stability. There would be no point debating, for example, whether a stable fixed exchange rate system was better than an inflationary system or whether inflation targeting was better than fixing a currency to an unstable anchor.

That early agreement had the merit of focusing the debate on the relevant and debatable issues. Similarly, the IMF could improve the quality of its advice not by knee-jerk rejection of fixed exchange rates but by engaging in serious research on which of three or more systems of maintaining monetary stability are likely to be preferable. What is best for the United States – perhaps inflation targeting – is not necessarily best for other countries.

Which system of targeting works best? There is no single answer that is right for all countries. The choice has to be made in the context of a country's situation and its history. Size, geography and history are all relevant. The United States cannot fix its currency to the Mexican peso or Canadian dollar and thereby expect to achieve stability,[6] but a fixed exchange rate zone in North

America, maintained primarily by Canada and Mexico, is an option worth considering.

2.5 MONETARY RULES AND STABILIZATION STRATEGIES

The choice of targets for stabilization is also a function of initial conditions, including the inflation rate itself. Hyperinflation, with rare exceptions, is caused by excessive monetary growth.[7] If monetary growth cannot be reduced, the resultant inflation cannot be stopped. A *sine qua non* of stopping high inflation is ensuring that monetary growth is an instrument, not impossibly tied to the finance of excessive government spending. The cause of the monetary expansion – e.g., the finance of budget deficits – must at the same time also be removed.

Monetary targeting is a sufficient technique when the inflation rate is very high; it has the advantage of being unambiguous and readily implemented, but only to the extent that there are wide swings in the ratios of the growth rates of monetary aggregates, or between any of these and the growth of money income or the inflation rate. It is a clumsy and inexact instrument. At lower rates of inflation – say below 30 percent a year – it is almost certainly better to shift from monetary targeting to the more refined method of inflation targeting.

Inflation targeting adjusts monetary policy to bring about, or maintain, a given inflation rate. It is, however, easier said than done. Monetary policy works with a lag. This means that the current inflation rate is determined by past monetary policy, and it is too late to change it. At best, current monetary policy can affect the future inflation rate.[8]

Monetary policy must therefore be based on inflation forecasts. For this reason, 'inflation targeting' is an incorrect term. It should be called 'inflation-forecast targeting'. It requires a model that specifies the effectiveness of monetary policy and the lags associated with it. But it is not very exact, and for that reason, monetary policy committees engaged in inflation-forecast targeting rarely come to unanimous recommendations. Bi-weekly (as in the European Central Bank) or tri-weekly (as in the Federal Reserve System) meetings are held at which the governing boards or committee members discuss whether to raise, lower or leave unchanged the key monetary variables.

2.6 STABILIZATION POLICIES AND THE PROBLEM OF OVER-VALUATION

A distinction should be made between static and dynamic inflation targeting. In static inflation targeting, the inflation rate is already at its equilibrium level and the objective of policy is to maintain it without change. In dynamic inflation targeting, the objective is to change the inflation rate to a new level, raising or lowering it to the desired equilibrium rate. The latter is more complicated than the former because it involves shifts in the demand for real money balances.

Dynamic inflation targeting has had only mixed success. It seems to be fairly successful in reducing inflation rates in the range between 30 percent and 5 percent. But most of the theory of the subject addresses a closed economy, whereas all economies in the real world are open. Stabilization of an open economy has to deal with the problem of exchange rates.

Small changes in rates of monetary expansion shift inflation expectations and asset preferences, leading to substantial effects on the exchange rate, which in turn reverberate back to the real economy and trade balances. Disinflation – the process of bringing down the inflation rate by tighter monetary policies – is rarely a smooth process and typically results in an appreciation of the real exchange rate above its long-run equilibrium. It is for this reason that disinflation processes typically end with a crisis and sharp devaluation. Exchange rates, when allowed to float, have to adjust to the vicissitudes of speculative capital movements, and are the most sensitive and flexible of all prices.

The stages of disinflation mirror somewhat the early stages of inflation. Just as the run-up to higher inflation rates involves over-shooting and under-valuation of a currency, so the rundown to lower inflation rates involves under-shooting and over-valuation. Tight money to lower inflation rates also raises interest rates, attracts capital, worsens the current account and appreciates an exchange rate above its long-run equilibrium value. When the incipient inflation finally settles down to its equilibrium rate, the associated current account deficit has to be reversed and the involved currency has become over-valued. More than likely, this adjustment will be anticipated and a currency crisis will result.

A good example of this process was the disinflation in Canada between 1987 and 1992, which first saw a steady appreciation of the Canadian dollar, followed by a very sharp depreciation – without much inflation – below the level from which the appreciation had started.[9] Similar examples can be found during the ERM crisis of the European Monetary System in 1992, when countries like Britain and Italy used the DM as a nominal anchor to get their inflation rate down, only to be forced to change into depreciation after the disinflation policy had proved successful.

2.7   STABILIZATION OF THE EXCHANGE RATES

Some countries (e.g., the United States) are not candidates for exchange rate stabilization. But most other countries are potential or actual candidates for it.

Assuming that there exists a suitable anchor currency (or basket of currencies), exchange rate stabilization can be the most effective means for small countries to maintain monetary stability. An exchange rate fix has the advantage that it is unambiguous and easy to implement, and if it is credible, it gives the fixing country more or less the inflation rate of the anchoring currency area.[10]

A credible fixed exchange rate will produce interest rates equal to the interest rates in the anchor currency area. Stabilization of exchange rates, however, will only be successful if certain conditions or prerequisites are met:

1. The first is that the fix be a 'hard fix' in the sense that the adjustment mechanism is allowed to preserve equilibrium in the balance of payments. This requires a commitment of monetary policy to the objective of making the exchange rate remain at an equilibrium rate. A *sine qua non* is non-sterilization of the monetary effects of changes in the central bank's international assets-of-payments adjustment process. A good example of this problem was the sterilization of reserve losses by the Bank of Mexico in the summer of 1994, leading to the fiasco at the end of the year.[11]

2. A second consideration is a commitment not to change an exchange rate except under very special circumstances. A change in an exchange rate should not be left up to a mere government decision, but should require a strong majority in legislative assemblies.

3. A third requirement is fiscal solvency. In the absence of fiscal solvency, high and rising debt levels will lead to expectations that the budget deficit will have to be financed by the central bank, leading to a breakdown of the adjustment mechanism and a currency crisis. A good example of this situation is Argentina during the winter of 2002. Argentina's stability broke down not because its currency board system was at fault, but rather because Argentina allowed itself to become fiscally insolvent.

4. A fourth requirement is a correct choice of exchange rate at the time of stabilization. Too high a rate (value of the domestic currency) would lead to deflation and probably a recession; too low a rate would lead to excessive inflation and possibly speculation that the real exchange rate will become over-valued. A good example of this problem was Estonia's choice of eight krooni per DM for its currency board system in 1992.

5. A fifth requirement is strong and united leadership. Policymakers from the top executive through the minister of finance to the head of the central bank have to be committed to making the stabilization policy work and the fixed exchange rate stable for the foreseeable future. This is a difficult requirement for countries where the supply of financial and economic leadership expertise is insufficient, but it is nevertheless essential.[12]

6. A sixth requirement is endorsement of the policy by the other members of the currency area. It would be a mistake for a country to fix its currency to,

say, the dollar or the euro, without endorsement by the United States (either the Treasury or the Federal Reserve System, or both) or the EU (either ECOFIN or the European Central Bank, or both), if for no other reason, including courtesy, because the larger country could easily obstruct the fix if it chose to do so. The exchange rate of the dollar or euro with the currency of country X belongs to the United States or the EU as well as to country X. While it is hard to imagine circumstances under which either anchor area would object to the relationship, it would be a mistake not to enter into consultations on the subject.

Indeed, the anchor leaders could play a more positive role in an exchange rate fixing process. The most successful and durable international currency area in the years since World War II has been the CFA franc area in francophone Africa, where (now) 14 countries have kept their exchange rates fixed to the French franc or, since 1999, the euro.[13] Its success was due in large part to an automatic adjustment process and the underwriting of the exchange rates by the French Treasury. In the future one should hope that both the ECB and the FRB would develop separate departments to deal with other present and prospective members of the euro and dollar areas.

A final comment can be made with respect to stabilization policies. It has been argued that, starting from a high-inflation situation, a country embarking on stabilization should start with monetary targeting, and its central bank with announcements of its intentions, so that the public will have a material basis for forming expectations. After inflation has been brought down below, say, 30 percent, the country should shift to inflation targeting as a more sophisticated technique. The inflation targeting approach can be continued until the inflation rate gets down to, say, 5 percent. But by the time the inflation rate has been brought down to this level, dynamic inflation targeting will have achieved its disinflation success partly by over-valuing the currency. It will be extremely important, therefore, to manage the final stages of the disinflation process either to avoid a crisis, or to use a crisis as the opportunity for putting into place the new fixed exchange rate system.

To repeat, inflation targeting achieves its effect primarily by over-valuation of the exchange rate, with the result that the exchange rate is over-valued when the inflation rate equilibrium or threshold level of 5 percent has been achieved. An exchange crisis is therefore inevitable. There are two possible approaches; to pre-empt the crisis by putting into place currency stabilization plans at a new devalued exchange rate and with the announcement that monetary policy would now be on 'automatic pilot'. If this is not possible, an alternative would be to wait for the inevitable crisis to begin, and then use the emergency as a means of rallying support for the necessary devaluation and the accompanying measures.[14]

2.8   CURRENCY AREAS AND THE DOLLAR

Few events in international monetary history have been as poorly prepared as exchange rates. There had been little scientific work in theory, history or econometrics on how a generalized arrangement of flexible exchange rates would be likely to work. It was universally acknowledged that cleanly floating exchange rates would be a disaster, and the addition of the qualifying adjective 'managed' turned out to be a diplomat's dream; 'managed flexible … rates' could be taken to mean anything at all.

It is a pity that before the Second Amendment was adopted, which endorsed managed flexible exchange rates, there was no large preparatory Bretton Woods-style conference assessing whether it was a good idea and whether it suited the interests of any country except the United States. Repeated calls for a 'new international monetary order' fell on deaf ears.

In the abstract, a move to floating exchange rates – however managed – could have led to chaos. How flexible exchange rates would operate in practice depends on the size configuration of the economies involved. Imagine a world of 200 economies of identical size! What a calamity for trade and payments and chaos to financial markets! There would be '$^1/_2 \times 200 \times 199$' spot exchange rates alone, and complete chaos. The incentive to create a common international money, reactivate gold or form large currency areas would be irresistible.

What saved the regime from chaos was the presence of the dollar, which despite the resentment its dominance inspired gave coherence to the international payments mechanism. As long as countries were willing to use the dollar as the international currency, they would be close to a universal unit of account. Were it not for political considerations, seignorage and the possibility that the United States might impose an inflation tax on the rest of the world, a world currency system based on the dollar would be as close to an optimal system as a world lacking political integration could expect.

The *pons asinorum* of a global currency area based on the dollar would be the choice of monetary policy by the United States. Let us suppose the United States adopted an inflation target of, say, 1–3 percent for the United States and that the United States represents one-quarter of the world economy. Would that prove to be acceptable to the rest of the world? It would be hard to imagine a better international monetary system.

Of course, there would be problems. If the US grew very rapidly in its international sector relative to the rest of the world, its real exchange rate would have to appreciate, and if the required annual appreciation exceeded 3 percent, price levels would have to drop in the rest of the world. In the opposite case, if the US real exchange rate had to depreciate, prices in the rest of the world would have to rise more rapidly than in the United States. Yet, these problems would be minor compared to those that have arisen due to large gyrations in exchange rates.

By far the main problem, however, is the political issue of dominance. A global dollar standard would involve a substantial increase in the dominance of the US power position in the world economy. Once on a dollar standard countries would be more vulnerable to small changes in US policy. It is conceivable that the United States might take advantage of its quasi-monopoly position and raise its inflation rate, imposing an 'optimal inflation tax' on the rest of the world as it arguably did, whether intentionally or inadvertently, in the 1970s.

Patterns of dominance lead to friction, resistance and countervailing alliances. In the 1970s, the United States, festering from the psychological wounds of the Vietnam War, was not in a mood for a cooperative solution, even if one had been proposed. Vexing under the dollar standard, the Europeans sought protection in a countervailing alternative: what eventually became the euro.

2.9   THE ADVENT OF THE EURO

The significance of the euro lies in the fact that it has the potential to change the power configuration of the international monetary system and to vie with the dollar as an alternative unit of account and reserve currency. In this sense, it might be more important than the breakdown of the system in the early 1970s.

Upon its creation in 1999, the euro was instantly the number two currency in the world. By the middle of 2002, the physical currency and coins will have replaced the currencies of the 12 countries that make up the euro area, countries with a combined GDP of $6 trillion. When Sweden, Denmark and especially Britain join the Eurozone – as seems probable – the euro area will have a combined GDP of 75 percent of the dollar area (at current exchange rates). The admittance of the accession countries to the European Union and possibly the Eurozone will probably mean another dozen countries added to the euro area in the next decade, not to mention 13 CFA franc countries of West Africa that are already tied to the euro through the former connections of the euro with the French franc.

Counting a few other countries that are likely to tie their currencies to the Eurozone in the coming decade, we could expect that as many as 40–50 countries, with a population approaching 500 million and a composite GDP perhaps 20 percent larger than the United States, in the Eurozone or tied to the euro within the next decade. This will produce a basic change in the power configuration of the system, with some shift of monetary and trade power from the United States to the EU. Although the United States, with its military power and centralized decision-making processes, will continue to be the only superpower for the foreseeable future, the euro area will grow in relative importance, creating the prospect of a shift from active unilateralism to a more cooperative duopolistic relationship, with increased sharing of seignorage and power. A multi-polar power system will have a chance to develop.

Is this estimate of the importance of the euro exaggerated? The euro has some defects to contend with. One defect is its relative weakness since introduction. A second is the reluctance of Britain to throw its lot in with its continental partners. A third is the overall problem of a system with one currency, but 12 governments. A fourth is the problem of decision-making and governance. A fifth is the weakness caused by the accession of low-income countries. A sixth is the sluggishness of structural reform of labor markets, legislation controlling competition and tax systems. A seventh is the relatively slow penetration of information technology throughout Southern Europe. The important truth in these objections provides an agenda for reform in Europe in the years to come.

There is, nevertheless, a bottom line that the euro was all but a political necessity. It is the only game in town. Whenever factors tend to make it weak, countervailing forces will at the same time be set in motion to help it recover. That has happened time and again over the past three decades since the process of monetary integration began. There will be crises in the future to deal with, as well, but it is extremely unlikely that a solution will lie in disbanding an effort that has taken decades to build. The European Union is going to become bigger and more important in the world economy.

2.10   THE DEMONSTRATION EFFECT OF THE EURO

By 2012, the importance of the dollar and euro will probably be about equal and countries may want to hold about an equal proportion of dollars and euros. What are the implications? Given that most of the existing reserves are now in dollars, a balance between dollars and euros would mean little, if any, growth in demand for dollars over the next decade, but a substantial demand for euros. If the past is any indication, the global demand for reserves will double over the next dozen years, say from $1.6 trillion to $3.2 trillion.[15] With, say, three-quarters of reserves in dollars today and in 2012, there would be no room for dollar growth, but demand for euros would amount to $1.2 trillion – or $100 billion a year. With unchanged capital movements, this would involve a substantial turnaround in current account and trade balances, with the United States generating a smaller – and Europe a larger – deficit, or surplus. Most likely, the change in reserves would be split between changes in current accounts and capital movements. In any case, it would involve a downward long-run pressure on the dollar, and a factor for the long-run strength of the euro.

Another consequence of the euro needs to be considered. The euro will have an important demonstration effect, changing the way people think about flexible exchange rates and currency areas. Consider the fact that the International Monetary Fund and the United States have together been preaching to countries throughout the world for two-and-a-half decades about the importance of destabilizing their exchange rates, and the calamities visited on countries that failed to do so.[16]

Then suddenly the euro emerges, and it is seen to be a great success. Instead of the fixed exchange rates in the Eurozone creating speculative capital movements, they are eliminated completely; hedge funds cannot make a dime in the Eurozone. Interest rates, which in several EU countries were between 10 and 15 percent ten years ago, suddenly dropped below 5 percent. Europeans suddenly had a capital market of continental dimensions and a currency that is the second most important currency in the world. The success of the Eurozone has made smaller countries look anew at the exchange regimes sponsored by the IMF.

Why indeed? To understand the conventional wisdom, which looks upon fixed exchange rates as, at best, an aberration, it is necessary to glance at a mistake that has permeated international economics for more than two centuries. This mistake is the idea behind what is still called in textbooks the 'price-specie-flow mechanism'. This is the mechanism attributed to David Hume, the 18th-century Scottish economist who was instrumental in developing (if not exactly originating) the immensely important doctrine of the self-adjusting international mechanism of the balance of payments under specie (gold or silver) standards.

2.11   THE ADJUSTMENT MECHANISM UNDER FIXED EXCHANGE RATES

Starting with equilibrium, Hume would postulate a disturbance, such as an increase in the quantity of money, and then show that the consequent outflow of specie would be self-correcting. Later, writers interpreted Hume to mean that domestic prices would rise, shift expenditures onto foreign goods, create a balance of payments deficit, which would, in turn, reduce the money supply, and thus correct the initial disturbance, with opposite effects occurring in the foreign country. This came to be known as the 'price-specie-flow mechanism'.

This interpretation of Hume cannot, however, be correct, because Hume was careful to insist upon the inviolability of the 'law of one price'. Prices at home could not rise above prices abroad. To save the idea, theorists then interpreted the change in relative prices to mean a change in the terms of trade. But this idea could be quickly refuted. What about a country that was too small to change the terms of trade?

It was only in recent years that the problem has been cleared up, although the erroneous view still circulates in some textbooks. Changes in relative price levels are only incidental to the mechanism under fixed exchange rates. In general, they are not needed; when they are needed, they may move in either direction. An increase in the quantity of money would simply increase expenditures, and thus worsen the balance of payments at unchanged prices, leading to an outflow of gold and the required equilibrating reduction in the quantity of money. Yet, generations of economists had been brought up on the defunct economics of their teachers. It was straightforward for those economists to reject the adjustment mechanism of fixed exchange rates as an evil force that imposed deflation on deficit countries and inflation on surplus countries. How much better it would be to replace it with changes in exchange rates.

Most business persons and bankers strongly supported fixed exchange rates, against the advice of academic scribblers who had made a mistake in their logic. This is one case where practical business persons have had greater insight into policy than the faculty of the economics profession.

2.12   CURRENCY INSTABILITY IN EAST ASIA

Taking a look at the world today, we have three islands of stability; the dollar area, the euro area and the yen area – with these three areas making up 60 percent of the world economy. We can roughly say that by the decade of the 1990s, inflation has been stopped in all three areas. In the past decade, there has been no inflation in the United States, no inflation in Europe and no inflation in Japan. But we have hugely unstable exchange rates. If we have price stability in each area, why do we need unstable exchange rates? If we look at the DM/dollar rate, which can be looked on as the predecessor of the euro/dollar rate, we find that, in 1975, the dollar was at DM 3.5. Five years later, in 1980, it was half that, at DM 1.7. Five years later, in 1985, the dollar had doubled to DM 3.4. Seven years later, in the exchange rate mechanism crisis of 1992, the dollar had fallen to DM 1.35. Now it is DM 2.20! What violent instability! If it were matched by the dollar-euro rate in the future, it would crack 'Euroland' apart.

Alternatively, look at the yen/dollar rate, more familiar in Hong Kong. In 1985, the dollar was at 250 yen; ten years later, in April 1995, it was 78 yen; three years later, in June 1998, it was 148 yen. Speculators said it was going up to 200 yen. Instead, it fell to 105 and then recovered to 125. The rise of the dollar and the depreciation of the yen between 1995 and 1998 was a major cause of the Asian crisis. For all kinds of subtle reasons, the impact was not just the increased competitiveness of Japan. Whenever the yen goes down, foreign investment from Japan dries up. That happened in 1997, and it was a great blow to many of the economies of Southeast Asia.

A different story applies to China. In 1998, there was widespread speculation that China would devalue its currency. The black market rate, reflecting speculation against the renminbi (RMB), rose to more than 9 RMB. With the RMB about to be devalued, why would businesses in Japan want to invest in China? How much better to pick up bargains after the devaluation! Thus, investment in China dried up and the speculation against the RMB almost proved to be self-justifying. The lesson is that exchange rate uncertainty can be just as damaging as the reality of exchange rate changes.

To elaborate here somewhat on the persistent proposals from the IMF that China should widen its exchange margins; depending on whether the balance of payments were in surplus or deficit, their currency might initially appreciate or depreciate. But the ultimate result is inevitable depreciation. Given the inconvertibility of the RMB in capital account and exchange controls, the widening of margins would aggravate uncertainty about their commitment to parity and be looked upon as a prelude to devaluation.

There are special features of the monetary situation in China that need to be allowed for. China has an unusually high ratio of money to GDP (using a broad definition of money that really includes quasi-money). That ratio is not just huge, it is also growing rapidly. Remember that people in China cannot look upon land as owned wealth; land cannot be held on the basis of ownership, but only in lease. Some other outlet in which to invest savings is needed. The stock market can take some of it, but it is not suitable for vast numbers of small savers who do not have ready access to the knowledge needed to manage stock portfolios.

In any case, market capitalization in the combined Chinese stock exchanges is still not large enough to absorb much of the deposits that are put into banks. Money, therefore, represents the most important abode of savings. But if the currency starts to depreciate, confidence in this outlet for savings will be undermined, and there will be a flight from money into hoarding in the countryside of the type that led to such a panic in the late 1980s. It would be especially disturbing in the poorer western part of China that has not by any means shared fully in the prosperity of the coastal regions. A policy of devaluation, or even a widening of exchange margins would be looked upon as movement away from China's commitment to monetary stability, and create grave uncertainty about the future.

Yet another argument against devaluation – or widening of margins as a prelude to it – is that the United States (China's main market) with its large trade deficit with China might retaliate by imposing quotas on China's exports. This would be especially likely in a global slowdown.

The conclusion, therefore, is that China should not appreciate, depreciate, widen the band around its currency, announce a fixed parity or spend its foreign exchange reserves. The fact that China weathered the 'Asian crisis' without IMF funds or advice lends strong support to that conclusion.

2.13   NEW PROSPECTS FOR ASIA

During a meeting of the APEC Study Group Commission in Korea a new phrase, 'the Asia-IMF crisis', was heard! Both adjectives need to be justified. Was it an Asian crisis? Was it an IMF crisis?

It was not really an 'Asian' crisis. The real crisis was restricted to four countries: Thailand, Malaysia, Indonesia and South Korea. There was no real crisis in Singapore, Hong Kong, China, Taiwan or Japan except, of course, for the fact that bystanders are never unaffected by the plight of their neighbors. The countries that avoided crises had three things in common. The first was large foreign exchange reserves. The second was relatively low (or at least manageable) external debts, so they didn't have to draw on the IMF or follow its policy prescriptions. Speculators had no interest in taking on these countries. The third feature they had in common was a clear-cut, specific target for monetary policy. Singapore has a currency basket (with unspecified weighting) target that has worked almost like inflation targeting. Hong Kong had a currency board system.[17] China had a fixed exchange rate coupled with exchange controls. Both Taiwan and Japan had commodity basket targets.

Was it an IMF crisis? The IMF had programs in each of the countries at the epicenter of the crisis, but little or no exposure in the other countries. But this does not prove causation! There are a lot of sick people in hospitals too! A serious case, however, could be made that IMF policies have led to the rejection of fixed exchange rates as an anchor without replacing that monetary rule with an equally satisfactory alternative anchor.

The question that must be asked next is: 'does Asia need a common currency?' The answer depends on what the alternative to it is. If the alternative is the present system then the answer is 'yes, Asia needs a common currency'. The present system has serious flaws. If, however, the alternative to it is a global currency, which would possibly be the best solution, then the answer is 'Asia does not need a separate common currency'.

To form an idea of the needs of Asia in the field of currency reorganization, one needs to form a view of the outlook for Asia and its prospects in the world economy as it could conceivably evolve. In the 30 March 2000 issue of the *Asian Wall Street Journal*, the author wrote on a plan for building a world currency on the platform of a three-currency (G-3) monetary union of the dollar, euro and yen areas. There is no room in this chapter to go into the details, but you can think of achieving it with the five steps leading up to the euro area (without the third phase in which national currencies are scrapped). The five steps are as follows:

1. establish a common inflation target for the G-3 area;
2. establish a common price index to measure inflation in the area;
3. lock exchange rates;
4. form a monetary policy committee to establish the common monetary policy; and,
5. develop an arrangement to share seignorage.

Given the high degree of inflation convergence among the three currency areas, making monetary policy decisions should not be more difficult than for the European Central Bank inside the euro area. If that could be achieved, it would be a relatively simple matter to use the dollar–euro bloc as the platform for a world currency produced by the members of the IMF.

Notice the great advantages of such a monetary union for the world economy. Instead of having to cope with unstable exchange rates among the dollar, euro and yen, the rest of the world would have the option of stabilizing their own currencies relative to the mainstream world economy.

Of course, it is possible – some might say extremely unlikely – that an agreement to lock exchange rates and conduct a common monetary policy could be worked out among the United States, the EMU countries and Japan. The day is long past when all the major central banks – as in the postwar era – believed in a fixed exchange rate monetary system as an act of faith. The current fashion is to go to the opposite extreme and praise policies of benign neglect of exchange rates. For that reason, Asia should not indulge in wishful thinking, but find (possibly second-best) alternatives.

It is here that the author believes that the solution is an Asian currency. Not, however, a single currency for Asia. When one speaks of the desirability of a world currency, one is not talking about a single currency. The distinction between a common currency and a single currency has given rise to difficulties elsewhere, so to avoid misinterpretation the distinction is underlined below.

2.14   SINGLE VERSUS COMMON CURRENCY

In the final episode of the debate 'The Nobel Monetary Duel' between the author and Milton Friedman, Friedman chastised the author for advocating a single world currency. But the author has never suggested a single currency for the world and, moreover, has several times suggested there would be problems with it. Assuming the political conditions were appropriate, the optimal and equilibrium solution is for each (sufficiently large) country to retain its own national currency, but keep it fully convertible to the world currency.

In the author's vision for the world economy, every country can keep its own currency. All that is needed is for currencies to be produced as if they were a single currency. What model would this be like? Well, it could be the model of the Belgium–Luxembourg monetary union. Belgium and Luxembourg formed a monetary union in 1921. The Luxembourg franc has existed along with the Belgium franc all this time, but monetary policy was (before the advent of the euro) conducted by Belgium. Luxembourg had no independent monetary policy, but there are nevertheless a lot of Luxembourg francs in circulation, just as there have been Scottish pounds kicking around since the Act of Union with Britain in 1707. The equilibrium is stable as long as the supply of each national currency is kept below the global demand for it at the fixed parity by a margin large enough to discourage speculation.

So, to get back to the main theme, Asia needs a common currency, but it is neither possible nor desirable for it to have a single currency. Each state could keep its own currency, but that should be kept convertible into the common currency organized and run by a consortium of relevant states. Such an arrangement would be highly desirable to avoid a repetition of the currency storm that struck several countries in Asia in 1997–98, and from which one or two countries have not yet fully recovered.

Remember the meeting of the IMF in Hong Kong in September 1997? At that time, Japan proposed the organization of an Asian Monetary Fund. This proposal was decisively rejected by the United States Treasury. The fear may have been that an Asian Monetary Fund would take decision-making power away from Washington and that decisions made away from them would be worse than those made in Washington. What a pity! What followed in just a few weeks was the so-called 'Asian crisis'. Policy responses for an Asian solution could hardly have been worse than those that have emanated from Washington.

2.15   WHAT ANCHOR FOR AN ASIAN CURRENCY?

If there is to be an Asian plan – 'solution' is too strong a word – for an Asian currency, it is natural to ask: what currency, and what anchor? As already emphasized, the European model of a single currency would not work in Asia now because a single currency requires a substantial degree of political integration, much more than exists in Asia now or in the foreseeable future. The Asian currency would have to be a common parallel currency, used for international trade within Asia and with the rest of the world.

What would be the anchor for a parallel currency in Asia? At least at the beginning, it would have to be based on one of the existing global currencies.

The relevant choices are the dollar, euro and yen, and possibly the RMB. But the RMB would not suffice at present, because it is not a convertible currency. If China continues to grow as it has in the past, the RMB will be an increasingly important currency in Asia, but it would be a step backwards to use an inconvertible currency as an anchor, and this rules out the RMB as the anchor for the next several years.

What about the yen? Japan's economy has got into trouble recently, but its strengths are still legion. It has the world's largest creditor position, a situation it has built up with a high savings rate that has led to huge current account surpluses. Japan also has been more successful (one could even say too successful!) than any other country in recent decades in keeping inflation under control.

But against these advantages, the choice of the yen as an anchor has severe problems. Japan has not put its macroeconomic house in order. A first problem is that its banking system is in grave trouble, a problem that has stemmed from the excessive appreciation of the yen in the late 1980s. A second problem was that its mix of monetary and fiscal policy has been wrong for several years; fiscal expansion coupled with a high degree of capital mobility and a flexible exchange rate (a straightforward conclusion, of the Mundell-Fleming model!). A third related problem concerns the secular tendency of the yen to appreciate, reflected in long-term interest rates less than 2 percent. Until these problems are corrected, the yen could not be used as the basis for a currency area. Among other obstacles, there is also a widely perceived notion that Japan has unfinished business left over in making amends from its role in World War II.

Because the euro is not a serious contender as an anchor for the Asian currency, at present, we are left with the dollar – or a basket of the dollar, yen and euro. But a basket of the three currencies, however useful as a long-run unit of account, would not make a good medium of exchange. As long as the dollar, euro and yen rates fluctuate against each other, the basket value would be uncertain and it would not be an interesting anchor for Asian currencies.

One is left, of course, with the dollar. The US GDP is, at current exchange rates, somewhat less than two-and-a-half times that of Japan and ten times that of China. The dollar would be an excellent anchor for the Asian currencies. China already uses the dollar as its anchor, as does Malaysia and of course Hong Kong.

2.16 THE SPECIAL CASE OF HONG KONG

Hong Kong has become an important feature of the economy of Southeast Asia. Outside Tokyo, Hong Kong has the largest foreign exchange market in Asia. Even so, its policy could be improved by a policy change that would be better for itself, Mainland China, the rest of Asia and the world economy – reform that would replace Hong Kong dollars with US dollars! What would be the costs and benefits?

Start with Hong Kong. There are about $HK 100 billion in circulation that would have to be replaced, at the current exchange rate of $HK 7.80 = $US 1.00, by about $US 12 billion. With Hong Kong's vast reserves of about $100 billion, it would be a simple matter to finance. The only cost to Hong Kong would be the interest receipts foregone on this $US 12 billion. The benefits to Hong Kong would be enormous. The Hong Kong public would suddenly get a currency that is the most important in the world, with a history of stability stretching over the last century, second to none. Interest rates in Hong Kong would fall to New York levels. And Hong Kong would continue to get the rate of inflation of the United States, modified by a secular productivity change factor. Hong Kong's financial center would suddenly dominate the rest of Asia.

China would benefit. The RMB has been fixed to the US dollar since 1994. China would have on its doorstep a region using the most important currency in the world and it would have access to a world-class capital market and financial center. The continued existence of the Hong Kong dollar is completely unnecessary for China. Other advantages would be that Hong Kong would become the focal point for an Asian monetary fund and an 'Asian dollar'.

The existence of a great financial center based on the dollar, and with dollar interest rates, would be of immense benefit for the rest of Asia. The transformation of the Hong Kong currency into a rock of stability for all Asia would have far-reaching – and beneficial – implications for the currency reorganization of the world.

In the long run, the formation of a dollar-based currency area in Asia, including China, Hong Kong and most Asian countries, could be used as the platform for an independent Asian currency that could become the standard unit of account of an Asian Fund.

2.17   CHOICE OF CURRENCY AREAS

International monetary relations straddle economics and politics. An Asian currency area cannot be considered inside a political vacuum. It has been argued that a single currency monetary union cannot take place without a substantial degree of political integration. It must be within a security area, in the sense that the states are friends, rather than enemies, and not likely to make war on one another. To a lesser extent, the same argument holds for the formation of currency areas and multiple currency monetary unions.

A necessary condition for the formation of a monetary union in Europe was the end of the Franco-German enmity that had soured relations for 200 years. It could not be said that the European Union is tightly integrated politically, yet there is nonetheless a substantial degree of governance exerted by the European Commission, such groups as ECOFIN and the periodic inter-governmental meetings of heads of state. The degree of political integration is, moreover, increasing as a result of the pressure to create a governance system that will work with additional accession countries.

Asia's political integration is a long way from that of Europe. But it is surprising how quickly it could develop if the conditions were right. At the present time, the most likely Asian currency area would start with the 'APT' (ASEAN Plus THREE) group, made up of the (newly expanded) ten ASEAN countries and Japan, Korea and China.

Another important issue in currency area formation is the system of governance, which is affected importantly by the relative power positions of the states involved. It goes without saying, for example, that the proposed North American Monetary Union comprising the same countries as NAFTA, would be dominated by the United States, a country whose economy is at least 11 times larger than Canada's and 20 times larger than Mexico's. Mercosur is heavily dominated by Brazil, with 180 million people, checked by Argentina, with 35 million, and the two much smaller states of Paraguay and Uruguay.

In the APT area, the dominant powers are Japan and China, complementary to one another in political as well as economic dimensions. The political viability of an APT currency area would depend critically on how well these countries got along, and on whether or how well the other 11 countries accepted their governance.

A key element in an APT currency area would be the choice of an anchor. For reasons already discussed, the only feasible single currency anchor at the present time would be the US dollar. The currencies of China, Hong Kong and Malaysia are already fixed to the dollar so that if Japan were to fix the yen to the dollar, the most critical steps in forming an APT currency area would have been hurdled.

It would be a mistake, however, to not recognize that the dollar itself may not be a safe anchor in the long run. Over recent years, it has been strong; but in the future, it could be weak. The fluctuations of the dollar against other major currencies pose a major problem for countries adhering to the dollar alone. Over the past 30 years, the dollar has been involved in large fluctuations against the Special Drawing Right (SDR). Thus the dollar started out as 1 SDR in 1970; it fell to an average low of SDR 0.76 in 1980; it rose to SDR 0.98 in 1985; it fell to SDR 0.66 in 1995 and rose to SDR 0.99 in 2001. While stabilization around the dollar would be the best step in the short run, the SDR might be a better long-run anchor. Currently the weights in the four-currency basket SDR are as follows: dollar = 39 percent; euro = 32 percent; yen = 18 percent; pound = 11 percent.

If political conditions made an Asian currency area based on the APT group unfeasible, an alternative might be available in the larger framework of APEC. This group, which has set a target of some kind of free trade area by 2015, comprises the entire Pacific Basin, including among others, China, Japan, the United States, Russia, Canada, Indonesia, Mexico, Peru, Australia, New Zealand and Chile. Its combined GDP is over $22 trillion, over half of world GDP.

An APEC currency area would have much to recommend it. Indeed a basic core for it already exists, with the United States, China, Hong Kong and Malaysia. If Japan fixed the yen to the dollar, other countries might be encouraged to do the same, creating the basis for a platform that could be used as the anchor for a global currency.

NOTES

1. One of the first casualties of the new dispensation was Mexico, which had had a fixed exchange rate at 12.5 pesos: $1 from 1954 until 1976. The 1976 devaluation and flexible exchange rates inaugurated a period of monetary instability from which Mexico has not yet recovered. The destabilization of Mexico was soon followed by IMF-sponsored destabilization of the currencies of many other countries in Central America.

2. Parenthetically, it should be noted that the author was a member of the staff of the IMF when the 1962 *Annual Report* came out, and he objected to some of the arguments used to attack flexible exchange rates and support fixed exchange rates, largely because the drafters of the report had not taken into account the important issue of currency areas, along the lines of R.A. Mundell (1961), 'A Theory of Optimum Currency Areas', *American Economic Review*, 51 (November): 509–17.

3. Per Christianen of Sweden in the 1760s and Thomas Attwood of Britain after 1815, where both advocated stabilization of a domestic price level rather than the gold price.

4. For a fairly up-to-date review of Friedman's (and the author's) view, see 'The Nobel Monetary Duel', debate between Milton Friedman and the author in the *National Post of Canada*, December 2000, available on the Internet.

5. The answer was sought in a joint float of the European currencies against the dollar. This idea had been first broached after 15 August 1971, when President Nixon took the dollar off gold, but European countries could not at that time agree on which of the European currencies – the major candidates were the pound, the mark and the franc – could act as a pivot. The issue came up again in the spring of 1973. But even at that stage the British and French were unwilling to acknowledge that the mark had become the second most important currency in the world and would be the natural and most effective pivot for a joint float. At that time, an Economic Study Group (of which the author was a member) had been set up in 1973 by the European Commission to advise on the monetary union project and was asked whether a joint float could be organized without naming one of the three main candidates as leader. The group's answer was yes, but while it was not incorrect as a theoretical matter, it was not a practical alternative in the time period involved. The major political problem, acknowledgement of the dominant role of the mark, was not finally acknowledged by France until the mid-1980s.

6. The United States could, of course, fix its dollar to a basket of currencies in the rest of the world, or a basket of currencies of stable countries in the rest of the world, and it would always pay for its monetary authorities to utilize the information from such an index, even if it were not strictly used as an object of fixing. The US economy, with 25 percent of the world economy, is the largest, but in a globalized world it might be preferable to stabilize the dollar in terms of a basket containing all the world's goods and services and not just 25 percent.

7. Hyperinflation can also be caused by the disappearance of any demand for money, an occurrence that frequently happens in a country or region that has lost a war. But most cases of very high inflation are produced by excessive issues of money.

8. Of course, earlier anticipations of current monetary policy can affect the current inflation rate.

9. Brazil's devaluation in February 1999 represents another example.

10. This is subject to qualifications due to imperfections in the information market, different weights in national price indexes, and differences in the rates of productivity growth in domestic and international industries.

11. In the absence of sterilization, a (say) purchase of foreign exchange to thwart appreciation of the currency (because of a balance of payments surplus) leads to additional money creation, which sets in a process of increasing domestic spending on goods and assets that brings about a correction of the balance of payments surplus. This mechanism was at the heart of the gold standard adjustment process and is in every country the means by which balances of payments are kept in equilibrium between different provinces or regions of a common currency area. If, on the other hand, the central bank nullifies this mechanism by selling an equal amount of domestic assets, preventing increased monetary expansion, the disequilibrium stays in effect, reserves continue to flood in, and speculation that the exchange rate is going to be changed leads to a crisis.

12. In this respect developing countries were much better served in the decades after World War II when countries could rely on IMF advice for assistance in exchange rate stabilization regimes.

13. The CFA franc zone is composed of two groups of countries: the West African Economic and Monetary Union (WAEMU) – composed of eight countries, and the Central African Economic and Monetary Community (CAEMC) composed of six countries. From 1948 until 1994, the French franc was fixed at 50 CFA francs. In 1994, the rate was doubled to 100 CFA francs per one French franc. In 1999, the euro replaced the French franc as the anchor at an exchange rate of CFA francs 655.957 per euro.

14. In the new arrangements, a policy of strict budget balance on the part of the government is desirable if not absolutely necessary, and a policy of adding domestic assets to the balance sheet of the central bank should be strictly limited to the objective of changing the level of the foreign exchange reserves, adding domestic assets when reserves are excessive, and selling domestic assets when reserves are too low.

15. More probably, however, the demand for reserves will grow at a considerably slower rate if not absolutely decline. This is because the global demand for reserves is a function of the number of currency areas, diminishing as larger currency areas are formed.

16. Guillermo Ortiz, the Governor of the Bank of Mexico, when he spoke at the World Economic Forum in Davos in the year 2000, was only expressing the new conventional 'wisdom' when he said something to the effect that if the Asian crisis taught us anything, it was that fixed exchange rate systems do not work.

17. It is true that Hong Kong got into a little trouble when the newly-created Hong Kong Monetary Authority threatened to depart from the rules of the system in order to support the stock market, but the punishment in the form of outward speculation was severe and the HKMA quickly corrected its mistake.

3. One country, two monetary systems: Hong Kong and China

Shu-ki Tsang

3.1 INTRODUCTION

One country, two monetary systems, or multiple monetary systems, has a number of precedents in China. The country had this during the civil wars of the 1930s and 1940s. Even communist occupied areas had their own (temporary) currencies, as these pockets of land were separated by nationalist armies. Anyway, the currencies were mostly short-lived, and were later unified by the renminbi in 1948–49 (Wu, 1998). The foreign exchange certificates (FECs), to be used exclusively by foreigners inside China before they were abolished by the reforms of 1994, could also be regarded as a pseudo-currency, despite the fact that they had a parity value with the renminbi. In the development of the four special economic zones (SEZs) in the 1980s, there were also discussions of setting up an SEZ currency (Chan and Tsang, 1985). The author, for one, was supportive of such an idea, along with other SEZ officials and scholars, but nothing emerged at the end of the day.

At present, China actually has 'one country, three currencies'; the renminbi, the Hong Kong dollar, and the pataca in Macau (which has continued to circulate after Macau became the second special administrative region (SAR) of China in 1999, after Hong Kong in 1997). Of course, Macau has been Hong Kong 'dollarized' to a marked extent for a long time, despite its history as a Portuguese colony. But you can still use the pataca in Macau today (which is pegged to the Hong Kong dollar at the rate of 1.03). If Taiwan ever re-unifies with Mainland China, there may be a situation of 'one country, four monetary systems'.

What seems interesting about the case of Hong Kong and Mainland China is perhaps the circumstances under which the two separate currencies emerged and then developed, and the 'asymmetry' between that SAR and the sovereign economy. Hong Kong is an international financial center that has roughly the fourth highest GDP per capita in the world; while China has undergone a very impressive process of economic reforms, albeit from a very low level of development and having had to deal with much socialist institutional rigidity. The gap between the two economies has been rapidly narrowing in the past two decades. Moreover, the integrative process between them – in terms of trade and investment – as well as controlled population flows, has generated tremendous impact on both sides, particularly on Hong Kong. The transformation of Hong Kong into a service economy with massive relocation of manufacturing industries into southern China is a case in point. Still, few would recommend a hasty monetary union, even after the renminbi achieves full convertibility some time in the future.

In any case, when monetary union does occur, it will be a very interesting experiment. Hong Kong is practicing a currency board system, with the Hong Kong dollar – a fully convertible hard currency – pegged to the US dollar at the rate of 7.80 (Tsang, 1996a; 1996b; 1999a). The renminbi had achieved 'Article VIII convertibility' by the end of 1996, according to IMF standards, and is under a managed float (Tsang, 1997). The convergence process, if deemed feasible and desirable, would pose challenges for monetary and economic management. Of course, one may argue for a long-term coexistence of these two currencies (Barandiaran and Tsang, 1997).

Section 2 of this chapter will first look at the facts about 'one country, two monetary systems'. Then the theories about separate currencies and monetary union will be reviewed in the changing circumstances of Hong Kong and China. Some empirical findings are reported in section 4. Section 5 speculates about the scenarios of a future monetary union. Section 6 concludes.

3.2   THE MEANING OF 'ONE COUNTRY, TWO MONETARY SYSTEMS'

Under the framework of 'one country, two systems', the Hong Kong special administrative region (SAR) is to decide its own monetary policies in accordance with Articles 110 to 113 of the Basic Law, the SAR's mini-constitution. Post-1997 monetary relations between Mainland China and Hong Kong were officially defined – in the words of Joseph Yam, Chief Executive of the Hong Kong Monetary Authority (HKMA), the territory's central bank – as 'one country, two currencies, two monetary systems and two monetary authorities which are mutually independent' (Yam, 1996). This characterization was openly endorsed by Chen Yuan, a Deputy Governor of the People's Bank of China (PBC), the country's central bank. Chen (1996) emphasized that '(t)he Hong Kong dollar and the renminbi will circulate as legal tender in Hong Kong and the mainland respectively. The Hong Kong dollar will be treated as a foreign currency in the mainland. Likewise, the renminbi will be treated as a foreign currency in Hong Kong'.

Reality has certainly been driven by more practical considerations and the existence of the Hong Kong dollar as a convertible currency served China well. As much as one-quarter to one-third of Chinese foreign exchange earnings was said to have been derived from Hong Kong. Of course, Hong Kong at that time being a British colony, nothing could have been done by China on the Hong Kong dollar anyway.

Hong Kong assumed a new role with the launching of the economic reform, as an important trading partner and 'external investor' for the mainland, as well as an important bridgehead for other foreign traders and investors. After more than two decades, Hong Kong is still the largest trading partner with China, and is the busiest port re-exporting goods in and out of the country.

As Table 3.1 shows, the SAR is the country's biggest 'foreign' investor, accounting for over 50 percent of total foreign capital. The second is the US and the third is Japan. However, it is widely believed that the second largest investor should be Taiwan, much of whose capital has been channeled to Mainland China through Hong Kong because of the restrictive policies of the Taiwan government.

In many ways, China has been benefiting from the continued existence of the Hong Kong dollar, given the fact that the renminbi is not yet a fully convertible currency (Tsang, 1997). Other than using Hong Kong as a source of foreign

Table 3.1   Cumulative investment of registered foreign enterprises in China (as of end-1998)

	Billions of US$
Hong Kong	410.18 (53.0%)*
US	68.76 (8.9%)
Japan	51.50 (6.7%)
Singapore	39.13 (5.1%)
Taiwan	37.50 (4.8%)
UK	20.24 (2.6%)
South Korea	16.96 (2.2%)
Germany	13.80 (1.8%)
Macau	11.92 (1.5%)
France	9.80 (1.3%)

Note: * Bracketed figures represent relative percentages to total foreign direct investment in China.

Source: *China Foreign Economic Statistical Yearbook 1999*, China Statistics Press.

exchange earnings, citizens and enterprises, especially those in southern China, have been hoarding Hong Kong dollars for transactions as well as store-of-value purposes. Table 3A.1 in Appendix A gives a rough estimate of the amount of extra-territorial circulation of the Hong Kong currency in China.

In the earlier years of reforms, hoarding might have been driven by a fear of devaluation of the renminbi, and therefore can be regarded as a form of 'currency substitution'. The situation has been quite different in recent years, particularly after the Deng whirlwind of 1992, when paramount leader Deng Xiaoping urged the country to accelerate its reforms and the pace of growth. Emboldened by the success in the transformation of some of its state-owned enterprises, China expanded its own stock markets in Shanghai and Shenzhen, and allowed a growing number of enterprises to be listed in Hong Kong. That resulted in an explosion of Chinese stocks traded in Hong Kong. At the present, the company with the largest market capitalization in the SAR stock exchange is China Mobile. Together with two other Chinese stocks, China Unicom and CNOOC, the three accounted for about 20 percent of the whole market's capitalization in 2001! There are also others that are called 'red chips' (Hong Kong companies built by Chinese capital) and 'H-shares' (Chinese enterprises listed in Hong Kong), which took another 6 percent of the share in the same year. In short, about one-quarter of the market value of Hong Kong's stock exchange belongs to Chinese-owned or directly related companies. Ten years ago, this was totally unimaginable.

On the other hand, because of the impact of the East Asian financial crisis, Hong Kong plunged into its deepest recession on record. Asset and consumer prices adjusted rapidly, but not deeply enough. Consumer goods, durable and otherwise, plus services in southern China, have become increasingly attractive. A new trend has emerged that Hong Kong people spend their free time consuming in Shenzhen and the Pearl River Delta. Despite the official position (since 1994) that foreign currencies are not allowed to circulate in China (Tsang, 1995), Hong Kong dollars are still easily accepted in daily transactions, at least in the Pearl River Delta, but with a major difference from the past. That is, in retail transactions (particularly in Shenzhen just north of the SAR in Mainland China), Hong Kong dollars are often traded at parity with the renminbi, implying a devaluation of the SAR currency (which is pegged to the US dollar at the rate of 7.80, while the renminbi's exchange rate against the US dollar has been hovering around 8.20–8.30 since 1995). In bulk transactions, though, the prevailing exchange rate is still used.

In other words, the situation is less of currency substitution than 'transaction convenience'. While the credibility of the renminbi has been on the increase, the higher degree of economic integration of Hong Kong and Mainland China reduces transaction costs for Chinese nationals to accept and to store Hong Kong dollars. The other side of the story must also be told; the renminbi is also increasingly accepted for transaction purposes in Hong Kong. Unlike China,

Hong Kong of course allows the circulation of foreign currencies, although the Hong Kong dollar is the only legal tender.

One interesting episode during the East Asian crisis was that Chinese authorities, including no less authoritative a figure than Premier Zhu Rongji, had to declare that the renminbi would not be devalued in order to ward off speculative pressure against the Hong Kong dollar, as if the fate of the two currencies were intertwined. The problems actually had more to do with Hong Kong's own economic development (Tsang, 1994; 1998c) and the defects in Hong Kong's own currency board system (Tsang, 1996b; 1998a, b, c; 1999 a, b). Nevertheless, one is easily reminded of Gresham's Law. But which is the good money? Which is the bad one? One has to be open-minded about it, particularly in the long run.

3.3   THEORIES BEHIND THE STATUS QUO

As Barandiaran and Tsang (1997) argue, supporting the status quo of 'one country, two monetary systems' mirrors a critical assessment of the arguments for monetary unification, the alternative to the coexistence of the two currencies. The situation cannot be compared directly with Europe's ongoing economic integration and monetary unification because of the differences in the political systems. In Europe, monetary unification has been advanced as an instrument of political integration. Nor can it be compared with the reunification of Germany, where the two economic systems were hardly related before the collapse of communism in Eastern Europe, and where monetary unification was a prerequisite for absorbing East Germany rapidly into the West German economic entity. Furthermore, it is unlike the unification of Germany in the 19th century under Bismarck, when political centralization spearheaded by Prussia over the various German states went ahead of monetary and fiscal union (James, 1997). Hong Kong, under the 'one country, two systems' framework, enjoys full autonomy from China except for two things: defense and diplomacy. After all, it is an SAR.

The economic arguments for monetary unification are mainly related to (1) the transaction costs of currencies and (2) the risk posed by exchange rate variations. As far as Mainland China and Hong Kong are concerned, unification would reduce the transaction costs and risk of exchange rate variations only between the Hong Kong dollar and the renminbi, but not between the renminbi and other currencies. The transaction costs and risk between the Hong Kong dollar and the other currencies, on the other hand, are generally perceived to be relatively small.

For China, the value of these benefits is determined mainly by the relative importance of trade and capital flows between China and Hong Kong, being rather high, but not overwhelming. For Hong Kong, though, their value would depend mainly on the impact on trade and capital flows between Hong Kong and countries other than China, which in turn would depend on perceptions about the quality of the renminbi. Only if the renminbi were a perfect substitute for the Hong Kong dollar, would there be no impact. This is unlikely to be the case in the short run.

In conclusion, both the economic benefits and costs of unification are likely to be low in the near term. Moreover, for Hong Kong, the net benefit could be negative. While there is no good economic justification for unifying the two currencies, the questions are how they may coexist and what the Chinese government should do to facilitate any particular form of coexistence.

Three forms of coexistence are distinguished by Barandiaran and Tsang (1997): (1) spontaneous competition; (2) legal competition; and (3) monopoly. The first two forms imply that both currencies may be used by residents of the respective geographical areas for their domestic transactions. Spontaneous competition means that only the renminbi is the legal tender, but at least in some areas of China, residents use both currencies in some domestic transactions and use the Hong Kong dollar in some transactions with Hong Kong counter-parties (and perhaps with other non-residents). Legal competition means that both are legal tender at least in some areas of China (e.g. Shanghai or Shenzhen). Monopoly assumes the strict enforcement of the prohibition of the Hong Kong dollar (or any foreign currency) to circulate in China.

We characterized the situation in 1996–97 as one of spontaneous competition. As it turns out, of course, the situation now is still that of 'spontaneous competition', at least in the Pearl River Delta. But as analyzed above, the competition is now less related to 'currency substitution', than to 'transaction convenience'.

In hindsight, the failure of options (2) and (3) to prevail should not be surprising. With rising confidence about the Chinese economy and concern about 'political correctness', option (2) could not even be brought to the agenda, particularly after the transition of 1997. Monopoly is the official stance. Nevertheless, given the difficulties of strict implementation and the informal benefits of transaction convenience, in some localities at least, it is rather unnecessary to crack down on spontaneous competition, when no harm is done to the renminbi.

3.4   HONG KONG – MAINLAND CHINA: AN OPTIMUM CURRENCY AREA (OCA)?

Given two neighboring countries or territories, each with its own currency, there are two forces conditioning the extent to which the two currencies are used and demanded in both areas. First, the degree of market integration between the two economies conditions the transaction demand for the currencies (i.e., their demands as means of payment). Second, if the two economies are closely integrated, the differences in the quality of the two currencies as determined by the stability of their values and their convertibility into other foreign currencies condition the asset demand for the currencies.

The degree of economic integration between China and Hong Kong is very high in the Pearl River Delta in the Guangdong Province of south China, but it declines rapidly when one moves further north inside the country. On the surface, the process of economic integration between Hong Kong and southern China has been phenomenal; one may ask whether the coexistence of two currencies within a highly integrated economy is beneficial. Nevertheless, one needs to look at the microstructure of integration. In terms of trade, for example, the following table shows some interesting features.

Table 3.2   Shares of China and the US in Hong Kong's external trade

%	1981		2000		2000 (adjusted)*	
	China	US	China	US	China	US
Domestic exports	3.6	36.3	29.9	30.1	10.5	38.4
Re-exports (origin)	19.3	11.5	61.4	4.7	27.2	8.8
Re-exports (destination)	30.7	9.7	35.1	22.3	21.4	27.1
Imports	21.3	10.4	43.1	6.5	13.6	10.3

Note: * The adjustments for year 2000 are to net out the portions estimated by the Hong Kong Census and Statistics Department for outward processing that Hong Kong performed in China, taken from China's figures, and the total of exports and imports in calculating the relative shares of the market by China and the US.

Source: *Hong Kong Monthly Digest of Statistics*, Census and Statistics Department.

If one neglects the phenomenon of outward processing, under which Hong Kong manufacturers take advantage of the cheap labor and other production costs in southern China, one would conclude that China has replaced the US as Hong Kong's number one trading partner. However, adjusted for outward processing, Hong Kong's dependence on the US as the largest market for end products has actually increased, not decreased!

Appendix A, on the other hand, gives estimates of the circulation of the Hong Kong currency (notes and coins) in China. The figures for 1998–2000 are subject to the noise of the East Asian financial crisis and the problems of Y2K, which led to large increases in currency issuance in Hong Kong. Given the rather simplistic methodology that the author has adopted, it tends to exaggerate the increase in extra-territorial circulation. Taking into account other anecdotal evidence, it seems safe to conclude that such circulation has stabilized at about 2 percent of Hong Kong's GDP. In other words, Hong Kong is not winning, and Mainland China is not losing in the process of 'spontaneous competition'.

Ma and Tsang (1999) also attempted some more formal tests on whether Hong Kong and China constituted an 'optimum currency area' (OCA) (Mundell, 1961). Appendix B highlights the major results. In a nutshell, the answer is 'no', not even for Hong Kong and eastern China, which supposedly have had the closest economic ties.

Hence, the empirical conclusion seems quite clear. There is no case for a monetary union any time soon. Since the present situation is not heavily manipulated by government policies, and it reflects, to a large extent, the interplay of economic forces, 'one country, two monetary systems' appears to be the optimal choice.

3.5 OPTIMAL EXIT STRATEGY FOR HONG KONG AND FUTURE MONETARY UNION: A PARADOX

What if we look further, perhaps much further ahead to a time when the renminbi becomes a fully convertible, internationally accepted hard currency, and when the economic integration between Hong Kong and Mainland China turns even more intimate, with a very high degree of factor mobility?

Then how would a monetary union be implemented? The major complication is that Hong Kong practices a currency board system with the Hong Kong dollar pegged to the US dollar, while the renminbi is a floating currency. Politically, reality dictates that the Hong Kong dollar should re-peg and then merge into the renminbi. How should the process be managed?

The unfolding experience of East European currency board regimes, e.g., Estonia and Lithuania – which are applying to join the EMU and the Eurozone – is an interesting reference. Exit from the currency board system becomes quite well defined. One may even argue that it is not really an exit (to some uncertain future or to a 'land of freedom', e.g., re-pegging or floating) but a 're-tracking', i.e., shifting from one track to another track, to take a railway metaphor (Tsang, 2000a).

One possibility is to implement what Lithuania has planned to do. The initial choice of pegging to the US dollar (rather than the German mark) created some problems. As the intention of joining the European Union and the eventual monetary union was made clear (Bank of Lithuania, 1997), a two-currency basket was proposed as a transitional measure to re-tracking (Niaura, 1998). However, the stability of the exchange rate between the euro and the US dollar, among other factors, led the Bank of Lithuania to announce that instead of a basket transition, the litas would be pegged to the euro in the second half of 2001 (Bank of Lithuania, 1999). Eventually, it was declared that the exchange rate would be decided on 1 February 2002 (Bank of Lithuania, 2001).[1]

In any case, there are uncertainties and costs associated with the re-tracking process (e.g., Keller, 2000). First of all, exchange rate uncertainty exists even after unilateral pegging to the euro by aspiring currency board regimes. (In Lithuania's case, it seems to have had the blessing of the European Central Bank (ECB) for the timing of its horizontal re-pegging.) Re-negotiation of the central rate against the euro may be required to reach an agreement for joining the monetary union. Depending on the perceived size of the required rate realignment, which could range from zero to something rather significant, speculative capital movements might emerge. Given that EU and then EMU membership will involve the fulfillment of many criteria, the re-tracking cost, i.e., costs incurred to facilitate the process by potentially painful fiscal, monetary and other economic policies, could also be substantial; various measures might not be fully consistent with each other. Finally, a currency board regime is a fixed exchange rate system, but the euro floats. There will therefore be other technical and behavioral adjustments that an economy making such an exit (entry) has to go through.

Can Hong Kong go the Lithuanian way, some time in the future, as an intermediate step to join the renminbi-zone? Probably yes, and the convergence problems may be easier to handle, if both Hong Kong and China work from a position of strength. Nevertheless, feasibility is one issue, desirability is another. On the latter, much more complicated issues of optimum currency areas are involved, ranging from trade, real and nominal convergence, risk sharing mechanisms as well as factor mobility, which are outside the confines of this chapter (see Tsang, 2002).

Assuming that the conditions for monetary union could be attained in the long run, a more troublesome problem with near-term impact for Hong Kong is the transition period required for that future end state. Despite the East Asian financial crisis, which led to deep deflation in Hong Kong, the SAR remains very expensive as an operating hub and an international financial center. Critics are widely calling for the abolition of the peg and the abandonment of the currency board system. They regard devaluation or re-floating as the best way to restore competitiveness for the SAR economy.

This is a vastly controversial subject. The author will only deal with one aspect of it here, taking some hints from what Argentina announced recently during the gathering financial storm and introduce a little 'innovation', if only in concept: an 'irrelevant currency paradox'.

As shown in Appendix C, one way for a currency board regime to reduce pain arising from a misaligned peg (in the fundamental sense) is to shift to a basket including an 'irrelevant currency'. The euro fulfils to a certain extent such a requirement for Hong Kong (though not in the case of Argentina because Europe is the country's second largest trading partner after Brazil). So if necessary, Hong Kong can announce a re-peg to a two-currency basket (the US dollar and the euro) with equal weights (50–50), and hope for a weakening euro to save the day for the domestic economy.

The trouble, though, is that this short-term expedient measure, even if it is viable, comes into conflict with Hong Kong's long-term objective: a future monetary union with the Chinese renminbi. A US\$ – euro basket peg would make life rather complicated, should Hong Kong want to move to a merger with the renminbi.

3.6   CONCLUSIONS

The experiment of 'one country, two monetary systems' as practiced in Hong Kong under Chinese sovereignty is a rather unique one, given the institutional differences and the developmental asymmetry. However, China is catching up fast, indeed very fast. Therefore, although there is still scant argument for a monetary union between Hong Kong and China any time soon, one may be tempted to be a futurologist, inclined to observe closely and, if possible, to draw some lessons from the convergence problems of East European currency board regimes in their entry to the Eurozone. The proposal of a two-currency basket transition is also worthy of looking into. One caveat is of course that Hong Kong is not eager to form a monetary union with Mainland China, nor vice versa.

APPENDIX A

Following the method of Asian Monetary Monitor (1990), we model the normal pattern of currency-to-GDP (C/GDP) ratio in Hong Kong as the economy matures. Any 'above normal' amount of currency in circulation (notes and coins) may then be interpreted as extra-territorial demand, i.e., circulation in southern China (and Macau, which we neglect here to simplify our analysis). International experience shows that a currency-to-GDP ratio of about 4 percent is a norm for a mature economy. We first fitted various equations of the form:

$$Y = a + b/X^n \qquad (3.1)$$

where Y is the actual currency-to-GDP ratio over the years, a is constrained to 0.04, and X is a time trend variable (66 representing the year 1966, 67 representing 1967 ... etc.). As X becomes larger, b/X^n will approach zero. Y will then come close to 0.04. We found that the equation:

$$Y = 0.04 + 187364000/X^{5.1} \tag{3.2}$$

gave the best fit for the period of 1966–87. The R^2 statistic was 0.9104. The equation was then used to extrapolate the value of Y for 1988–2000. The fitted values of Y in those years represent what currency-to-GDP ratios should have existed in Hong Kong if there had been no extra-territorial circulation of Hong Kong currency in (southern) China during those years. Table 3A.1 summarizes the simulation results.

Table 3A.1   Estimates of Hong Kong currency circulating in China

Year	(1) Actual C/GDP (%)	(2) Fitted C/GDP (%)	(1)–(2) Extra-Hong Kong C/GDP (%)	Estimated (HK$ million)	
1988	7.49	6.32	1.18	5437	
1989	7.57	6.19	1.38	7246	(35.50%)
1990	7.43	6.07	1.36	7896	(9.00%)
1991	7.36	5.97	1.40	9334	(18.20%)
1992	7.85	5.88	1.99	15518	(66.20%)
1993	8.01	5.80	2.25	20187	(30.10%)
1994	7.72	5.72	2.05	20747	(2.80%)
1995	7.39	5.64	1.80	19947	(−3.90%)
1996	7.31	5.43	1.88	22408	(12.30%)
1997	7.00	5.38	1.62	21446	(−4.30%)
1998	7.34	5.31	2.03	25564	(19.20%)
1999	10.10	5.24	4.86	59664	(133.40%)
1999*	8.24	5.24	3.00	36830	(44.10%)
2000	8.32	5.18	3.14	39780	

Note: * The 1999 figure is adjusted using normal year-end cyclical pattern in lieu of the Y2K effects.

The estimated amount of HK$15.5 billion for the year of 1992 is indeed very close to that of HK$15 billion in Yam (1994), which does not specify the exact year to which the estimate applies. The findings for 1992–93 show evidence that there was an increase in the extent of currency substitution (of the renminbi by the Hong Kong dollar) in China, as the quality of the renminbi deteriorated.

However, the situation was reversed in 1994–97, when the successful effects of the 1994 reforms surfaced and the Chinese currency achieved 'Article VIII convertibility' in late 1996 (Tsang, 1997).

The figures from 1998 onwards are difficult to interpret. First, the Hong Kong dollar was under unprecedented attacks from October 1997, and speculation spread to the stock market in 1998. As a result, the government had to make a historic move to intervene in the stock market in August 1998. In any case, Hong Kong plunged into the deepest recession since reliable statistics were available in the early 1960s, and a serious process of asset deterioration as well as deflation set in. Moreover, the 'Y2K' problem at the end of 1999, when banks deliberately 'overstocked' cash, also clouds any meaningful analysis.

APPENDIX B

Ma and Tsang (1999) implemented some formal tests on whether Hong Kong and China constituted an optimum currency area (OCA) (Mundell, 1961). Two major empirical tests were used: (1) the variance method, and (2) the shocks decomposition method. Tables 3B.1 and 3B.2 sample just two of the major findings that returned a negative answer, as yet.

The first approach focuses on the deviations of key variables between Mainland China and Hong Kong, as well as those between major regions in the Mainland and Hong Kong. Most variables such as GDP and investment growth rates can be modeled by conventional analysis. Table 3B.1 presents the results on real GDP growth.

The second analytical technique applies a principal components analysis to decompose common shocks to economic variables in different regions into symmetric and asymmetric shocks. This is complementary to von Hagen and Neumann's (1994) individual shock approach. One example of this approach is Caporale (1993), which Ma and Tsang (1999) adapted and extended. The mainstream view is that if the symmetric contributions outweigh the asymmetric contributions for a particular economy in a region, it would constitute evidence that the economy would derive net benefit by being a member of the region, i.e., the region has the potential to form an OCA. If asymmetric contributions of common shocks predominate, an OCA would then be regarded as undesirable. As shown in Table 3B.2, where both variance and decomposition results are presented, asymmetric shocks prevailed in Hong Kong, even when compared to the coastal regions of China, with which it has had the closest economic relationship.

Table 3B.1   Annual real GDP growth of 28 regions of Mainland China and Hong Kong from 1978 to 1995

Region	Standard Deviation	%
Beijing	0.049719	(+5.5)
Tianjin	0.064501	(+36.9)
Hebei	0.039888	(−15.4)
Shanxi	0.051596	(+9.5)
Inner Mongolia	0.045992	(−2.4)
Liaoning	0.040040	(−15.0)
Jilin	0.052028	(+10.4)
Heilongjiang	0.046250	(−1.9)
Shanghai	0.036820	(−21.9)
Jiangsu	0.049079	(+4.1)
Zhejiang	0.048911	(+3.8)
Anhui	0.056235	(+19.3)
Fujian	0.052644	(+11.7)
Jiangxi	0.041745	(−11.4)
Shandong	0.039777	(−15.6)
Henan	0.049455	(+4.9)
Hubei	0.043099	(− 8.6)
Hunan	0.036184	(−23.2)
Guangdong	0.046012	(−2.4)
Guangxi	0.051775	(+9.9)
Sichuan	0.040462	(−14.1)
Guizhou	0.045991	(−2.4)
Yunnan	0.043089	(−8.6)
Shaanxi	0.045444	(−3.6)
Gansu	0.053316	(+13.1)
Qinghai	0.059695	(+26.7)
Ningxia	0.046769	(−0.8)
Xinjiang	0.043000	(−8.8)
Hong Kong	0.057156	(+21.3)
Mainland China (excluding HK)	0.047126	

Note: * The period under investigation is 1978–95. The figures in brackets represent the percentage divergence of the standard deviation from China's national average (excluding HK). Due to the insufficiency of observations, the principal component analyses cannot be conducted for the annual series, and because of data unavailability, Hainan and Tibet are not included.

Table 3B.2   Annual real GDP growth rates of 11 coastal regions of Mainland China and Hong Kong from 1978 to 1995*

	Standard Deviation	%	Shocks Decomposition		
			Symmetric	Asymmetric	Total
Beijing	0.055146	(+23.1)	100.000	0.000	100.00
Tianjin	0.063840	(+42.5)	74.476	25.524	100.00
Hebei	0.041415	(−7.6)	100.000	0.000	100.00
Liaoning	0.042949	(−4.2)	95.303	4.697	100.00
Shanghai	0.035176	(−21.5)	100.000	0.000	100.00
Jiangsu	0.046599	(+4.0)	100.000	0.000	100.00
Zhejiang	0.042396	(−5.4)	80.207	19.793	100.00
Fujian	0.043754	(−2.4)	81.306	18.694	100.00
Shandong	0.035165	(−21.5)	56.606	43.394	100.00
Guangdong	0.040867	(−8.8)	65.559	34.441	100.00
Guangxi	0.045643	(+1.9)	67.603	32.397	100.00
Hong Kong	0.058990	(+31.6)	29.862	70.138	100.00
Coastal regions (excluding HK)	0.044813				

Note: * The figure in brackets represents the percentage divergence of the standard deviation from China's national average. Due to data unavailability, Hainan is not included in this table.

APPENDIX C

Optimal exit strategy from a currency board through a basket: The 'equivalence condition' and the 'irrelevant currency paradox'. (Ma and Tsang, 1999)

Thanks are due to Yue Ma for alerting the author to the equivalence issue, which was implicit in the author's previous studies (Tsang, 1996a; 1999a). They have collaborated in working out the 'equivalence condition' presented here. However, the 'irrelevant currency paradox' is the author's own addition and extension.

Suppose there are two currencies: the domestic one is the peso, the foreign counterpart is the US$. Initially, the peso is pegged to the US$ under a currency board regime. Now to get out of a misaligned peg (e.g., the strength of the US$ is generating unbearable pain on the domestic economy), a temporary basket peg, even for a currency board, may be an 'optimal' strategy. But other foreign currencies to be introduced to the basket have to be 'irrelevant'. Moreover, they should be weak currencies, tending towards depreciation against the US$. This is the gist of the 'irrelevance paradox'.

To take an example that has realistic implications (without any intended paradoxical meanings). Let us imagine a shift from a single currency peg (to the US$) to a two-currency peg under a currency board system. The 'irrelevant and weak currency' is the euro. In the true spirit of the 'AEL model', the model of Argentina, Estonia and Lithuania (Tsang, 1998b; 1999b), can arbitrage hold the basket peg? Why not?

First let us prove that the shift to the two-currency basket is equivalent to a shift to an implicit index peg only under certain conditions. We call that the 'equivalence condition'.

What the government needs to do is to assign weights to the two currencies at day one of transition:

$$1 \text{ peso} = a.\text{US\$} + b.\text{US\$} \tag{3.3}$$

where the weights sum up to one: i.e. $a + b = 1$. This implies that:

$$\text{US\$/peso} = a + b.\text{US\$/euro} \tag{3.4}$$

This is what Argentina has announced that it would do, when US\$/euro = 1.0, i.e. parity.[2]

To look at the matter from an index perspective, if the authority is going to defend the weighted-average index of the two-currency basket (compared with Tsang, 1999a), we have the general formula:

$$c.\text{peso/US\$} + d.\text{peso/euro} = \text{Io} \tag{3.5}$$

where c and d are again relative weights ($c + d = 1$), and Io is the initial index value.

Multiply (3.5) by US\$/peso, we have

$$c + d.\text{US\$/euro} = \text{US\$/peso.Io} \tag{3.6}$$

Hence,

$$\text{US\$/peso} = c/\text{Io} + (d/\text{Io}). \text{ US\$/euro} \tag{3.7}$$

It is obvious that equation (3.7) and equation (3.4) will be identical if $a = c/\text{Io}$ and $b = d/\text{Io}$ simultaneously. Only then will the peso/US\$ exchange rate be the same under either weights assignment and index peg. Now for the sake of political acceptance, the shift better not involve any change in the peso/US\$ rate in day one. Given that constraint, this 'equivalence condition' will be obtained if the authority starts the shift for the peso from the single peg to the two-currency basket peg when the exchange rate of euro/US$ equals one. That is what Argentina said it would do. Then Io must be unity and a = b; c = d. If in day one, euro/US$ (or trivially, US$/euro) is not on parity, equivalence will not hold. If monetary authority wants to stick to equivalence, c and d will have to be changed frequently, assuming that Io is more difficult to be modified.[3] Such changes of index weights may create confusion in the market. This could be one of the reasons why Argentina said that the shift would take place only when parity is achieved.

The merit of having continued equivalence is basically that of simplicity and transparency. In a nutshell, the two arrangements, assigning weights to the two currencies and the defense of an index, are then identical. Pegging the domestic currency to two foreign currencies with assigned weights is equivalent to pegging to their weighted-average index.

This shift may be a viable exit strategy for a currency board regime (Tsang, 2000a) because the effective domestic purchasing power under the convertibility undertaking (from one peso to one US$ to one peso equal to half US$ and half euro) is guaranteed. The trouble is that the regime has to wait for the arrival of the parity, which is uncertain. (Argentina has been using tariffs and subsidies to achieve the de facto effect, but that is another story.)

So much for the equivalence condition. The trick for the currency board regime is this: whether the 'equivalence condition' holds or not, the peso/US$ exchange rate will 'dance to the tune' of the euro/US$ (cf. Tsang, 1996a; 1999a), over which it has no control. Assuming that the currency board regime could make the transition politically acceptable through the equivalence condition, the 'exit' from the misaligned single peg to an excessively strong US$ lies in its expectations about the future euro/US$ exchange rate. After day one, for example, if the euro depreciates against the US$ (i.e. euro/US$ increases in magnitude, or US$/euro decreases in magnitude), the peso/US$ exchange rate will also depreciate, no matter whether we look at equation (3.4) or equation (3.7), and irrespective of their equivalence! The trouble is that the expectations of a weak euro may not materialize.

In any case, it is also obvious from both equations that the peso will appreciate against the euro in both systems. That is exactly why the euro has to be 'irrelevant' (which is actually not the case for Argentina). The reason is that the currency board regime then has no need to worry about the negative effects of the depreciation of the euro on the domestic economy, for example, undermining competitiveness or importing deflation (or inflation, depending on the economic structures and relationships), etc. In other words, with a weak euro, the peso will strengthen against the euro but weaken against the US$, although the basket index remains the same. But if the domestic country has very little trade and other economic exchanges with the Eurozone, but a lot with the US$-zone, this basket peg would represent a de facto devaluation against US$.

One crucial question is the loss of immediacy and transparency in a basket peg. So far, no currency boards have pegged to more than a single currency; and regimes that peg to a basket usually do not announce the weights and the formula – and they are not very different from crawling pegs or dirty float, from the perspective of foreign exchange market participants.

Modern analysis of currency board regimes (particularly the AEL model) has emphasized the use of market forces (instead of government intervention) to hold the spot exchange rate, just like under the old gold standard (Tsang, 1996a,b; 1998b; 1999b). Even Hong Kong, with very deep pockets in terms of foreign exchange reserves, had to partially adopt the model in the 'seven technical measures' of September 1998 by providing a firm, albeit one-way convertibility undertaking, so that market arbitrage could be done (Tsang, 1998c; 2000b). Can arbitrage efficiency be strong enough to hold a basket peg under a currency board regime? In normal times, theoretical three-way arbitrage could do the job, and there should not be serious problems. In crises, it may be a challenge (see e.g. Taylor [1989] for a general treatise of arbitrage).

Moreover, if the euro is irrelevant to the economy, it may also be irrelevant to different sectors and citizens to various degrees. How would they respond to the basket shift and how should they hedge against the risk in the changes of the euro/US\$ exchange rate? These are open questions that it is not possible to venture into here.

In any case, the author's 'paradox', largely pedagogical in nature, is just an intuition about a possible way to exit from a currency board: choose a weak, and *irrelevant* currency to be incorporated into the basket when you have been 'wrongly' pegged to a single strong one. You may with some justification say that you are sticking to a currency board, particularly as you still defend the effective purchasing power of the convertibility undertaking, although in effect you are half-exiting from the peg to that irritating US\$!

NOTES

1. The litas was pegged to the euro at 3.4528 on 2 February 2002, in accordance with the euro/US\$ exchange rate announced by the ECB on 1 February.
2. Post-conference note: the Argentine currency board system later collapsed without any shift to a basket. Parity between the US\$ and euro did not materialize before the collapse anyway.
3. Of course, if the authority wants to ensure equivalence at all costs, it can always change the peso/US\$ rate in day one as well. With two unknowns in two equations, equivalence will obviously hold forever for equations (3.4) and (3.7). However, changing the peso/US\$ exchange rate immediately is a rather dramatic 'exit', further undermining the image of the continuation of the currency board. Here we start from the premise that the original single peg rate is not changed in day one. This is equal to introducing a third equation (a constraint) that peso/US\$ = k, k being the original peg rate.

REFERENCES

Asian Monetary Monitor (1990), 'An Estimate of HK's Currency Circulating in Guangdong Province', *Asian Monetary Monitor*, July–August, pp. 37–44.

Bank of Lithuania (1997), *The Monetary and Policy Framework for 1997–99*.

Bank of Lithuania (1999), *Statement of the Bank of Lithuania*, 13 October.

Bank of Lithuania (2001), *On the Litas Peg to the Euro*, News Releases, 28 June.

Barandiaran, Edgardo and Tsang Shu-ki (1997), 'One Country, Two Currencies: Monetary Relations Between Hong Kong and China', in Warren Cohen and Li Zhao (eds), *Hong Kong under Chinese Rule: The Economic and Political Implications of Reversion*, Cambridge University Press, pp. 133–54.

Caporale, G.M. (1993), 'Is Europe an Optimum Currency Area? Symmetric versus Asymmetric Shocks in the EC', *National Institute Economic Review*, **144**, pp. 95–103.

Chan Man-hung and Tsang Shu-ki (1985), *Shenzhen Pou Xi (Anatomy of Shenzhen)*, Hong Kong, CERD Consultants (in Chinese).

Chen Yuan (1996), '*Monetary Relations between China and Hong Kong*', speech at Bank of England Seminar on Hong Kong Monetary Arrangements through 1997, London, 10 September.

von Hagen, J. and Neumann, M.J.M. (1994), 'Real Exchange Rates within and between Currency Areas: How Far Away is EMU?', *Review of Economics and Statistics*, **126**, pp. 236–44.

James, Harold (1997), 'Monetary and Fiscal Unification in Nineteenth-Century Germany: What can Kohl Learn from Bismarck', *Princeton Essays in International Finance*, **202**.

Keller, Peter M. (2000), *Recent Experience with Currency Boards and Fixed Exchange Rates in the Baltic Countries and Bulgaria and Some Lessons for the Future*, paper presented at the Seminar on Currency Boards – Experience and Prospects, Eesti Pank, 5–6 May, Tallinn: posted on www.ee/epbe/en/seminar_2000_05_05-06/.

Kwon, Goohoon (1997), 'Experience with Monetary Integration and Lessons for Korean Unification', *IMF Working Paper*, WpP/97/65.

Ma, Yue and Tsang, Shu-ki (1999), *Do Hong Kong and China Constitute an Optimum Currency Area?*, mimeo.

Mundell, Robert A. (1961), 'A Theory of Optimum Currency Areas', *American Economic Review*, **51**, pp. 657–65.

Niaura, Janos (1998), '*The Experience of Lithuania in Adopting and then Exiting from the Currency Board System (Monetary Reforms in Lithuania)*', keynote speech delivered at the International Conference on Exchange Rate Stability and Currency Board Economics, Hong Kong Baptist University, 28–29 October.

Taylor, Mark P. (1989), 'Covered Interest Arbitrage and Market Turbulence', *Economic Journal*, **99**, June, pp. 376–91.

Tsang Shu-ki (1994), 'The Economy', in Donald McMillen and Man Si-wai (eds), *The Other Hong Kong Report 1994*, Hong Kong: The Chinese University Press, 1994, pp. 125–48.

Tsang Shu-ki (1995) 'Financial Restructuring', in Lo Chi Kin, Suzanne Pepper and Tsui Kai Yuen (eds), *The China Review 1995*, Hong Kong: The Chinese University Press, chapter 21.

Tsang Shu-ki (1996a), *A Study of the Linked Exchange Rate System and Policy Options for Hong Kong*, a report commissioned by the Hong Kong Policy Research Institute, October (not published).

Tsang Shu-ki (1996b), 'The Linked Rate System: through 1998 and into the 21st Century', in Nyaw Mee-kau and Li Si-ming (eds), *The Other Hong Kong Report 1996*, The Chinese University Press, 1996, chapter 11.

Tsang Shu-ki (1997), 'Towards the Full Convertibility of the Renminbi?', in Maurice Brosseau, Kuan Hsin-chi and Y.Y. Kueh (eds), *The China Review 1997*, Hong Kong: The Chinese University Press, chapter 7.

Tsang, Shu-ki (1998a), *The Hong Kong Government's Review Report: An Interpretation and a Response*, paper posted on the website www.hkbu.edu.hk/~sktsang.

Tsang, Shu-ki (1998b), 'The Case for Adopting the Convertible Reserves System in Hong Kong', *Pacific Economic Review*, **3**(3), pp. 265–75.

Tsang, Shu-ki (1998c), *Welcome on Board the AEL Model, Hong Kong, but ...* , paper posted on www.hkbu.edu.hk/~sktsang.

Tsang, Shu-ki (1999a), *A Study of the Linked Exchange Rate System and Policy Options for Hong Kong*, Hong Kong Policy Research Institute, January.

Tsang, Shu-ki (1999b), 'Fixing the Exchange Rate through a Currency Board Arrangement: Efficiency Risk, Systemic Risk and Exit Cost', *Asian Economic Journal*, **13**(3), pp. 239–66.

Tsang, Shu-ki (2000a), *Commitment to and Exit Strategies from a CBA*, paper presented at the Seminar on Currency Boards – Experience and Prospects, Bank of Estonia (Eesti Pank), 5–6 May, Tallinn: posted on www.hkbu.edu.hk/~sktsang.

Tsang, Shu-ki (2000b), *The Evolution and Prospects of the Hong Kong CBA*, paper presented at the Bank of Estonia, 8 May, Tallinn: posted on www.hkbu.edu.hk/~sktsang.

Tsang, Shu-ki (2002), 'From "One Country, Two Systems" to Monetary Integration?', *HKIMR Working Paper*, No. 15, Hong Kong Institute for Monetary Research, 28 pages.

Wu Chouzhong (1998), *Zhong Guo Zhi Bi Yan Jiu (A Study of Chinese Currency Notes)*, Shanghai: Shanghai Old Books Publishing Company (in Chinese).

Yam, Joseph (1994), 'Monetary Developments in China and Implications for Hong Kong', in *The Practice of Central Banking in Hong Kong*, Hong Kong Monetary Authority.

Yam, Joseph (1996), '*Hong Kong's Monetary Scene: Myths and Realities*', speech at Bank of England Seminar on Hong Kong Monetary Arrangements through 1997, London, 10 September.

4.   The role of the yen in East Asia

Takatoshi Ito

4.1   INTRODUCTION

The impact of the new currency, the euro, has been assessed by East Asia as a symbol of new Europe as a second-largest economy, the place Japan had maintained for more than a decade. The euro is expected to become, if not already, a key currency in the global currency market, rivaling the US dollar. Although the Japanese yen had been the currency of the second largest country, the use of the yen was not as widespread as one could expect. An interesting question is whether the Japanese yen is being adversely affected by the emergence of the euro or not, as the euro is becoming an alternative to the US dollar, or is it helped by it as a part of the alternatives to the US dollar together with euro. This remains to be seen. The interest of this chapter is more narrowly focused on the use of the yen in East Asia, since the influence of the yen is expected to be stronger in neighboring regions. The objective of this chapter is, however, twofold. First, the international use of the yen as a currency is reviewed. The so-called internationalization of the yen will be discussed. Second, the exchange rate policy of East Asian countries will be discussed. The role of the yen in their exchange rate movements, or so-called basket currency regimes, will also be examined.

A currency is said to be used internationally when large shares of trades are denominated and settled in the currency, and asset and debt instruments denominated in the currency are held outside the country. According to these criteria, the internationalization of the yen is far behind the US dollar in the global market. In East Asia, the use of the Japanese yen is higher than that in the global arena. However, the degree of the use of Japan's currency in East Asia is much lower than expected from its influence in trade and investment.

One of the reasons that the Asian countries fell into currency crises was that East Asian countries had inappropriately adopted the *de facto* dollar peg. Most currencies in East Asia were floated after the crisis. However, their exchange rates were not completely left to market forces. Monetary, fiscal and intervention policies have been employed to limit the volatility of exchange rates. This is understandable because exports are still an important engine of Asian economies, and large volatility is known to harm trade and investment. Then, what kind of guiding principle should a country follow in allowing flexibility, while some stability in exchange rates is also sought? It will be argued that a policy to stabilize the *real effective* exchange rate is important. This will imply that for East Asian countries, the weight of the yen in the basket should increase. This point will be elaborated on in later sections.

4.2   INTERNATIONAL USE OF THE YEN

4.2.1   Definition

Many economists have studied the use of this currency in global markets. A currency is said to be used as an important international currency, when trade and investment are denominated and settled in that currency, and assets denominated in the currency are held by foreign nationals as a regular portfolio. Table 4.1 summarizes several aspects of the international usage of currency, sorted by role. By any measure, the yen seems to be under-used compared to its economic might, the second largest economy in the world or the third largest economy if the euro-currency area is considered as one national entity.

Table 4.1   Conditions for the international currency

	Private Sector	Public Sector
Unit of account	Invoice currency	Currency peg
Settlement	Settlement currency	Intervention peg
Storage of value	Portfolio investment	Foreign reserves

Source: Krugman (1984).

4.2.2   Invoice Currency

The following regularities in invoicing practices of international trade have been observed from Table 4.2:[1]

1.   Trade between industrial countries is denominated mainly in the exporter's currency, much less so in the importer's currency, and rarely in a third currency.

2. In trade between an industrial and developing country, the currency of the industrial country, or the third currency (mainly the US dollar) is used.
3. The currency with high inflation is less likely to be used than the currency with low inflation.
4. Commodities are invoiced in US dollars (and much less in sterling).
5. The US dollar is the only currency that is used much more than its indigenous trade value.

Figure 4.1 and Table 4.2 show the invoice currency of Japanese exports and imports (surveyed by the Ministry of International Trade before 1998, and the Ministry of Finance, after 2001). The yen-denominated export ratio peaked at 43 percent in 1993, and then declined to 34 percent in 2001, while the yen-denominated import ratio has been stable since 1995 at around 20–24 percent. The yen ratio of exports is consistently higher than the yen ratio of imports, which is consistent with a general tendency of the currency. Both exports to, and imports from, the United States are mostly denominated in US dollars. This is also a tendency observed in other currencies.

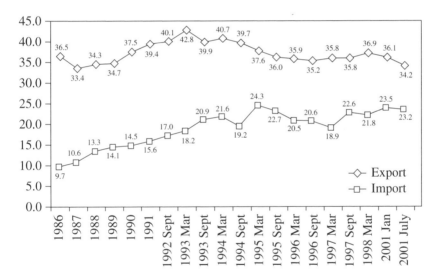

Figure 4.1   Ratio of yen-invoiced exports and imports

What is peculiar in the case of the yen is that the yen ratio of exports to and imports from Southeast Asia remains relatively low. According to general economic principles, trade between an advanced country (such as Japan) and developing countries (such as those in Southeast Asia) should be denominated in the advanced country's currency (the yen), but in reality, the ratio of the US

East Asia's monetary future

dollar is equal (in the case of exports) or greater (in the case of imports) than the ratio of the yen in this trading. The yen is clearly under-used in trade between Japan and Asia.

Table 4.2   Invoice currency of Japan by region

Exports %	World			US			EU			East Asia		
	Yen	US$	*	Yen	US$	*	Yen	US$	*	Yen	US$	*
1992 Sep	40.1	46.6	13.1	16.6	83.2	0.1	40.3	11.1	48.4	52.3	41.6	5.9
1993 Sep	39.9	48.4	11.7	16.5	83.3	0.2	41.0	7.5	51.5	52.5	44.3	3.2
1994 Sep	39.7	48.3	12.0	19.0	80.8	0.2	36.6	9.0	54.4	49.0	47.9	3.1
1995 Mar	37.6	51.5	10.9	17.5	82.3	0.2	37.2	11.3	51.5	47.2	49.9	2.9
1995 Sep	36.0	52.5	11.5	17.0	82.9	0.1	34.9	12.2	52.9	44.3	53.4	2.3
1996 Mar	35.9	53.1	10.9	15.9	83.9	0.2	36.1	12.5	51.3	44.1	53.5	2.3
1996 Sep	35.2	53.3	11.5	14.5	85.4	0.1	33.3	12.4	54.4	46.3	51.3	2.4
1997 Mar	35.8	52.8	11.3	16.6	83.2	0.2	34.3	13.4	52.3	45.5	51.7	2.7
1997 Sep	35.8	52.1	12.1	15.3	84.5	0.2	34.2	12.3	53.5	47.0	50.2	2.7
1998 Mar	36.0	51.2	12.9	15.7	84.1	0.1	34.9	13.2	51.9	48.4	48.7	2.9
2001 Jan	36.1	52.4	11.5	13.2	86.7	0.1	33.5	13.0	53.5	50.0	48.2	1.8
2001 Jul	34.2	53.0	12.8	12.5	87.4	0.1	30.4	12.8	56.8	49.0	48.9	2.1

Imports %	World			US			EU			East Asia		
	Yen	US$	*	Yen	US$	*	Yen	US$	*	Yen	US$	*
1992 Sep	17.0	74.5	8.5	13.8	86.0	0.2	31.7	17.9	50.4	23.8	73.9	2.3
1993 Sep	20.9	72.4	6.7	13.8	86.1	0.1	45.0	18.2	36.8	25.7	72.0	2.3
1994 Sep	19.2	73.9	7.0	13.3	86.4	0.3	38.6	21.9	39.5	23.6	74.2	2.2
1995 Mar	24.3	68.9	6.8	18.4	80.9	0.6	40.6	20.2	39.2	34.1	64.2	1.7
1995 Sep	22.7	70.2	7.1	21.5	78.4	0.2	44.8	16.1	39.2	26.2	71.9	2.0
1996 Mar	20.5	72.2	7.3	17.5	82.7	0.1	40.9	15.3	43.0	23.9	74.1	2.0
1996 Sep	20.6	72.4	6.9	16.4	83.2	0.4	46.1	12.5	41.5	24.0	73.8	2.3

Imports %	World			US			EU			East Asia		
	Yen	US$	*	Yen	US$	*	Yen	US$	*	Yen	US$	*
1997 Mar	18.9	74.0	7.1	14.2	85.6	0.2	41.3	17.0	41.7	23.3	74.9	1.7
1997 Sep	22.6	70.8	6.6	22.0	77.8	0.2	49.3	13.1	37.7	25.0	73.0	1.9
1998 Mar	21.8	71.5	6.7	16.9	83.0	0.1	44.3	14.3	41.4	26.7	71.6	1.7
2001 Jan	23.5	70.7	5.8	20.8	78.7	0.5	49.7	17.5	32.8	24.8	74.0	1.2
2001 Jul	23.2	70.4	6.4	20.5	78.8	0.7	48.1	16.9	35.0	24.2	74.5	1.3

Note: * Means other currencies. East Asia includes ASEAN countries, Korea, Taiwan, Hong Kong, India, Pakistan, Sri Lanka, Maldives, Bangladesh, East Timor, Macao, Afghanistan, Nepal and Bhutan.

Source: MITI (up to 1998); Ministry of Finance (after 2001).

4.2.3 Foreign Exchange Transactions

Once every three years, the Bank of International Settlements conducts a survey of foreign exchange transactions; this includes transaction volumes in each financial center, their currency compositions and other statistics. Tables 4.3 and 4.4 show the total size of foreign exchange transactions and their currency pairs from 1989 to 2001. According to the most recent survey (April 2001), the daily transaction volume of foreign exchange amounts to 1.2 trillion dollars, down from 1.5 trillion dollars in 1998. Of the currency pairs in transactions, 90 percent of the transactions involved US dollars on one side of the transaction. The euro had 38 percent (higher than the German mark, with 30 percent in 1998); the yen with 23 percent (up from 20 percent in 1998, but lower than 27 percent in 1989), while the pound sterling showed 13 percent (up from 11 percent in 1998). (Note that the total is 200 percent, since one transaction involves two currencies.) In fact, the ratio of the yen had declined from 1989 to 1995, and then increased slightly to the level of 1992.

Table 4.3   Global foreign exchange market turnover, daily averages, April

Turnover Item (US$ billions)	1989	1992	1995	1998	2001
Spot transactions	317	394	494	568	387
Outright forward	27	58	97	128	131
Foreign exchange swaps	190	324	546	734	656
Estimated gaps in reporting (**)	56	44	53	60	36
TOTAL 'traditional' turnover	590	820	1,190	1,490	1,210
Turnover at April 2001 exchange rates (*)	570	750	990	1,400	1,210

Note: Adjusted for local and cross-border double counting. Single asterisks (*) denote non-US dollar pegs of foreign currency transactions were converted into original currency amounts at average exchange rates for April of each survey year and then reconverted into US dollar amounts at average April 2001 exchange rates. Double asterisks (**) means estimated by BIS.

Source: Bank of International Settlements, October 2001. See also Bank of Japan, www.boj.or.jp/siryo/stat/glo0104.htm.

Table 4.5 shows currency transactions by financial centers. London is the largest, with transactions of 637 billion dollars a day, followed by New York with 351 billion dollars. Third place goes to Tokyo, but the status of Tokyo as the international money center is also threatened. Transaction volumes of Tokyo have declined from 161 billion dollars a day in 1995 to 136 billion dollars a day in 1998, giving third place to Singapore. The volume of transactions in Tokyo recovered to 147 billion dollars a day in 2001, regaining the third place in the world financial centers.

Table 4.4   Currency distribution – percentages of average daily turnover, global foreign exchange market, April

Currency	1989	1992	1995	1998	2001
US dollar	90.00	82.00	83.30	87.30	90.40
Euro	–	–	–	–	37.60
German mark	27.00	39.60	36.10	30.10	–
Japanese yen	27.00	23.40	24.10	20.20	22.70
Pound sterling (UK)	15.00	13.60	9.40	11.00	13.20
French franc	2.00	3.80	7.90	5.10	–
Swiss franc	10.00	8.40	7.30	7.10	6.10
Canadian dollar	1.00	3.30	3.40	3.60	4.50
Australian dollar	2.00	2.50	2.70	3.10	4.20
ECU and other EMS currencies	4.00	11.80	15.70	17.30	–
Others	22.00	11.60	10.10	–	–
Total	200.00	200.00	200.00	200.00	200.00

Note: Because two currencies are included in each transaction, the sum of the percentage shares of individual currencies totals 200 percent instead of 100 percent. The figures relate to reported 'net-net' turnover, i.e., they are adjusted for both local and cross-border double-counting, except for 1989 data, which are available only on a 'gross-gross' basis.

Source: BIS, Central Bank Survey of Foreign Exchange and Derivatives Market Activity in April 2001: Preliminary Global Data, Press Release, 9 October 2001.

Table 4.5   Geographical distribution, global foreign exchange market turnover – daily averages, April, US$ billions and percentages

Country	1989		1992		1995		1998		2001	
	$Bil.	(%)	$Bil.	(%)	$Bil.	(%)	$Bil.	(%)	$Bil.	(%)
UK	184	25.60	291	27.00	464	29.50	637	32.50	504	31.10
US	115	16.00	167	15.50	244	15.50	351	17.90	252	15.70
Japan	111	15.50	120	11.20	161	10.20	136	6.90	147	9.10
Singapore	55	7.70	74	6.90	105	6.70	139	7.10	101	6.20
Germany	–	–	55	5.10	76	4.80	94	4.80	88	5.50
Switzerland	56	7.80	66	6.10	87	5.50	82	4.20	71	4.40
Hong Kong	49	6.80	60	5.60	90	5.70	79	4.00	67	4.10
France	23	3.20	33	3.10	58	3.70	72	3.70	48	3.00
Canada	15	2.10	22	2.00	30	1.90	37	1.90	42	2.60
Total	718	100.00	1,076	100.00	1,572	100.00	1,958	100.00	1,618	100.00

One of the reasons for Tokyo's decline from 1995 to 1998 – not only relative to New York and London, but also to Singapore – is that its currency transactions are skewed toward yen/dollar trade. Other centers, including Singapore, deal with many currencies. However, Singapore probably suffered from decline in foreign exchange transactions in the wake of the Asian currency crises in the period after 1998. Several Asian currencies, including the Thai baht, Indonesian rupiah and Malaysian ringgit, de-internationalized their currencies, that is, restricted transactions of non-deliverable forward contracts in offshore markets, including Singapore.

4.2.4 Foreign Reserves

The monetary authorities hold foreign reserves for several reasons, including a safeguard against too-volatile fluctuations in exchange rates. Unless the country exercises a completely free float, monetary authorities will reserve that right, and will also tend to intervene in the exchange market from time to time, especially in periods of high volatility. Foreign reserves are held in portfolios of foreign government securities from hard-currency nations. Although the currency compositions of foreign reserves are typically not disclosed publicly, the IMF reports once a year the composition of aggregate foreign reserves of its member countries. At the end of 1999, the share of the US dollar was 66 percent, up from 50 percent in 1990. The euro share was 12.5 percent, a similar number to the share of the German mark a year earlier. The share of the yen was 5 percent in 1999, down from the peak of 8.5 percent in 1991. The long slide in the popularity of the yen among central banks in the world is puzzling. It is still the third-largest economy's currency, after the United States and the EU. The value of the yen fluctuated widely in the 1990s: from 160 yen/dollar in 1990 to 80 yen/dollar in 1995, to 145 yen/dollar in 1998, and then to 100 yen/dollar in 2000. However, the share of the yen did not respond to these fluctuations, and has shown steady decline.

4.3   PROMOTION OF THE USE OF THE YEN

4.3.1   Motivations to Expand the Role of the Yen

The Japanese government has made it clear that it is pursuing the 'internationalization of the yen'. Promoting the international use of the yen is based on three reasons. First, the Asian currency crisis, which started with the baht devaluation in July 1997, was blamed partly on the adoption of the dollar peg by Asian countries. As the currency being pegged to the US dollar, the yen depreciation vis-à-vis the US dollar from April 1995 to 1996 hurt the

Table 4.6   Foreign reserves, IMF members by currency composition, %

End-Year	1976	1980	1985	1990	1991	1992	1993	1994	1995	1996	1997	1998	1999	2000	2001
All Nations															
Yen	2.0	4.4	7.3	8.0	8.5	7.6	7.7	7.9	6.8	6.0	5.2	5.4	5.5	5.2	4.9
US$	76.5	68.6	55.3	50.6	51.1	55.3	56.7	56.6	57.0	60.3	62.4	65.9	68.4	68.1	68.3
DM	9.0	14.9	13.9	16.8	15.1	13.3	13.7	14.2	13.7	13.1	12.9	12.2	–	–	–
GBP	1.8	2.9	2.7	3.0	3.2	3.1	3.0	3.3	3.2	3.4	3.7	3.9	4.0	3.9	4.0
FF	1.6	1.7	0.8	2.4	2.9	2.7	2.3	2.4	2.3	1.9	1.4	1.4	–	–	–
ECU	–	–	11.6	9.7	10.2	9.7	8.2	7.7	6.8	5.9	5.0	0.8	–	–	–
Euro	–	–	–	–	–	–	–	–	–	–	–	–	2.7	13.0	13.0
Other	9.1	7.5	8.4	9.5	9.0	8.3	8.4	7.9	10.2	9.4	9.4	10.4	9.4	9.8	9.8
Industrial Nations															
Yen	1.8	3.3	7.6	8.8	9.7	7.6	7.8	8.2	6.6	5.6	5.8	6.6	5.8	–	–
US$	87.0	77.2	50.1	45.5	43.6	48.8	50.2	50.8	51.8	56.1	57.9	66.7	68.3	–	–
DM	6.2	14.3	16.7	19.8	18.3	15.1	16.4	16.3	16.4	15.6	15.9	13.4	–	–	–
GBP	0.8	0.8	1.6	1.7	1.8	2.4	2.2	2.3	2.1	2.0	1.9	2.2	2.3	–	–
FF	0.5	0.7	0.1	2.5	3.1	2.9	2.6	2.4	2.3	1.7	0.9	1.3	–	–	–
ECU	–	–	20.1	14.5	16.6	16.7	15.2	14.6	13.4	12.0	10.9	1.9	–	–	–
Euro	–	–	–	–	–	–	–	–	–	–	–	–	11.0	–	–
Other	3.6	3.7	3.9	7.2	6.9	6.5	5.6	5.4	7.4	7.0	6.7	7.9	12.6	–	–
Developing Nations															
Yen	2.2	5.4	6.8	6.4	6.6	7.7	7.5	7.6	7.0	6.5	4.7	4.5	4.7	4.4	4.5
US$	68.8	59.9	62.5	61.1	62.8	64.5	64.3	63.1	62.4	64.3	66.2	65.3	64.6	64.2	64.1
DM	11.4	15.4	9.8	10.7	10.0	10.8	10.5	11.9	11.0	10.6	10.3	11.3	–	–	–
GBP	2.6	5.1	4.3	5.7	5.3	4.0	4.0	4.4	4.3	4.8	5.1	5.2	5.3	5.2	5.5
FF	2.5	2.7	1.9	2.4	2.4	2.3	2.0	2.4	2.3	2.0	1.8	1.5	–	–	–
ECU*	–	–	–	–	–	–	–	–	–	–	–	–	–	–	–
Euro	–	–	–	–	–	–	–	–	–	–	–	–	14.2	15.0	15.3
Other	12.4	11.5	14.8	13.7	12.9	12.7	13.3	11.9	14.4	13.0	12.8	13.4	12.1	–	–

Note: *ECU is not differentiated as a currency in 1976, 1980.

Source: IMF, Annual Reports, 2002 (for 1992–2001) and other issues (for other years).

competitiveness of Asian products. Exports from Asian countries plummeted in late 1995 and 1996. For example, gross exports from Thailand were growing at the pace of 20 percent per year in the first half of the 1990s, but the export growth rate plummeted to 0 percent in 1996. Deterioration in exports and resulting slowdown in economic growth made Asian currencies vulnerable to speculative attack (in the case of Thailand) and crisis contagion (in the cases of Indonesia and Korea). In order to allow a more stable foreign exchange rate regime to emerge in Asia, the role of the yen has to increase.

When an Asian country wants to adopt a currency basket system, which is considered more robust to external shocks, the basket should include not only the US dollar, but also the yen and the euro as important components. Removing costly regulations and taxes, the yen would become easier to be traded and owned by Asian governments and corporations. This would help stabilize international finance in the region. Timing is important, in that for Asia, the next 12 months will be important in exploring new regional efforts to find a stable financial arrangement.

Second, as the euro has come into circulation, the combined GDP and population that is created by the European Union becomes comparable to that of the United States. The euro has become a natural alternative to the US dollar if a country or investors want to diversify their portfolio. As the euro has emerged as the second key currency, the status of the yen will decline in relative terms. Once a ranking is lost, it will be difficult to enjoy the economies of scale. Currency is like language. You use it because others are using it. Therefore, timing is important. The yen has to be there to be used efficiently if it wants to remain a globally traded currency.

Third, the 'big bang' of the Japanese financial system is rapidly changing the Japanese financial institutions. The Tokyo market will become open to global institutions, and the Japanese markets will be integrated into global markets. In order to benefit fully from the 'big bang', foreign exchange markets have to be efficient, too. Although foreign exchange laws were completely revised to allow most transactions for most market participants, there remain some costs to transactions and regulations on accessibility to yen assets. Again, now is a good time to push the agenda of yen internationalization in order to support the spirit of the 'big bang'.

4.3.2   Measures to Promote the Usage of the Yen

The Japanese government has taken several measures to promote usage of the yen in the past several years. Important measures were taken in December 1998 to promote its usage; first, withholding taxes on treasury bills (TBs) and finance bills (FBs) were eliminated. Then the Ministry of Finance started to auction FBs, as well as TBs, which had been auctioned previously. For non-residents, withholding tax for government long-term bonds (JGBs) became exempt. Also, JGB trading and settlement was improved. In general, reforms in the JGB market are supposed to invite more foreign nationals to purchase and hold JGBs. Unfortunately, interest rates on JGBs have been extremely low (below 2 percent most of the time since 1998), so foreign nationals have not been enticed to invest in them. Other measures are soon to be introduced. It is said that the benchmark medium-term government bond should be developed to promote foreign investment. Five-year JGBs have been issued instead of four-year and six-year bonds. Other proposals include issuance of JGB STRIPs.

4.4   THE DEMAND FOR THE YEN IN ASIA

4.4.1   Role of Exchange Rate Regimes in the Asian Currency Crisis, 1997–98

Prior to the Asian currency crisis, Asian countries had adopted *de facto* dollar peg exchange rate regimes. Their destinations of exports and origins of imports, however, were diversified, being the United States, Japan, Europe and neighboring Asian countries. The fluctuations in the yen have had strong impact on their export competitiveness. When the yen appreciated, Asian exports rose sharply, and vice versa.

Another problem was also caused by fixed exchange rate regimes of emerging market economies with liberalized capital accounts. Capital flows were liberalized, while exchange rates were de facto fixed, prompting capital to become sensitive to interest rate differentials. For example, when interest rates associated with the Thai baht were higher than the US interest rate, Thai banks and corporations had an incentive to borrow in US dollars, and invest in projects denominated in the Thai baht. Thai financial institutions and corporations therein developed currency mismatches.

Borrowers (local corporations and banks) and lenders (foreign banks and investors) of short-term loans did not realize that there would be a devaluation risk premium in the baht interest rate. Borrowers thought that dollar-denominated loans were cheaper than local currency loans. Lenders tended to think that borrowers with high growth performance were safe and free from default risk. It was only after devaluation that borrowers realized their debts were becoming unsustainable, and lenders realized that borrowers were defaulting in the midst of currency crises.

4.4.2   Impossible Trinity

It is impossible to pursue the following three policies together:

1.   fixed exchange rate;
2.   free capital mobility; and
3.   independent monetary policy.

Henry Wallich (1972) was the first to spell out the policy implications of this impossible trinity. Many Asian countries pursued these policies in the late 1980s and 1990s and ended up in the crisis of 1997–98. The combination of (1) and (2) means that interest rates cannot differ from international interest rates, where monetary policy becomes subject to the influence of the key currency. The more credible the fixed exchange rate regime becomes, the less independent monetary policy becomes. A currency board like that adopted by Hong Kong is a way to abandon monetary policy by design of a monetary rule.

There are three ways to get out of the impossible trinity:

1. floating exchange rates;
2. capital controls; and
3. abandoning independent monetary policy.

After the currency crisis, Asian countries each adopted at least one of these three measures. These problems that confronted them are schematically analyzed in Table 4.7.

Table 4.7 The impossible trinity

	Fixed Exchange Rate	Free Capital Mobility	Independent Monetary Policy	Example
Impossible trinity	Yes	Yes	Yes	Pre-crisis Asia a CRISIS!
Floating	No	Yes	Yes	Post-crisis Korea, Indonesia, Thailand, Philippines
Capital controls	Yes	No	Yes	China Malaysia (Sept 98–Sept 99)
Currency board	Yes	Yes	No	Hong Kong

4.4.3 Two-corner Solution

Many researchers and policymakers advocate the two-corner solution: either (1) free-floating exchange rate system, or (2) a currency board can be stable, but anything in between is unstable. Is this true?

Advocates of the two-corner solution would say that the floating exchange rate regime will keep the exchange rate broadly consistent with balanced current accounts. The floating exchange rate regime will keep investors and borrowers keenly aware of exchange rate risk. The problem of too much capital inflow is less likely to take place under a free-floating exchange rate regime. Currency crises would not happen under a free-floating exchange rate regime.

Critics of the two-corner solution would say that the floating exchange rate system does not automatically balance the current account. This is obvious from the experience of advanced countries (US, Japan, European countries). The exchange rate would be subject to capital account movements rather than current account movements. With free capital mobility, capital flows tend to overreact to news. The excessive inflows and outflows, which may not be deterred, but rather encouraged by exchange rate movements, will present difficult policy problems.

Therefore, under a free (non-intervention) floating exchange rate regime, exchange rates may fluctuate beyond a desirable range. The exchange rate fluctuation may discourage inward investment and manufacturing investment.

Note that many Asian countries' currencies (except the Thai baht) collapsed several months after moving to a floating exchange rate regime. In other words, their most difficult time came when their currencies were already under floating exchange rate regimes. When capital wants to leave the country, a floating exchange rate regime will not be particularly helpful. The free-floating exchange rate regime is not a panacea. When contagion from neighboring countries threatens to spread, free-floating regimes would cause a downward spiral of regional currencies. A devaluation of a currency would bring down the currencies of trade- and investment-related countries. Those who praised China as a barrier to stop contagious devaluation throughout the region by maintaining its fixed exchange rate should also be advocating some sort of managed float in times of crisis.

Advocates of the currency board system cite its high reputation against speculative attacks. Confidence in the system is backed by large foreign reserves, enough to pay for all withdrawals of cash or even an (M1) flight out of the country. The currency board in Argentina withstood attacks well in the wake of the Mexican crisis (at the beginning of 1995). Hong Kong fended off speculative attacks well in the fall of 1997. No modern currency board has collapsed under any speculative attack except in Argentina in 2001.

One particular aspect of the pure currency board arrangement is that there is no need to have a central bank, because money supply is automatically decided by capital inflows and outflows, and interest rates should be equivalent to those of the key currency the emerging market currency is pegged to.

However, Hong Kong found that the currency board is not a panacea. When investors attacked Hong Kong foreign exchange and stocks simultaneously by taking short positions on both markets, investors positioned themselves to gain either from the devaluation of the currency or the decline of stock prices (which is likely from defending an exchange rate by increasing interest rates). The so-called 'double play' was discovered in October 1997, but was planned on a massive scale in the spring-summer of 1998. That was why Hong Kong monetary authorities intervened to purchase stocks in addition to the Hong Kong dollar in August 1998.

4.4.4 Real Effective Exchange Rate Consideration in Asia

If the two-corner solution is not the answer for all countries – that is, there is no 'one-size-fits-all' solution – each country must then select its own exchange rate regime. One criterion for selecting the regime is to stabilize the real effective exchange rate. Loss of export competitiveness is dangerous for a small open economy, as shown in the experience of the Asian currency crisis. It becomes a reasonable policy goal to prevent extreme volatility in the real effective exchange rate, while allowing some flexibility to absorb internal and external shocks to fundamentals. For Asian countries that trade with the United States, Japan and other Asian neighbors, maintaining the real effective exchange rate implies that Asian currencies have to respond credibly to movements in the Japanese yen. The role of the yen in Asian exchange rate regimes is an important factor in the avoidance of a future currency crisis in Asia.

4.5 BASKET CURRENCY PROPOSAL FOR ASIA

4.5.1 Middle Ground

Since the two-corner philosophy is not a panacea, a multilateral-trading country has to explore a middle ground. There are several other regimes in the middle grouping, including:

1. basically a free-floating exchange rate regime, with some occasional interventions to smooth out fluctuations;
2. a crawling peg;
3. a target zone (hard/soft band, wide/narrow band, explicit/implicit, or mutual/unilateral, to decide the central rate); and
4. a basket currency regime (basket peg, or a band around it).

The first option has been adopted by the three major currencies, the US dollar, the yen and the deutschemark (now the euro). The second option is 'crawling peg', which is basically a fixed exchange rate with pre-announced depreciation. There could be a band around the central rate, which could be continuously adjusted. The crawling peg was adopted by Mexico before the 1994 crisis and by Indonesia before the 1997 crisis. The target zone is another variant of the fixed exchange rate with a band around the central rate. The band could be narrow (±2.5 percent) or wide (±15 percent). The band could be hard (defended with a strong commitment) or soft (might or might not be defended, depending on the situation). The existence of a target zone might be announced or kept secret. A target zone could be mutually committed or unilaterally exercised. A target zone with a moving central rate is similar to a crawling peg with a band.

In the rest of this section, one particular proposal of the middle ground, namely the basket regime with a band, is recommended to Asian countries. This is based on the relationship with Japan as well as the United States. In order to mitigate impacts from yen/dollar fluctuations on their export competitiveness, the currencies of Asian countries should float partly with the yen. The role of the yen in the basket is important.

4.5.2 Basket System

Benassy-Quere (1999), Ito, Ogawa and Sasaki (1998) and Williamson (2000), to name a few, have proposed a basket currency regime as a desirable exchange rate regime for emerging market economies with diverse trading partners. The proposal implies that Asian countries should allow their exchange rate to fluctuate against the US dollar, the yen and the euro, with varying weights of trading partners' exchange rates. On average, the fluctuations in the real effective exchange rate are minimized. There are pros and cons in adopting a basket currency regime and concerning details in implementation, such as the width of a band and disclosure of the band, where there are several options.

A successful implementation of a basket system depends on the choice of the weights and the width of the band. The basic idea of the basket system is to keep the real effective exchange rate stable, so that trade weights are a good approximation of optimal weights. Table 4.8 shows a tentative calculation of optimal weights based on trade weights and price competitiveness, according to Ito, Ogawa and Sasaki (1998), as compared to the actual peg estimated by Frankel and Wei (1994). It is evident that Thailand and Korea should have chosen a much higher yen weight than they did in reality before the crisis. That flexibility may have helped avert a crisis by not causing exports and GDP growth first to boom and then to crash in the period of 1993–97.

Table 4.8   Optimal weight for currency basket of East Asian countries

	Actual weight early-1990s*		Optimal weight mid-1990s**	
	US$ (%)	Yen (%)	US$ (%)	Yen (%)
Thai baht	91	5	35.3	64.7
Indonesian rupiah	95	16	77.9	22.1
Korean won	96	−10	45.7	54.3
Taiwan dollar	96	5	7.3	92.7
Singaporean dollar	75	13	51.0	49.0
Philippine peso	107	−1	72.8	27.2

Source: (*) Frankel and Wei (1994) and (**) Ito, Ogawa and Sasaki (1998).

Ito, Ogawa and Sasaki (1998) did not explicitly consider the question of choosing the width around the optimal basket, or the appropriateness of defending the ceiling and floor of the basket band. However, the basket proposal is nevertheless based on solid reasoning.

4.5.3 Nash Equilibrium Problem

Ito, Ogawa and Sasaki (1998) used the model where there are only two destinations of exports of an Asian country: Japan and the United States. However, in the real world, intra-regional trade in Asia is as important as that destined to Japan or the United States. When the basket is calculated, neighboring countries' exchange rate regimes do matter.

One particular problem in this implementation of the basket is the treatment of neighbors' exchange rates. Ogawa and Ito (2002) have pointed out a coordination problem for a group of emerging market economies in their efforts to stabilize real effective exchange rates. For example, in the calculation of the Thai real effective exchange rate, the neighbor's exchange rate – say, Malaysia's currency value – should be included. Similarly, in the calculation of Malaysian real effective exchange rate, the Thai exchange rate should be included.

If Malaysia decides to adopt a dollar peg (for political reasons), like it did in September 1998, the *de facto* dollar weight in calculating the Thai baht real effective exchange rate suddenly increases, and the baht will start moving more closely with the dollar than before. Therefore, Malaysia and Thailand should solve the joint problem of choosing the weight on major currencies, excluding each other's exchange rates. A joint decision would produce a better result than uncoordinated solutions.

For example, if Indonesia, Singapore, Malaysia and the Philippines were adopting the *de facto* dollar peg, Thailand would be well advised to adopt a dollar peg, because the weight of the US dollar, through the rupiah, Singapore dollar, ringgit and peso would increase. However, if neighboring countries adopted a dollar–yen–euro basket system, then Thailand would also be well advised to adopt that basket system. The situation is symmetrical to neighboring countries. The reaction function of Thailand is defined as a relationship that would determine the Thai dollar weight (WT) in the basket as a function of the Malaysian dollar weight. Similarly, the reaction function of Malaysia is defined as a relationship where the Malaysian dollar weight is determined as a function of the Thai dollar weight. Therefore, 'equilibrium' is determined by the intersection of the reaction functions. A rigorous model is presented by Ogawa, Ito and Sasaki.

Figure 4.2 shows the example of optimal weights of interdependent countries; when Malaysia uses the dollar peg (WM = 1), then the reaction function of Thailand states that Thailand should also adopt the dollar e.g. (WT = 1). Then this is an equilibrium. However, if WM is less than one but above 0.5, then the Thailand reaction function states that Thailand would put less weight on the dollar than the WM, in turn that will prompt Malaysia, through its reaction function, to lower its weight on the dollar. The equilibrium is at WT = 0.5, and WM = 0.5. This illustrates the need for coordination in their setting exchange rate policies.

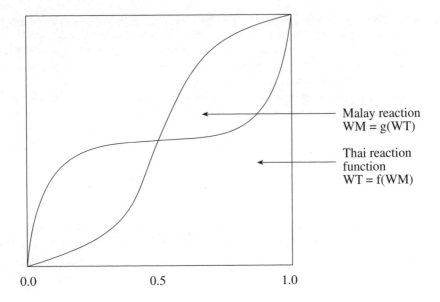

Figure 4.2   Thailand dollar weight (WT)

4.5.4   Regional Cooperation

What would be an appropriate form of regional coordination and cooperation with respect to an exchange rate regime? The regional cooperation is very important because the optimal exchange rate regime of Thailand depends on the exchange rate regime of NIEs and ASEAN. The three major economies in Northeastern Asia – Japan, Korea and China – will benefit from mutually understanding each other's exchange rate policies, and discuss what would be a better exchange rate arrangement in the region. The following steps are important in implementing a basket system in the Asian region:

1. Study the structures of exports and imports of Asian countries and encourage intra-regional trade and investment.
2. Study exchange rate elasticities of exports and imports of Asian countries.

3. Set objectives in exchange rate and foreign reserve policies. Minimize current account fluctuations? Maximize exports? Maximize capital inflow incentives?
4. Calculate optimum basket weights.
5. Coordinate exchange rate policies with trade-linked neighboring countries: common currency unit as a reference rate? Common basket? Joint floating?

It would be great if researchers and policymakers of the three countries could make some progress toward research on this topic, and use research on their policies.

4.6   CONCLUSION

In this chapter, the role of the yen in East Asia was reviewed. First, the degree of yen internationalization was examined. It was shown in one statistic after another that the yen weight in the international currency scene did not increase during the 1990s. It is now the third most important currency in the world, after the US dollar and the euro. However, the use of the euro may not be as important as its economic size, just like the yen. Therefore, the lack of use of the yen may be due to the unusual strength of the US dollar, rather than an unusual weakness of the yen. In the future, however, the use of the euro may spread rapidly among other countries. The Japanese economy has to recover its growth potential and increase imports from Asian countries to promote the use of the yen in the region.

One of the lessons from the Asian currency crisis was the importance of exchange rate regimes. The *de facto* dollar peg that was adopted by Asian economies before 1997 had side effects. When the yen appreciated vis-à-vis the US dollar, export booms occurred in Asian economies, sometimes leading to overheating. When the yen depreciated, it resulted in a burst of overheating in Asian countries having strong trade and investment. The boom and bust cycle in the 1990s, along with the yen–dollar exchange rate fluctuation, had weakened the fundamentals of the Asian economies, and had become one of the reasons for the Asian currency crisis of 1997.

One way to avoid the boom and bust is for Asian emerging market economies to collectively adopt a basket exchange rate regime, possibly with a band, and to avoid excessive volatility in – and to maintain the stability of – real effective exchange rates. Important questions to be considered are what would be a reference rate for appropriate real effective exchange rates, and what would be an appropriate coordination among Asian emerging market economies? The role of the yen will remain important for its Asian neighbors.

NOTE

1. See, for example, Philipp Hartmann (1998), 'The Future of the Euro as an International Currency', *Journal of the Japanese and International Economies*, **12**(4), pp. 424–54.

REFERENCES

Benassy-Quere, Agnis (1999), 'Optimal Pegs for East Asian Currencies', *Journal of the Japanese and International Economies*, **13**, pp. 44–60.

Calvo, Guillermo A. and Reinhart, Carmen M. (2000), 'Fear of Floating', *NBER working paper*, **7993**, November.

Frankel, J.A. and S.J. Wei (1994), 'Yen Bloc or Dollar Bloc? Exchange Rate Policies of the East Asian Economies', in T. Ito and A.O. Krueger (eds), *Macroeconomic Linkage: Savings, Exchange Rates, and Capital Flows*, Chicago: University of Chicago Press.

Hartmann, Philipp (1998), 'The Future of the Euro as an International Currency', *Journal of the Japanese and International Economies*, **12**(4), pp. 424–54.

Ito, Takatoshi, Ogawa, Eiji and Sasaki, Yuri N. (1998), 'How did the Dollar Peg Fail in Asia', *Journal of the Japanese and International Economies*, **12**, pp. 256–304.

Krugman, P. (1984), 'The International Role of the Dollar: Theory and Prospect', in J.F.O. Bilson and R.C. Marston (eds), *Exchange Rate Theory and Practice*, Chicago: University of Chicago Press.

Ogawa, Eiji and Ito, Takatoshi (2002), 'On the Desirability of a Regional Basket Currency Arrangement', *Journal of the Japanese and International Economies*, **16**(3), September, pp. 317–34.

Wallich, Henry C.(1972), *The Monetary Crisis of 1971 – The Lesson to Be Learned*, Washington DC: Per Jacobsson Foundation.

Williamson, John (2000), *Exchange Rate Regimes for Emerging Markets: Reviving the Intermediate Option*, Washington, DC: Institute for International Economics, September.

5. The dollarization debate: is it over?

Ricardo Hausmann

5.1 INTRODUCTION

Once upon a time, there was a debate about a bi-polar option in the choice of exchange regimes. The point was that intermediate exchange rate regimes were likely to be blown away by currency speculators.[1] Countries would either have to allow their currencies to float freely – and move to the flexible pole – or they would have to peg very rigidly their exchange rate through currency boards or full 'dollarization' or 'euroization'.[2] Today, Argentina's crisis seems to have eliminated one of the poles from the world of intellectual respectability. It seems that the shortcoming of hard pegs in complex economies should be strongly discouraged. Nevertheless, the issue is of obvious importance in Europe, especially for the accession countries to the East. Moreover, countries such as Ecuador and El Salvador have recently dollarized, and others in Central America are giving the option serious consideration.

To be fair to conventional wisdom, the bi-polar view never really existed. It was really a view about the convenience of floating regimes for emerging markets, but with an escape clause to make room for Hong Kong and Argentina. That was the thrust of the G-7 declaration in Cologne in 1999, where those leading countries pledged not to provide financing to strengthen the ability of countries to defend 'unsustainable' exchange rates.[3] This preference for floating regimes stems from two radically different views: one based on virtue and the other on vice. The virtuous critique would argue that dollarization or currency boards have such a long list of prerequisites – a sound banking system, a high stock of international reserves, a solvent government and a flexible labor market – that few countries can actually qualify. The ones that can do not need to surrender monetary policy; if they can do all that, they can surely run a decent central bank.

The other view, based on vice, would say that convertibility is a solution for hopeless countries. If a nation cannot hope to create credible institutions, it may be better off importing them, even if the foreign variety is not a perfect fit. All other countries should attempt to create their own institutions. If you do not share Argentina's hyperinflation history and its *de facto* dollarization of financial assets, you have little to learn from the experience. Look at Brazil, Mexico, Chile and even Colombia. In spite of their checkered history, they have been able to bring inflation down while keeping the degrees of freedom offered by their monetary autonomy.

Argentina's defense of the currency board has been based more on vice than on virtue. Critics would say that the currency board was a desperate solution adopted in 1991 in a country with few remaining options. After three consecutive bouts of hyperinflation, no credibility in its monetary and fiscal institutions and massive capital flight, just providing a stable currency became so large a challenge that it overwhelmed all other considerations.

But such a regime was never a good long-term fit. It is hard to find a country that scores lower in the traditional optimal currency area (OCA) criteria – deep trade integration, factor mobility and common shocks. On the trade front, Argentina is too closed and too distant from the US to share a currency. Sooner or later the US currency would appreciate, or interest rates would rise, just when the opposite would suit the Argentine macro balance. And what could happen in theory actually has taken place in practice; the dollar's strength and the weakness of the Argentine real after its devaluation in January 1999 have caught Argentina between a rock and a hard place. While massive liability dollarization makes devaluation unpalatable, the alternative – deflation – is not without its problems; it keeps real interest rates high, hurting growth and fiscal solvency. In the end, so the argument goes, the system lacked the degrees of freedom it needed. When their currency collapsed, default on dollar debts became inevitable as the dollar value of their GDP dwindled to a third of its original level. Should the world copy Argentina, or is the Argentine experience only relevant for desperate countries like Bulgaria or Ecuador?

So, are hard pegs or dollarization the monetary equivalent of a platypus? Is it a wrong turn, an evolutionary dead-end in the process towards economic modernity? Or is it, on the contrary, a futuristic prelude of things to come?

It will be argued in this chapter that there is more logic to the move towards dollarization than is suggested by this introduction. It will also be claimed that the alternatives are less appealing than they are now thought to be, and to emphasize the point, an overview of the history of the debate will be provided. The author admits that his rendition is probably affected by concerns that characterized the Latin American experience in exchange rate arrangements. Other regions of the world typically perceive Latin America as overly concerned with financial instability. Unfortunately, that seems to be a predicament Latin America must bear.

5.2 EXCHANGE RATE POLICY: A BRIEF OVERVIEW OF THE TRADITIONAL DEBATE

One of the troubling conundrums in economic theory is that there is no role for money in a world of complete markets, such as mentioned by Arrow-Debreu. Briefly (1954), in a model without imperfections, it is impossible to make money matter. People would never demand it, and even if they did, they could see through all nominal variables and focus only on their real implications. Monetary policy cannot help stabilize the economy but it can do a lot of damage if people distrust the government's intentions. In order to make money matter, some economic flaw has to be put into the model. This is very unsatisfactory, because it makes the whole monetary debate hinge on what the assumed relevant market flaw is, how exogenous or endogenous the imperfection is to the whole theoretical enterprise, and how likely it is to go away with the right policy framework.

The traditional solution is to assume some nominal rigidity. The most common assumption is rigidity in nominal wages.[4] From this assumption you get the implication that flexible exchange rate regimes can restore the flexibility in relative prices that is thwarted by wage rigidity. As Milton Friedman (1968) argued, when a real shock hits, it is easier for the exchange rate to move than for millions of individual contracts to change. Flexible exchange rates can compensate for nominal rigidities.

Wage rigidity is a relatively simple and elegant assumption, although what causes this rigidity is not altogether clear. These days, macroeconomists tend to hide behind the fact that there are so many papers published in leading journals that have used this assumption that it has become an accepted building block. Nevertheless, accepted does not mean understood. For example, it is common practice among theoretical papers that compare the characteristics of alternative exchange rate regimes to assume that the degree of nominal or even real wage rigidity is independent of the exchange arrangement.[5] This is grossly inadequate, both for theoretical as well as empirical reasons. Assume for example, that an employer and a trade union are negotiating over the setting of future wages. Would they not try to anticipate expected future changes in nominal variables when they discuss the nature of the deal? Would they not choose the duration of the contract based on their perception of nominal uncertainty? Would they not opt for some form of wage indexation if inflation is expected to be high and uncertain? Are all these expectations not affected by the exchange arrangement?

Empirically, Hausmann, Gavin, Pagés-Serra and Stein (1999) studied the degree of responsiveness of nominal wages to price and exchange rate innovations and found radically different elasticities even for the same country, across different exchange arrangements. Moreover, the policy implications that emerge from the assumption of nominal rigidity are without much foundation in either theory or evidence. For example, it is often argued that countries that want to peg or dollarize require a very flexible labor market so as to limit the costs caused by nominal rigidities. This sounds intuitively true. But what if anything is the relationship between the assumed nominal rigidity and labor market policies? Is it the nature of collective bargaining? Is it minimum wage legislation? Is it severance payments? What would happen if the real source of nominal rigidities is small menu costs? These issues are seldom discussed because nominal rigidities are more an assumption than a testable hypothesis in need of the kind of detailed analysis of its causes that could inform policy.

5.3 MONETARY POLICY AND THE OPTIMAL CURRENCY AREA ARGUMENT

So, at the most fundamental level, we really are uncertain about the question of why money matters and how its mattering is related to the exchange regime. But let us set aside that issue and suppose that there is a role for monetary policy, and that this role is the conventional one. Assume that economies are hit by real shocks, and that the world is such that the use of exchange rate flexibility and control over interest rates may facilitate the adjustment. This makes monetary autonomy and exchange rate flexibility a better alternative. However, economies are also hit by shocks of demand on their currencies, the so-called nominal shocks. In this case, flexible regimes will cause movements in relative prices, which are just inefficient noise that is best avoided. A sudden increase in the demand for money under a floating regime would cause an appreciation that would move resources around in an uncalled-for manner. Instead, central banks should simply supply the additional money demanded by the market. Under a fixed exchange regime, or a currency board, this would happen naturally. Hence, the Frankel (1980) argument: if the shocks are mostly real, then float. If they are mostly nominal, then fix.

The noise caused by unexpected and inefficient movements in relative prices may hinder trade, and if this is important to growth, it may actually have important growth implications. According to Rose (1999), countries that share a currency, trade three times more than otherwise expected, given their economic characteristics. Moreover, Frankel and Rose (2000) find large implied effects of currency unions on long-term income through their impact on trade. In addition, they argue that this effect is not caused by trade diversion; they show that countries that belong to a currency union do not trade less with non-members. This literature has been extended to look at possible spillover effects (Rose and van Wincoop, 2001) caused by trade diversions. The effect has also been estimated using adoption and abandonment of currency unions in order to focus on the time-series, instead of the cross-country effects (Glick and Rose, 2001). This goes on to the question of what would be the trade effects of adopting a currency union in a given context. The estimated effect is that it would increase trade by some 90 percent. In general, these results have survived a long list of critiques.[6]

On the other hand, if nominal rigidities hinder an effective adjustment to real shocks, this will generate real losses. Levi-Yeyati and Sturzenegger (2001) provide evidence that on average growth in floating-rate countries has been lower than in fixed-rate countries.

The traditional literature on optimal currency areas inaugurated by Mundell (1961) took as a given precondition that there were both benefits and costs of having an autonomous monetary policy. However, it made the important point that if two countries are deeply integrated through trade or factor movements, then real shocks are likely to be shared, i.e., a boom in one country will spill over to the other. Business cycles will be highly correlated. In this case, if countries adopted their own monetary policy, they would be trying to do very similar things with it anyway. This forms them into an optimal currency area (OCA): they would be better off just sharing a currency, adopting a common monetary policy and enjoying the benefits of a more stable monetary environment to support trade without the costs caused by harmful and noisy nominal shocks, or any other form of transaction cost caused by the multiplicity of currencies.

If we add the two strands of literature together, then it becomes obvious that the optimal currency area criteria are not exogenously given, but may in fact become endogenous to the choice of exchange arrangement, among other factors. If countries sharing a currency do trade more, and if more intense trade improves the OCA criteria, then countries that initially fail the test may actually meet it *ex post* as a consequence of the currency union (Frankel and Rose, 1998).

5.4 MONETARY POLICY IN A WORLD OF CREDIBILITY PROBLEMS

With the advent of time-inconsistency and credibility (Kydland and Prescott (1977), Calvo (1978), Barro and Gordon (1983)), the flexibility benefits derived from monetary policy have to be weighed against the credibility problems that a monetary authority may encounter vis-à-vis its inflationary commitments. Flexibility may be able to reduce unnecessary output fluctuations, but it can be abused. Since the market will anticipate this abuse, higher equilibrium inflation will ensue. Countries with low credibility would pay a cost of higher inflation if they followed this course of action and should probably opt for renouncing the discretion that flexibility entails. Adopting somebody else's currency is one way out.[7]

However, this is not the only solution. The alternative is to delegate the discretion to an institution that does not have the incentives to abuse it, such as an autonomous central bank with a clear mandate to target inflation. This may in fact move the flexibility-credibility frontier out and allow the country to enjoy more of both. That is the challenge offered by the new focus on floating exchange rates with inflation targets (IT). It is argued by many that this is just a more efficient option. It may take some time to build the credibility of the central bank, but not that much time, after all. Look at the single digit inflation rates in Chile, Colombia and Mexico…three countries with quite a checkered inflationary past. It can be done and it is worth doing.

5.5   A FIRST BALANCE OF THE ARGUMENTS

By all of this logic, the bulk of the emerging market countries should float. Their economies are subject to very large and quite idiosyncratic real shocks and business cycles are not very correlated. They could benefit significantly from the flexibility provided by monetary autonomy and exchange rate adjustments. When hit by an adverse shock, they could let the exchange rate take the hit by lowering interest rates.

Australia during the East Asian and Russian crises is a good example of this. As shown in Figure 5.1, their monetary authorities lowered the policy interest rate several times while also allowing exchange rates to depreciate. Under these circumstances, the export sector was protected from external deflation while the domestic economy benefited from lower interest rates. This is why emerging market countries should float.

Or should they? Let us look at how floating rates in Mexico dealt with a similar circumstance. Figure 5.2 shows exchange rates and interest rates for the same period. The difference could not be starker. When the crisis hit, putting pressure on exchange rates, the monetary authorities reacted with a drastic increase in interest rates from 17 percent to over 50 percent, and rates were left above 35 percent for over five months! A similar pattern could be observed in other Latin American countries; floaters jacked up interest rates much more than did fixers, contradicting the idea that such regimes can have a more subdued interest rate policy because the exchange rate helps in the adjustment process. This comes as a bit of a surprise. After all, many argued that abandoning pegged exchange rates would also avoid having to increase interest rates too much because central banks would not be forced into such a painful and ultimately unproductive strategy.

What explains this behavior? In fact, if the foundations of the analysis were the ones presented so far, why have we historically observed so little floating? What explains the 'fear of floating' (Calvo and Reinhart, 1999) that seems to characterize emerging markets that have adopted *de jure* floating regimes?[8] In fact, what makes some countries want to dollarize at all?

Figure 5.1   Floating at its best: Australia

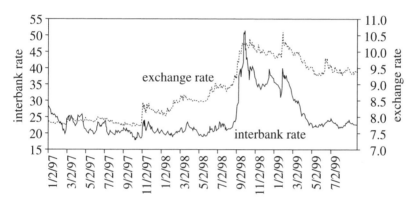

Figure 5.2   Floating Latin style: Mexico

The issue is not just a trade-off between stability of output and inflation. Something is missing from the picture ... but what? Two considerations come to mind. The first is the need to avoid crises, i.e., those catastrophic disruptions of the economic order. The second has to do with the cost of capital. As we shall see, both are related.

5.6   WHICH IS WHICH? THE PUZZLE OVER INTEREST RATES

Imagine two countries. Country A has a public debt to GDP ratio of 120 percent; it has a primary fiscal deficit of 4 percent and has an anemic GDP growth of

0 to 1 percent. Country B has a public debt to GDP ratio of 50 percent; it has a primary fiscal surplus of 3 percent and has a moderate GDP growth of 3 to 4 percent. Which country will pay the higher interest rates on its public debt?

The answer is straightforward. Simple inter-temporal debt sustainability considerations suggest that country A is in serious trouble. Even at a low interest rate of 5 percent, the overall fiscal deficit would be 10 percent of the GDP (i.e., $4 + 1.2 \times 5$). Moreover, the lack of growth means that the increase in the debt burden greatly surpasses the growth in the capacity to pay it. Surely, the markets will understand that holding this debt is highly risky. A 5 percent rate is unlikely to be a sustainable one. But the interest rate should be higher to compensate for the imminent default risk.

Country B is clearly in a much better situation. At a 5 percent interest rate, it would have an overall surplus of 0.5 percent of GDP. The stock of debt would be falling while the economy is growing. Even at a real rate of 10 percent, the overall deficit would be only 2 percent of the GDP, which would keep the debt to GDP ratio constant if the denominator, i.e., the nominal GDP were to grow at 4 percent. This means that a 10 percent real interest rate is just too attractive, given the alternative low-risk investments in today's world. It is unlikely to be equilibrium. The market rate should be lower. Right?

Not really. Country A is a stylized representation of Japan, where 10-year bonds trade at an interest rate of about 2 percent! Country B is inspired from Brazil where 10-year bonds in local currency do not exist. At one-year maturities, interest rates in local currency are about 25 percent. Interest rates on dollar-denominated bonds yield upwards of 14 percent. Obviously, if Brazil were to have all its debt at 25 percent, its fiscal deficit would be 9.5 percent and thus clearly unsustainable, justifying the high interest rates.[9]

This discussion is meant to indicate that we really do not understand what determines the interest rate on public debt in an economy, at least not in a way that can account for the real world.[10] Almost any interest rate can be rationalized, *ex post*. Granted, it is really hard to explain Japan. At a low interest rate, a primary surplus of 3 percent looks more than enough to stabilize debt ratios for a country with a debt to GDP ratio of 50 percent like Brazil. For a country like Turkey with a debt to GDP ratio of 80 percent, a primary surplus of 5 percent should be enough. But it has not been enough to generate reasonable interest rates in either case. You could blame the low credibility in the sustainability of the primary fiscal surpluses and say that these are not real, but only projected. After all, the market is not sure that they will actually be delivered and that keeps the interest rate high. Yes, but if the interest rate remains high, the primary surplus will be hard to deliver and the financial ratios will deteriorate, making matters worse over time.

In this context, the impact of the choice of exchange rate regime on interest rates becomes of paramount importance. The Italian lira and the Spanish peseta were the weakest currencies of Europe. Obviously, the inflationary history and the high debt ratios of those two countries justified higher interest rates. But these in turn lead to fragile public finances and weak currencies. Joining the European Monetary Union caused interest rates to decline and this had tremendous salutary effects on fiscal accounts.[11] This then justified lower interest rates. Hence, at least in those cases, monetary union led to an improvement of public finances, which then justified stronger currencies.

All this suggests that lurking at the bottom of this problem is a multiple equilibria story. In fact, more than one story too! The next section will create a path towards dollarization as a step-by-step process of avoiding bad outcomes in consecutive multiple equilibria stories.

5.7   THE ROAD TO DOLLARIZATION IS PAVED WITH GOOD INTENTIONS

The last decade has been characterized by a nasty sequence of crises. When the decade started, it was a common belief that crises had relatively similar causes, being due to profligate macro policies. But the experience of the 1990s showed that there are many ways in which you can get into serious trouble, even while you think you are getting your house in order. Avoiding crises involves choices that impact the monetary regime and its properties.

5.7.1   Step 1: Avoid Short-term Nominal Public Debt: It Can Kill You

If a country has a sufficiently large stock of public debt denominated in domestic currency, and if this debt is sufficiently short-term, or indexed to a short-term interest rate so that movements in interest rates actually impact fiscal outcomes, then the economy can be subject to self-fulfilling inflationary crises (Calvo, 1989). If the public has high (or low) inflation expectations, interest rates will be high (or low). But this would cause a large (or small) fiscal deficit, which, given the fact that taxation is distortionary, would lead to the need for larger (or smaller) monetization, thus justifying the initial inflationary expectations. In fact, if the government were to resist pressures to monetize, high *ex post* real interest rates would lead to the kind of unpleasant monetary arithmetic that would eventually cause a later and larger monetization.

This is probably the mechanism that caused the hyperinflations of Argentina in the late 1980s. It is a process that could equally well get triggered in Brazil or Turkey today, given their current debt structure. It is a potentially explosive situation that depends to a large extent on unclear factors that make the market choose one equilibrium over the other. Adopting policies that focus markets on good outcomes seems paramount.

One way to do this is to credibly commit to a low inflation policy. This is easier said than done, but credible pegs such as currency boards often have this in mind. Another way out of this particular form of crisis is to dollarize the public debt. Through this mechanism, expectations about inflation do not affect the dollar interest rate on public debt, eliminating the mechanism that generates this type of crisis.

5.7.2   Step 2: But Short-term Debt in Foreign Currency Can Also Kill You

As is well known from models of bank runs, mismatches in the maturity structure of assets and liabilities can also trigger self-fulfilling crises. If others decide to roll over maturing debt, it makes sense for each individual investor to do so as well. However, if investors fear that others might not roll over, it is optimal for individual investors to be the first to head for the exits (Diamond and Dybvig, 1983).

The logic in this type of situation was clear during the 1984 Mexican crisis. It could be argued that the 1997 Korean crisis also had important elements of this story. When investors realized that there was a large stock of dollar-linked short-term debt (the so-called *tesobonos* in Mexico and the bank credit lines in Korea) well in excess of international reserves, a panic ensued.

Obviously, the solution to this kind of situation involves a careful monitoring of the liquidity position of the government and banks. Governments are well advised to significantly lengthen the maturity of the public debt and adopt a policy of pre-funding their financial requirements, so that they do not become dependent on markets being open at all points in time. On the banking side, they should adopt a systemic liquidity policy through a combination of significant international reserves at the central Bank, and a remunerated liquidity requirement on bank liabilities.[12]

5.7.3   Step 3: Dollar Debts Can Kill You

If nominal debt can kill you, does dollarizing the debt avoid crises? Certainly, it avoids one type of crisis. However, it can create others. According to Chang and Velasco (1999), a banking system is not subject to liquidity crises if it has a floating exchange regime and domestic currency liabilities. In this context, the central bank – acting as lender of last resort – can credibly commit to guarantee the liquidity of the short-term liabilities denominated in a currency that it can issue, thus eliminating the bad equilibrium. However, they also show theoretically that this is not the case if there are dollar liabilities.

Moreover, if liabilities are dollarized and the currency floats, it is possible to have a situation of self-fulfilling crises. If people expected the currency to weaken significantly, then borrowers, public or private – who earned pesos and owed dollars – would have trouble servicing their obligations. In anticipation of such an event, investors would attack the obligations of the government and banks, precipitating a large depreciation that they feared. The crises in Indonesia and Ecuador clearly had this dynamic component as a central element. In general, the lesson is an important one; floating exchange rates and liability dollarization are a mix that may expose countries to crisis.

5.7.4 Step 4: Even If They Do Not, Currency Mismatches Thus Generated Make Monetary Policy Less Effective

In fact, even if they do not kill you, dollar liabilities create important balance sheet effects that severely diminish the advantages of floating regimes toward inflation targets.[13]

To see this point, it is useful to consider the typical Mundell-Fleming model with floating exchange rates and inflation targeting (Svensson, 1998). In such a model, interest rates are assumed to operate through two channels. First, they directly affect aggregate demand through their impact on consumption and investment decisions (i.e., the 'IS' curve). Secondly, the interest rate affects the interest parity condition. An unexpected reduction in interest rates should, *ceteris paribus*, depreciate the exchange rate. This depreciation is assumed to have a positive effect on aggregate demand through its effect on net exports.[14] However, if balance sheet effects are important, this latter channel may operate in the opposite direction; a weaker currency may hurt firms with dollar liabilities and cause a contraction in demand (Aghion, Bacchetta and Banerjee, 1999; Cespedes, Chang and Velasco, 1999; Velasco, 2001). Under these conditions, interest rates have either a smaller expansionary impact or perhaps a contractionary impact on aggregate demand.

In this context, inflation targeting may be problematic. If the net effect of interest rates on aggregate demand is positive but small, interest rates would have to move a lot to affect aggregate demand, making interest rates very volatile. Alternatively, if the effect were negative, interest rates would need to move in the opposite direction; i.e., raising interest rates and appreciating the currency, instead of lowering them in bad times. The high volatility of interest rates and their pro-cyclical nature is a common feature of floating, emerging markets as has been documented in Calvo and Reinhart (2000) and in Hausmann, Stein and Panizza (2000).

In fact, the previously mentioned recent experience of Latin American floaters is illustrative of this point. During the Russian crisis, countries were forced to increase interest rates much more than Argentina or Panama, in spite of the fact that they could supposedly have let part of the hit be taken by exchange rates.[15] Later on, during their recoveries in 2000, both Brazil and Mexico lowered interest rates, while during the 2001 slowdown, they were forced to raise them again. This pro-cyclical monetary policy calls into question the purported benefits of the scheme. If the alternative to a-cyclical implicit hard pegs and 'dollarizers' is a pro-cyclical policy, the benefits of floating may be quite limited.

In short, to be a successful floater, you better not have too many dollar liabilities lying around. But remember, short-term domestic currency liabilities can also get you in trouble through self-fulfilling inflationary expectations.

5.8   WHY SO MANY DOLLAR LIABILITIES? THE ORIGINAL SIN ASSUMPTION

According to a commonly held view, unhedged dollar liabilities are the consequence of currency pegs (e.g., Burnside, Eichenbaum and Rebelo, 1999). The private sector feels protected by the government's commitment to keep the peg, or its willingness to bail out borrowers, if it does not. Hence the private sector does not buy insurance against the possibility of devaluations. When there are such occurrences, pandemonium ensues. The obvious solution is to let the currency float. Under such circumstances, people will not want to take unhedged loans in foreign currency, and this will limit the accumulation of currency mismatches.

The problem with this story is that there are an awful lot of floating rate countries that do all their external borrowing in foreign currency, unhedged, while there are only a few non-G10 countries that borrow internationally in their own currency. The empirical evidence suggests that very few countries borrow internationally in their own currency. The large majority of countries – including essentially all developing countries, meaning their governments, their banks and their non-financial corporations – do not borrow internationally in their own currency.

One approach is to assume that they do not borrow, not because they do not want to, for reasons of moral hazard, but instead, because they cannot: the market just does not exist. Figure 5.3 shows a measure of original sin taken from Hausmann, Stein and Panizza (2000). It measures the ratio of debt issued internationally in the currency of a given country to debt issued in any currency by residents of that country. Countries with original sin get a low number. The ratio can exceed one as there may be more debt issued in a given currency (e.g., US$) relative to debt issued by residents of that country (e.g., American residents), as others use that currency to denominate their debts. As can be observed, original sin seems to be a shared characteristic of all emerging markets, with very few exceptions; South Africa is the most notable example.

Whatever the reasons for original sin, the important point is that the reasons may not be directly related or influenced by the choice of exchange rate regime, or other areas of feasible macro policy; they are not just a consequence of pegging. In fact, all countries included in Figure 5.3 formally float their currencies.

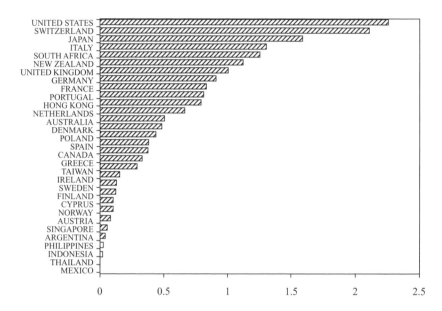

Figure 5.3   Index 3 of original sin

What causes original sin is an interesting question in itself, and is generating a growing literature in this area.[16] As far as macro policy is concerned, there may have been unclear causes in the past, but the current generation is nevertheless presented with stark choices. Eve may, or may not have been duped by the snake, but men have to work and women go through childbirth with pain.

Original sin is an assumption of a certain type of market incompleteness and, as such, has important implications for monetary policy, because, as we mentioned before, it is the market incompleteness that gives monetary policy its impact. So this opens three questions. What are the potential causes of this phenomenon? What are the monetary consequences of this form of market incompleteness? How does it affect the choice of the exchange regime?

5.9   ON THE CAUSES OF ORIGINAL SIN

The causes of original sin are not well understood, and it is not easy to learn from the few countries that have achieved 'redemption'. It is too global a phenomenon to be explained by Latin American-style fiscal or macro- economic peccadilloes. It affects virtuous Chile and prudent East Asia as much as it does the lesser credits. Here are a set of possible explanations.

First, assume a country has a net foreign debt. If it were in domestic currency, the residents would benefit from depreciations. Hence, net creditors would not want to lend in a currency that the borrower can manipulate. However, if a country is a net creditor, this logic would not apply.

Second, political economy considerations may also play a role. For example, in countries where the median voter does not benefit from maintaining the real value of local currency assets, foreigners may not be willing to denominate their claims in that unit.

Third, consider the network effects of money. There may be forces that create economies of agglomeration. The larger the market, the more liquid it is and the greater the incentives for both issuers and investors to use it. A disproportionate amount of debt is issued in G-3 currencies.

Fourth, it may also be related to the fact that the gains from portfolio diversification decrease rapidly with the number of assets. Such plurality may justify 10 currencies in the portfolio, but not 30 or 180.

Fifth, as shown by Chamon (2001), if the risk of default and depreciation are correlated, and if after borrowing in local currency a firm can later increase its foreign currency debt, investors may not want to denominate their claim in a unit that would lose value relative to other investors when a bankruptcy cum devaluation occurs.

Finally, as shown by Chamon and Hausmann (2002), there may be multiple equilibria in the choice of currency denomination and monetary policy. If investors choose to denominate their debts in dollars, central banks will choose to make the exchange rate stable vis-à-vis the interest rate, making their original choice the safer one. The converse would also be true if investors choose to borrow in domestic currency.

The point is that any of these six potential causes are not necessarily endogenous to the choice of exchange regime, as in the moral hazard story. We must then figure out the implications of this.

5.10   CONSEQUENCES OF ORIGINAL SIN

The central point is that because of original sin, capital importing countries will have large currency mismatches in their balance sheets. If an original sin country has a net external debt, it will have a net currency mismatch, as that debt will be denominated in foreign currency.

The consequences for monetary policy appear to be quite clear and powerful. Floaters with original sin will be less able to use monetary policy in a stabilizing manner than can their more virtuous fellow floaters. They will try to prevent large currency movements, because these will have a negative impact on the balance sheet of companies and hence on their capacity to borrow and invest. In order to prevent these currency fluctuations, central banks will have to raise interest rates when there is pressure on the currency, and let them come down when the pressure is reduced. They do so more than in economies with hard pegs because the central bank cannot signal to the market its commitment to defend its *de facto* currency target. This will cause monetary policy to be used pro-cyclically and in a destabilizing manner.

The empirical evidence in Hausmann, Stein and Panizza (2000), indicates that when countries with original sin float, they do so with more international reserves than countries with currency boards, such as Argentina, which have little *de facto* exchange rate flexibility and very unstable interest rates.

Dollarization of liabilities at the corporate level may in fact be much larger than the effect caused only by the net external debt. For the reasons argued above, it may not make as much sense for foreigners to lend in domestic currency.[17] However, it also does not make that much sense for residents to save only in domestic currency, especially in floating rate countries. This is so for the following reason.

If the expectation is that the domestic currency will be strong in good times and weak in bad times, then it makes little sense for residents – whose income is mainly tied to how well the economy is doing – to save in domestic currency. In bad times, savings will be worth less, when they are most needed. Said differently, the correlation between shocks to national income and movements in the exchange rate cause a positive correlation between national income and returns on financial assets, which makes it less attractive to hold domestic assets. Ideally, risk-averse households will want to hold assets whose return is negatively correlated with their income. This logic might explain why dollarization of savings is so entrenched in Latin America. While in many countries *de facto* dollarization accelerated during bouts of high inflation, in no country was the process reversed after the return to low inflation (Rojas-Suarez and McNellis, 1996). Exchange rate flexibility may provide an added impetus to this logic. If the idea is to stimulate the economy in bad times with a weaker currency and to slow it down in good times with a stronger currency, this will create precisely the incentives for the further dollarization of savings.

5.11   IMPLICATIONS FOR EXCHANGE RATE POLICY: TOWARD A SECOND 'IT' BUBBLE?

What does all this mean for the choice of exchange rate regime? Disappointment is rampant these days in many camps. The reform effort in many countries has paid off less spectacularly than once expected. Information technology (IT) was supposed to usher in a period of unencumbered prosperity. Instead, the NASDAQ (National Association of Securities Dealers Automatic Quotation System) has registered a quite remarkable collapse, led by the rising stars of the information revolution. The Argentine Convertibility Law is increasingly under attack. The only system that has yet to receive such impacts these days is the other IT revolution: inflation targeting. If you read some of its most vocal supporters (Velasco, 2001), the jury is in. Latin American countries have gained enough credibility to run decent monetary policy anchored by inflation targets. The system is bound to be superior to any of the alternatives now on offer.

Given this background, it may be useful to bring to the table some of the things that may make this second IT bubble burst. After all, there are so many different types of crisis that it would be a surprise to find that this new system is immune to all of them.

Floating with original sin may have quite unsavory effects. Here are some conjectures about how a floating regime anchored by inflation targeting may operate in practice:

1. As argued above, floating will tend to accentuate the dollarization of domestic savings. It will create a positive correlation between national income and returns to domestic assets, thus increasing the incentives for residents to hold dollar assets as a risk diversification strategy.
2. Less demand for dollar-denominated loans. Exchange rate uncertainty will reduce the demand for dollar-denominated loans. This will not only limit the ability to use foreign savings, but will also reduce the intermediation of the portion of domestic savings that is denominated in dollars.
3. Pro-cyclical monetary policy. Original sin will force central banks to concern themselves with exchange rates. However, without the benefit of a clear anchor, they will need to signal their intentions by moving the interest rate. But this signal is not very transparent, forcing the monetary authorities into moving interest rates erratically and by larger amounts to achieve their goals. In good times, to prevent too much appreciation, they will lower rates. In bad times, to prevent depreciation they will raise rates, as we are seeing now in Mexico and Brazil. This will amplify business cycles.
4. Riskier banking systems. Volatile interest rates and pro-cyclical monetary policy make safe banking difficult. It is hard to gauge the solvency of a client if you do not know what the interest rate environment will be like. It is also hard to manage the credit booms and busts that go with a pro-cyclical monetary policy.[18]
5. Difficulty in developing long-term markets. With volatile short-term rates, it will be difficult to lengthen the maturity of obligations, unless these are indexed to the price level, as in Chile.

6. Less financial development. With no long-term markets in domestic currency and strong disincentives to borrow in foreign currency there will be less financial development.
7. Lower growth. To the extent you believe that financial development is important for growth, this follows from the previous point.
8. Risk of self-fulfilling crises. IT is not crisis free. Countries can get into types of crises that are inherent to systems with monetary discretion, such as inflationary self-fulfilling crises that are caused by short-term or floating rate nominal debt. They can also be attacked because of the presence of dollar liabilities. They can also get into types of crises that affect all systems.
9. Crises for all: types of crises that are not contingent on currency arrangements.

So, it may well be that after Argentina, the next major crisis will be in an inflation-targeting country. Here it is important to note that crises do not really depend on the exchange regime. After all, of the three countries that are now creating concerns – Brazil, Uruguay and Turkey – all have floating arrangements. In a certain reading of things, their crises appear remarkably similar to those faced by Argentina.

It was argued above that self-fulfilling attacks can be caused by nominal debt and inflationary expectations, by maturity mismatches with foreign currency debt and bank-like runs and by dollar debts and depreciation expectations. In all these crises, there is a monetary element to the story. You may be able to avoid the crisis if you have the right currency denomination or the right regime. The next section mentions two types of crises that are likely to affect emerging market countries, independently of these nominal considerations.

5.12   CONCERNS OVER FISCAL SOLVENCY CAN KILL YOU

If the market believes that a country might not be able to honor its debts, then interest rates will be high, in order to compensate investors for the high risk of default. However, if interest rates are high, investment and growth will be low. With low growth, the tax base does not expand, making continued debt service improbable. By contrast, if the expectations of default are low, this will engender an environment of low interest rates, which makes growth possible, leading to an expanding tax base with which to pay a lower debt burden. In fact, the author takes this to be the root cause of the current difficulties in Argentina.

Notice that this argument is quite unrelated to the currency regime. In fact, the same logic may apply to Brazil, in spite of its different currency regime. It is a real argument, not a monetary one. If markets become concerned again about debt dynamics in Brazil, the above logic will apply. In fact, in Brazil the situation could become even nastier as the types of crisis discussed above may further complicate matters. For example, a weakening currency may lead to self-fulfilling inflationary expectations. Or a depreciating currency may call into question the solvency of dollar debtors.

5.13   SUDDEN STOPS CAN KILL YOU

Financial integration was supposed to facilitate the absorption of shocks and make economies more stable. When an economy receives a shock, it can smooth the adjustment process by borrowing abroad. Fluctuations in income need not cause major changes in spending; the current account can take the hit.

Of course, a major assumption of this view is that countries face a relatively elastic supply of funds at an interest rate that is relatively stable. This is a major assumption! The country risk of emerging markets has exhibited an enormous volatility and great correlation across countries, suggesting that changes are highly influenced by international factors (Fernández-Arias and Hausmann, 2000). Moreover, financing availability has been highly pro-cyclical; capital flows and bond prices rise in good times and decline when they are most needed to finance the bad times. This means that instead of facilitating the management of other shocks, international finance has either amplified fluctuations or become a major new disturbance.

Shocks to the capital account or sudden stop can become self-fulfilling. Suppose a country is being financed to the tune of 4 percent of the GDP. If for some reason external financing were to stop, this would lead to a major domestic contraction and a real exchange rate depreciation (as demand for non-tradable falls and dollars become scarce). Those borrowing abroad would have trouble repaying their loans, thus justifying the collapse in finance.

5.14   A SECOND BALANCE OF THE ARGUMENTS

Monetary arrangements have to be designed taking into account the nature of the incompleteness of markets. After all, it is that incompleteness that gives monetary policy its real consequences. The traditional approach assumes that the incompleteness is related to unspecified nominal rigidities that can be circumvented by having a flexible exchange rate, but at the cost of generating undesired inflationary expectations. The traditional approach presents the issue as one of flexibility versus credibility, of more stable output versus more stable inflation.

However, the issue of financial fragility has become central to the choice of exchange rate regime for emerging markets. For some, pegged exchange rates are implicit guarantees that cause moral hazards, excessive risk-taking and crises. We have argued instead, that original sin makes all exchange rate arrangements problematic. If countries are unable to borrow internationally in their own currency and if they, as is often the case, also lack long-term markets, even domestically, all firms will face a very incomplete financial market. Either they borrow in dollars and expose themselves to undesired exchange rate risk, or they borrow short term in local currency and expose themselves to roll-over problems and liquidity crises. We take this incompleteness to be central to the exchange rate dilemma.

With original sin, central banks face very stark choices. When a negative shock hits, they fear letting exchange rates move because of the currency mismatches in the system. But the alternative – restricting the money supply and letting the interest rate rise – complicates the life of those with short-term debts and exposes them to the risk of liquidity crises. Empirical evidence suggests that countries with original sin that float restrict the benefits of exchange rate flexibility in order to avoid financial fragility; they exhibit fear of floating, accumulate massive reserves and use interest rates in a pro-cyclical manner.

In this context, dollarization exhibits some of its advantages. It does away with currency mismatches that underpin many of the problems caused by original sin. It eliminates currency mismatches by having a domestic currency that can be used to borrow internationally. It also facilitates the elimination of maturity mismatches. After all, many emerging markets that are able to place 30-year bonds in dollars have trouble issuing two-year bonds in local currency. These aspects may eliminate some of the problems that lead to financial fragility. In addition, if Andrew Rose and Eric Van Wincoop (2001) are right, dollarization may lead to more trade among the countries that share the same currency and to more total trade. This not only promises higher incomes, but it will tie together economies more closely, making them score better in the traditional optimal currency criteria of greater good and factor mobility and common economic cycles.

However, the world also has very large exchange rate volatility between the major countries. The dollar/yen and dollar/euro exchange rates have been remarkably volatile for a world of such low inflation differentials. This creates enormous challenges for countries that are not clearly tied to any currency area. East Asia and the Southern Cone of Latin America are two such regions. For them, G-3 exchange rate volatility represents very large real shocks to their economies. In fact, these shocks played an important role in the East Asian crisis and are a contributing factor in Argentina's travails today. Moreover, G-3 exchange rate volatility increases the volatility of commodity prices in world markets, further augmenting the importance of real shocks. All this favors more exchange rate flexibility.

But flexibility in a world of original sin is problematic. Having a national currency that cannot be used internationally is not the right solution. It may facilitate the management of certain shocks, but it exposes countries to financial fragilities of the kind that are at work today in Brazil. The real choice is between dollarization and redemption.

Dollarization does away with the problem of original sin by having foreign money become domestic currency. Redemption, i.e., the undoing of original sin, implies that the domestic currency becomes part of the acceptable global financial portfolio. This is obviously a superior solution in many respects. It eliminates the fragilities that come with original sin and it frees the hands of the central bank to use monetary policy in a more stabilizing manner. Moreover, if the foreign debt is denominated in the national currency and if this currency adjusts to shocks in the standard manner, then the debt burden takes on equity-like characteristics: it increases in value in good times and falls in bad times thus sharing the risks internationally and making the domestic economy more stable.

The problem is that we really do not know how to seek redemption. The view that attributes foreign currency borrowing to the moral hazard caused by pegs is clearly wrong. There are plenty of countries with original sin that float. Our ability to learn about the road to redemption is limited by the fact that there are very few countries that have changed status with respect to their ability to borrow internationally in their own currency. Australia and New Zealand are interesting cases. This is a critical new area of research that requires a much better understanding of the causes of original sin. In the meantime, we do not know how to proceed, nor for how long countries that embarked on this road would be exposed to financial fragilities or restricted from adequate access to international finance.

For countries like Britain or Switzerland, the choice between adopting the euro or keeping their national currency is obviously unrelated to original sin, a problem they do not confront. There the debate is more clearly one that involves the trade benefits of a common currency against the flexibility provided by a quite powerful monetary policy. For Turkey and the Czech Republic, the issue is quite different. By having a national currency, they not only limit their trade integration but expose themselves to financial fragilities; in exchange, they get a stunted monetary policy. These countries should get a bigger return out of adopting the euro.

But for the Czech Republic, joining the euro will eventually mean being a full member of its governance structure of the monetary system. That is not an option for Turkey, Ecuador, El Salvador or even Canada and Argentina. Obviously having some form of political representation is better than being excluded from it, but this point should not be exaggerated. European monetary policy will pay scant attention to the macroeconomic situation in Luxembourg or Ireland when setting interest rates. What may be more important for small peripheral countries that adopt a major currency are issues of seignorage and last resort lending. Moreover, beyond the setting of interest rates, there are many policy issues that need to be continuously analyzed and decided within a monetary regime, many of them unknown at present. Being excluded from any form of participation represents a source of risk. In this respect, the lack of interest on the side of the United States to create a framework for dollarization is a major problem.

In addition, there is an important issue for countries that, given their diversified trade and financial integration to the world, are importantly exposed to G-3 exchange rate volatility, as is the case in East Asia and the Southern Cone of Latin America. By choosing one of the major world currencies, they expose their economies to significant real shocks. Here an alternative is to opt for more than one international currency. If a country is not going to have its own currency, it might as well have more than one foreign one. This allows it to develop a monetary index that would be a basket of the major currencies designed to limit the problems caused by G-3 exchange rate volatility. Countries would be able to borrow internationally in any of the major currencies and hedge any exposure in the well developed international derivative markets, thus avoiding currency mismatches.

Monetary sovereignty is unlikely to have a long life. As the world becomes more integrated, more transactions involve citizens of different sovereigns. For those transactions, there is no such thing as monetary sovereignty, as each of the sovereigns involved can only affect half of the transaction, which is like half a bridge. As international transactions become a larger share of total transactions, the attractiveness of sovereign currencies with respect to common currencies diminishes.

But we are not there yet. In the meantime, the question for emerging markets is whether to seek redemption from original sin in order to fully exploit the flexibility provided by an autonomous monetary policy, or to start constructing the monetary arrangements of a world of common currencies.

NOTES

1. The argument was initially put forward by Andrew Crocket in 1993 at the annual Jackson Hole gathering of central bankers organized by the Federal Reserve Bank of Kansas City. For a recent restatement of this view see Fischer (2001), Frankel (1999) and Williamson (2000).
2. For the purpose of simplifying the terminology, the adoption of a currency other than one issued solely by the national authority will be labeled as dollarization, even if it involves the adoption of the euro or some other currency.
3. As is so often the case in this complex world, this commitment was soon broken when the Turkish exchange-rate-based stabilization program started to unravel at the end of 2000.
4. An alternative is small menu costs, but it has attracted much less policy attention.

5. See for example, Cespedes, Chang and Velasco (2000), Velasco (2001).
6. The debate can be followed in Andy Rose's website http://haas.berkeley.edu/~arose.
7. Alesina and Barro (2002) present a model in which the traditional Barro-Gordon framework is mixed with optimal currency criteria. They show that countries with a bigger credibility problem should adopt the currency of those with more credibility.
8. Evidence of lack of floating is discussed in Hausmann, Gavin, Pagés-Serra and Stein (1999), Calvo and Reinhart (1999), Hausmann, Stein and Panizza (2000).
9. In fact, the accounts would be close to balance if expected inflation were about 15 percent, but the market is expecting much less (about 7 percent), making the situation worse.
10. Japan and Brazil are not unique cases. Belgium or Italy could play the role of country A, while Argentina or Turkey could play the role of country B.
11. Granted, they did use the reduction in debt service to improve the fiscal balance instead of increasing spending.
12. Interestingly, Argentina was probably the most advanced emerging market in the management of its fiscal and financial liquidity.
13. See Aghion, Bacchetta and Banerjee (1999), Cespedes, Chang and Velasco (2000), Velasco (2001).
14. It may even have potentially positive aggregate supply effect as it lowers dollar wages.
15. See Hausmann, Gavin, Serra-Pagés and Stein (1999).
16. Among others, Aghion, Bacchetta and Banerjee (1999), Chamon (2001), Jeanne (2000).
17. This argument is made in Hausmann, Gavin, Pagés-Serra and Stein (1999) and shown more formally in Aizenman and Hausmann (2000).
18. In fact, contrary to a commonly held view, floating rate countries are not subject to fewer credit crunches (Braun and Hausmann, 2001) or banking crises (Arteta and Eichengreen, 2000).

BIBLIOGRAPHY

Aghion, P., Bacchetta, P. and Banerjee, A. (1999), 'Capital Markets and the Instability of Open Economies', *CEPR Discussion Paper*, **2083**, London, United Kingdom: Centre for Economic Policy Research.

Aizenman, J. and Hausmann, R. (2000), 'Exchange Rate Regimes and Financial-Market Imperfections', UCSC Department of Economics Working Paper, 493.

Alesina, A. and Barro, R.J. (2002), 'Currency Unions', *The Quarterly Journal of Economics*, May 2003, pp. 409–36 .

Arrow, Kenneth J. and Debreu, G. (1954), 'Existence of an Equilibrium for a Competitive Economy', *Econometrica*, **22**(3), pp. 265–90.

Arteta, C. and Eichengreen, B. (2000), 'Banking Crisis in Emerging Markets: Presumptions and Evidence', *Center for International and Development Economics Research Working Paper*, **C00-115**.

Barro, Robert J. and David B. Gordon (1983), 'A Positive Theory of Monetary Policy in a Natural-Rate Model', *Journal of Political Economy*, **91**(4), pp. 589–610, *Journal of Economic Literature*, **22**(1), March 1984.

Braun, Matias and Ricardo Hausman (2001), *Credit Crunches in Latin America and the World*, unpublished manuscript.

Burnside, Craig, Martin Eichenbaum and Sergio Rebelo (1999), 'Hedging and Financial Fragility in Fixed Exchange Rate Regimes', *NBER Working Paper*, **W7143**.

Calvo, G.A. (1978), 'On the Time Consistency of Optimal Policy in a Monetary Economy', *Econometrica*, **46**(6), pp. 1411–28.

Calvo, G.A. (1989), 'Servicing the Public Debt: The Role of Expectations', *American Economic Review*.

Calvo, G. and Reinhart, C. (1999), 'Capital Flow Reversals, The Exchange Rate Debate, and Dollarization', *Finance and Development*, **36**(3), pp. 13–15.

Calvo, G. and Reinhart C. (2000), '*Fear of Floating*', Paper presented to the Conference on Currency Unions, Hoover Institution, Stanford University.

Cespedes, Luis Felipe, Robert Chang and Andres Velasco (2000), 'Balance Sheets and Exchange Rate Policy', *NBER Working Paper*, **W7840**.

Chamon, Marcos (2001), *Why Firms in Developing Countries Cannot Borrow in their Own Currency Even When Indexing to Inflation*, mimeo, Harvard University.

Chamon, Marcos and Ricardo Hausmann (2002), *Why Do Countries Borrow the Way they Borrow?*, mimeo, Harvard University.

Chang, Roberto and Andrés Velasco (1999), 'Liquidity Crises in Emerging Markets: Theory and Policy', *NBER Working Paper*, **W7272**.

Diamond, D. and Dybvig, P. (1983), 'Bank Runs, Deposit Insurance, and Liquidity', *Journal of Political Economy*, **91**, pp. 401–19.

Eichengreen, Barry (1997), *Globalizing Capital*, Washington: Institute of International Economics.

Feldstein, Martin and Charles Horioka (1980), 'Domestic Savings and International Capital Flows', *The Economic Journal*, **90**, pp. 314–29.

Fernández-Arias, Eduardo and Ricardo Hausmann (2000), 'What's Wrong with International Financial Markets?', *IADB Working Paper*, **429**.

Fernández-Arias, Eduardo and Ricardo Hausmann (2001), 'Is FDI a Safer Form of Financing?', *Emerging Markets Review*, **2**(2001), pp. 34–9.

Fischer, Stanley (2001), 'Exchange Rate Regimes : Is the Bipolar View Correct?', *Journal of Economic Perspectives*, **15**(2), pp. 3–24.

Frankel, J.A. (1980), 'The Demand for International Reserves under Pegged and Flexible Exchange Rate Regimes', in *The Functioning of Floating Exchange Rates: Theory, Evidence, and Policy Implications*, edited by David Bigman and Teizo Taya, pp. 169–95, Pensacola: Ballinger.

Frankel, J.A. (1999), 'No Single Currency Regime is Right for All Countries at All Times', *NBER Working Paper*, **7338**.

Frankel, Jeffrey A. and David Romer (1996), 'Trade and Growth: An Empirical Investigation', *NBER Working Paper*, **W5476**.

Frankel, Jeffrey and Andrew K. Rose (1998), 'The Endogenity of the Optimum Currency Area Criterion', *Economic Journal*.

Frankel, Jeffrey and Andrew K. Rose (2000), 'Estimating the Effect of Currency Unions on Trade and Output', *NBER Working Paper*, **W7857**.

Frankel, Jeffrey, Sergio Schmukler and Luis Serven (2000), 'Verifiability and the Vanishing Intermediate Exchange Rate Regime', *NBER Working Paper*, **W7901**.

Friedman, Milton (1968), *Dollars and Deficits: Inflation, Monetary Policy and the Balance of Payments*, Englewood Cliffs, NJ: Prentice-Hall.

Galindo, Arturo (2001), 'Creditor Rights and the Credit Market: Where Do We Stand?', *IADB Working Paper*, **448**.

Glick, Reuven and Andrew K. Rose (2001), 'Does a Currency Union Affect Trade? The Time Series Evidence', *NBER Working Paper*, **W8396**.

Hausmann, Ricardo, Michael Gavin, Carmen Pagés-Serra and Ernesto H. Stein (1999), 'Financial Turmoil and Choice of Exchange Rate Regime', *IADB Working Paper*, **400**.

Hausmann, Ricardo and Roberto Rigobon (2001), *Self-Fulfilling Fiscal Expectations and The Argentine Crisis*, unpublished manuscript.

Hausmann, Ricardo, Ernesto H. Stein and Ugo Panizza (2000), 'Why Do Countries Float the Way they Float?', *IADB Working Paper*, **418**.

Helliwell, John F. and Ross McKitrick (1998), 'Comparing Capital Mobility across Provincial and National Borders', *NBER Working Paper*, **6624**.

Jeanne, O. (2000), 'Currency Crisis: A Perspective on Recent Theoretical Development', *Special Papers in International Economics*, No. 20. International Finance Section, Princeton University.

Kydland, Finn E. and Edward C. Prescott (1977), 'Rules Rather than Discretion: The Inconsistency of Optimal Plans', *The Journal of Political Economy*, **85**(3), pp. 473–92.

Levi-Yeyati, Eduardo and Federico Sturzenegger (2001), *To Float or to Trail*, unpublished manuscript.

Mundell, Robert (1961), 'Flexible Exchange Rates and Employment Policy', *Canadian Journal of Economics and Political Science*, **27**(4), pp. 509–17.

Rojas-Suarez, Liliana and Paul D. McNellis (1996), 'Exchange-Rate Depreciation, Dollarization and Uncertainty: A Comparison of Bolivia and Peru', *IADB Working Paper*, **325**.

Rose, Andrew K. (1999), 'One Money, One Market: Estimating the Effect of Common Currencies on Trade', *NBER Working Paper*, **W7432**.

Rose, Andrew K. and Eric van Wincoop (2001), 'National Money as a Barrier to Trade: The Real Case for Currency Union', *American Economic Review*.

Svensson, Lars E.O. (1998), 'Inflation Targeting as a Monetary Policy Rule', *NBER Working Paper*, **W6790**.

Velasco, Andre (2001), *Balance Sheets and Exchange Rate Policy*, unpublished manuscript.

Venables, Anthony and Steve Redding (2001), *Economic Geography and International Inequality*, unpublished manuscript.

Williamson, John (2000), *Exchange Rate Regimes for Emerging Markets: Reviving the Intermediate Option*, Washington, DC: Institute for International Economics.

6. The East Asian exchange rate dilemma and the world dollar standard

Ronald I. McKinnon

6.1 INTRODUCTION

In the realm of economics, the term 'globalization' refers to the growing interdependence among countries in cross-border flows of goods, services, capital and technical know-how. At first glance, the case for globalization in East Asia, as elsewhere, seems to be just a more general version of the case for freer trade. Moreover, we have persuasive theorems showing that welfare generally (although not necessarily that of particular individuals or firms) increases as the ambit of trade expands. Indeed, the formal theory underlying the advocacy of free trade has it that small countries are the biggest gainers. Outside the United States, why then should globalization make so many people in smaller countries – and even larger ones like China and Japan – so uneasy?

The enhanced hegemony of the United States is a prime source of international uneasiness in the new millennium – just as British military and financial hegemony made other countries uneasy with the spread of freer international trade in the 19th century. In today's military terms, there is just one superpower that sends gunboats – i.e., aircraft carriers – to keep the peace in faraway places, at least where its vital interests are concerned. There is also the invasive crass commercialism of multinational firms, mainly American, which non-Americans see as a threat to their traditional way of life – as when French farmers set fire to MacDonald's hamburger stands. Other countries, particularly regimes that force their people into subservience through a blinkered religion, see foreign influences undermining national cultures.

However, this chapter will approach the problem of American global hegemony in general, and the associated problem of crafting suitable exchange rate policies in East Asia in particular, quite differently – which at first glance might seem like an arcane exercise in monetary economics. In the absence of a common international money (such as gold in the 19th century), the ever-widening ambit of international trade and finance today accentuates an entirely natural asymmetry among national currencies. A strong central money (or key currency) becomes dominant, as the US dollar now dominates on a worldwide scale outside of Europe, and as the old Deutschmark dominated within Europe before its monetary unification with the advent of the euro. (In the 19th century, Britain was also resented as the world's dominant creditor country that kept the rest of the world somewhat in thrall to the London capital market. However, because Britain was then on the gold standard, more or less on a par with the other industrial countries, it had much less autonomy in monetary matters than does the United States in today's world of 'fiat' national moneys.)

We live in an inherently asymmetrical, and perhaps unfair, world because there can be only one central money for facilitating international exchange. In East Asia, the US dollar is the dominant vehicle currency in interbank foreign exchange transactions, and the currency of choice for invoicing the great bulk of commodity trade. Inevitably this leaves most countries' currencies on the periphery of that central money, where countries – particularly developing ones – have domestic financial systems that are naturally more fragile. They live with the ever-present threat of a currency crisis, i.e., a run from their peripheral money into the central one, the American dollar. Indeed, managing foreign exchange and financial policy is more difficult on the periphery than at the center. It is easier to be the US Secretary of the Treasury than to be the Korean, Argentinean or Thai Minister of Finance!

One important aspect of this asymmetry is the nature of currency risk in the foreign exchanges. The US economy is by far the biggest debtor to the rest of the world – something like $2.7 trillion of net indebtedness, which continues to increase with the current American trade deficit. Nevertheless, nobody thinks that the dollar could really be attacked, or that there could be a currency crisis in the ordinary sense. Insofar as American banks, insurance companies, and so on receive foreign funds as the counterpart of America's trade deficit, this build up of liabilities to foreigners is entirely denominated in US dollars.

So American banks have dollar-denominated liabilities both to foreigners and to domestic nationals, and they make dollar-denominated loans – largely to American firms and households. Because of this absence of foreign exchange exposure, American financial institutions can absorb this huge capital inflow without currency risk. There are other risks, but they are not associated with fluctuations in the dollar's exchange rate against other currencies.

However, if smaller debtor economies on the periphery of the dollar standard – such as Korea, Thailand, or any in Latin America – absorb foreign capital, typically the debts are denominated in another country's currency, i.e., mainly the US dollar, but also the yen or the euro upon occasion. The genesis of the great 1997–98 crisis was the huge short-term inflow of capital into the smaller

East Asian economies, but denominated in dollars or yen. This meant their banks and financial institutions were at risk if there were any exchange rate fluctuations. In particular, any devaluation made repaying these external dollar obligations from earnings on domestic assets denominated in won, or baht, or pesos, much more difficult.

Paradoxically, in the United States itself, there is surprisingly little appreciation of how today's world dollar standard actually works. Indeed, in the whole of postwar academic literature since 1945, the dollar standard has been little analyzed. As a consequence, American policymakers have had little clear guidance in their interactions with other countries, and in their relationships with agencies such as the International Monetary Fund, the World Bank, or the Asian Development Bank. What needs to be done to reform the 'international financial architecture', to make the world a financially safer place, thus remains in limbo.

The first part of this analysis provides a historical perspective on how the world dollar standard has evolved since World War II, with special concern for the developing countries and emerging markets on their periphery. Then, the second part focuses on East Asia. Specifically, 'the East Asian exchange rate dilemma' – including the current plight of Japan – will be linked to how the dollar standard now works.

6.2   THE WORLD DOLLAR STANDARD IN HISTORICAL PERSPECTIVE

How did this asymmetrical position of the dollar become established in the world economy? After World War II, the US had the world's only intact financial system. There were inflation, currency controls, and so on in Europe, as well as in Japan and most developing countries. Thus, in open foreign exchange markets, the dollar naturally became the world's vehicle currency for (private) interbank transactions, and the intervention currency that governments used for stabilizing their exchange rates. Under the Bretton Woods agreement of 1945, every country pegged to the dollar, and the US did not have a formal exchange rate policy, except for its residual tie to gold.

Given the history of the situation, this was quite natural. The US had the only open capital market, so countries could easily build up their dollar reserves and have a liquid market in which to buy and sell them. Similarly, private corporations in other countries all built up dollar reserves, as well, because their own currencies had exchange controls. Because of this accident of history, the US dollar became the intermediary currency in international exchange between any pair of 'peripheral' moneys.

6.3   THE DOLLAR AS FACILITATOR OF INTERNATIONAL EXCHANGE

But why does the dollar continue with this facilitating function even when most other industrial countries – such as Japan and those in Europe – no longer have exchange controls? A little algebra helps explain the continued dollar predominance. Suppose you have N currencies, say 150, in the world economy. The markets, themselves, would always pick one currency to facilitate international exchange. The reason for that is a big economy of markets.

If we think of a world of N countries with independent national moneys, then just from your basic high school probability theory, the total number of country pairs in the system is $N(N - 1)/2$. If foreign exchange dealers tried to trade across each pair, say, Swedish crowns against Australian dollars, or Korean won against Japanese yen, it would turn out that there would be a huge number of different foreign exchange markets. With 150 national currencies in the world ($N = 150$), if you tried to trade each pair, there would be 11,175 foreign exchange markets!

It is expensive for any bank to set up a foreign exchange trading desk, thus, rather than trading all pairs of currencies bilaterally, in practice just one currency, the Nth, is chosen as the central vehicle currency. Then all trading and exchange takes place first against the vehicle currency before going to the others. By having all currency trading against that one currency, you can reduce the number of markets in the system to $N - 1$. Thus, with 150 countries, we need to have just 149 foreign exchange markets instead of 11,175. Unlike the Bretton Woods system where all countries set official dollar parities, this result does not depend on any formal agreement among governments. In private markets today, choosing one currency like the dollar to be the intermediary currency is the most natural way of economizing on foreign exchange transacting.

However, history is important. If one country starts off providing the central money, as did the US in the late 1940s, then it becomes a natural monopoly because of the economies of scale. The more countries that deal in dollars, the cheaper it is for everybody to deal in dollars. If you're a Japanese importer of Swedish Volvos and you want to pay for the Volvos, you first get your bank to convert your yen into dollars on the open market, then use the dollars to buy Swedish crowns. Volvo Corporation receives the Swedish crowns and the importer gets the Volvos. However, the dollar is the intermediary currency.

Using the standard textbook classification of the roles of money, Table 6.1 summarizes our paradigm of the dollar's central role in the facilitating of international exchange. For both the private and government sectors, the dollar performs as medium of exchange, store of value, unit of account and standard of deferred payment for international transactions on current and capital account – and has done so from 1945 into the new millennium. It is a slight generalization of a similar table presented by Peter Kenen in 1983, but it remains as valid today as then.

Table 6.1   US dollar's facilitating role as international money – 1945 to 2000

	Private	Official
Medium of exchange	Vehicle currency	Intervention currency
Store of value	Banking	Reserves
Unit of account	Invoice	Parity fixing
Deferred payment	Private bonds	Sovereign bonds

First in Table 6.1, the dollar is a medium of exchange. Because foreign exchange markets are mainly interbank, the dollar is the vehicle currency in interbank transactions serving customers in the private sector. Thus, when any government intervenes to influence its exchange rates, it also finds it cheaper and more convenient to use the dollar as the official intervention currency. (The major exception to this convention had been within Europe prior to the advent of the euro, where for many purposes the old Deutschmark was the central money. Now, a fringe of small European countries to the east of 'Euroland' mainly use the euro as their central money.)

Second in Table 6.1, the dollar is an international store of value. Corporations and some individuals hold dollar bank accounts in London, Singapore and other 'offshore' banking centers – as well as in the US itself. For governments, international reserves are mainly in dollars – largely US Treasury bonds; Korea has $95 billion, Japan almost $400 billion, China nearly $200 billion, and so on. In fact, almost half of the US Treasury bonds outstanding are held by foreign central banks.

Third in Table 6.1, the dollar serves as a unit of account for much of international trade. Trade in primary commodities shows a strong pattern of using the dollar as the main currency of invoice. Exports of homogeneous primary products such as oil, wheat and copper all tend to be invoiced in dollars, with worldwide price formation in a centralized exchange. Spot trading, and particularly forward contracting, is concentrated at these centralized exchanges, which are usually in American cities, such as Chicago and New York, although dollar-denominated commodity exchanges do exist in London and elsewhere.

Invoicing patterns for exports of manufactured goods are more complex. Major industrial countries with strong currencies tend to invoice their exports in their home currencies. Before European Monetary Union, more than 75 percent of German exports had been invoiced in marks, more than 50 percent of French exports invoiced in francs, and so on. However, these illustrative ratios were dominated by intra-European trade. With the advent of the European Monetary Union, how much continental European countries will invoice their exports outside of Europe in euros remains unknown.

Within East Asia, however, foreign trade is invoiced mainly in dollars: Korean trade with Thailand is typically dollar invoiced. Even Japanese trade with other East Asian countries is invoiced more in dollars than in yen. Outside of Europe, the prevalence of dollar invoicing is also true in other parts of the world. For example, intra-Latin American exports are almost entirely dollar invoiced.

For pricing manufactures, more than pure invoicing is involved. Exporters everywhere outside of Europe typically opt to quote selling prices for their products in dollars, and then keep these dollar prices fairly constant in industrial catalogs and other published price lists. In effect, they price to the world market – and not just to the American one – in dollar terms. Thus, national central banks aiming to stabilize the international purchasing power of their currencies, often opt – either formally or informally – to peg against the dollar, and thus against the huge sticky-priced mass of internationally traded goods that it represents.

Fourth in Table 6.1, if we think of a standard of deferred payment – which is also a traditional role of money – private and sovereign bonds in international markets are largely denominated in US dollars, though some are now in euros. In international bond markets, US Treasury bonds are taken as the benchmark, or 'risk-free' asset. That is, dollar-denominated sovereign bonds issued by emerging markets the world over have their credit ratings (by Moody's, Standard and Poor's, or Fitch) measured relative to US Treasuries. Thus, risk premiums in interest rates on these bonds are typically quoted as so many percentage points over US Treasuries.

6.4   THE DOLLAR AS NOMINAL ANCHOR

Beyond facilitating international exchange, the dollar has a second and complementary international function. Foreign monetary authorities may better anchor their own domestic price levels by choosing to peg, officially or unofficially, to the dollar. By opting to keep their dollar exchange rates stable, foreign governments are essentially opting to harmonize – without always succeeding – their monetary policies with that of the United States. This monetary harmonization has two avenues: (1) international commodity arbitrage, i.e., the arbitrage avenue, and (2) the signaling avenue where other central banks take their cue from actions of the US Federal Reserve Bank.

The arbitrage avenue arises naturally out of the dollar's facilitating role in international finance. Because international trade in goods and services is largely dollar invoiced (including trade between countries outside of the United States), international arbitrage in the markets for goods and services through a fixed dollar exchange rate can be a powerful device to anchor any one country's domestic price level. Putting the matter more negatively, if other countries fail to prevent their dollar exchange rates from fluctuating, the degree of pass-through of these exchange rate fluctuations into their domestic prices is (ultimately) very high. (The one big exception would be countries in the large euro-area – whose domestic price levels are fairly well insulated from fluctuations in the euro's exchange rate against the dollar.)

Asymmetrically, because both American imports and exports are invoiced in dollars, America's own domestic price level is relatively insulated from fluctuations in the dollar's exchange rate. More generally, in the world at large, the dollar prices of internationally traded commodities are relatively invariant to fluctuations in the dollar's value against other currencies. So, as the Nth country in the system, the US alone can carry out an independent monetary policy to target its own domestic price level without being much disturbed by exchange rate fluctuations. For the other N–1 countries, however, direct international commodity arbitrage through a fixed exchange rate can help stabilize their own internal price levels.

In securing monetary harmonization with the United States, the signaling avenue can also be important. If any one national government resists upward pressure on its currency in the foreign exchanges, the resulting increase in its official dollar reserves signals the need for domestic monetary expansion – and vice versa. The national central bank can even take its cue directly from what the Fed is doing. For example, the Bank of Canada typically changes its own discount rate (interbank lending rate) relatively quickly in response to changes in the US Federal Funds rate.

However, for the dollar to function successfully as nominal anchor, two important conditions must be satisfied: (1) The American price level, as measured by a broad index of tradable goods prices, is stable and expected to remain so; and, (2) Most countries, and certainly neighboring ones, are on the same international standard, i.e., they also fix their exchange rates to the dollar. In the history of the postwar dollar standard, these two conditions were satisfied in some periods – but not so in others. Indeed, in contrast to the dollar's ongoing robustness as the facilitator of international exchange under either fixed or floating exchange rates, its function as a nominal anchor has been continually metamorphosed.

6.5 HIGH BRETTON WOODS, 1950 TO 1968

From the 1950s through 1968, the first panel of Figure 6.1 shows that the US price level for tradable goods prices – as measured by the US wholesale price

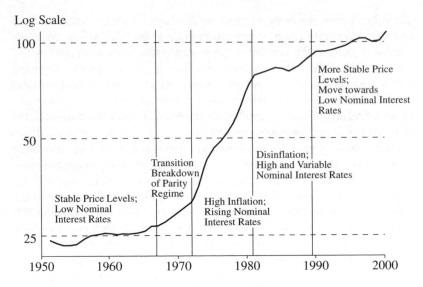

Log Scale

Source: International Financial Statistics, IMF (August 2001).

Figure 6.1   The world's nominal anchor: US wholesale prices (1951–2000)

index – was stable. In addition, interest rates on dollar assets were low and stable because of the absence of expected inflation. Therefore, under the old Bretton Woods par value system, all other countries willingly declared dollar parities, and kept their market exchange rates within a narrow band of 2 percent around these central parities, which were seldom changed. During this period of 'high' Bretton Woods, IMF member countries could use price stability in the center country as an anchor for their own domestic price levels.

Nevertheless, more than just the behavior of the center country was involved in this anchoring process. Because virtually all the major industrial countries were on the same fixed exchange rate regime, the 'world' price level was more secure. Precipitate devaluations (or appreciations) of any one country, which could impart deflationary pressure to a neighboring one, were avoided. In addition, potentially inflationary national macroeconomic shocks were dampened. The inertia or 'stickiness' in each country's price level was greater because all of them were committed to, and bound together under, a common monetary standard – albeit one ultimately dollar-based.

During this high Bretton Woods regime, even the American price level itself was more stable because of the generally fixed exchange rates. In the short and medium terms, the center country could benefit from commodity arbitrage with neighboring countries across the fixed exchange rates to dampen potentially inflationary shocks originating at home. In the end, however, the system could not survive persistent inflationary pressure in the center country – as we shall see.

Finally, as the initial panel of Figure 6.1 indicates, nominal interest rates in the industrial countries were low and remarkably stable in the 1950s and 1960s. Until the very late 1960s, the common rate of price inflation was so low that ordinary Fisher effects in interest rates were largely absent. In these immediate postwar decades, the perceived continued stability in exchange rates meant that cross-country interest differentials remained modest – despite the presence of capital controls in most of the industrial countries. This commitment to fixed dollar parities by the industrial countries finally collapsed in early 1973. However, the common monetary anchor undergirded that era's famously high real economic growth – not matched in the industrial world in any sustained way before or since.

For the less developed countries with immature domestic financial markets, having price and interest rate stability in the core industrial economies was particularly advantageous. They would have had great trouble controlling domestic inflation independently of stabilizing their dollar exchange rates. Instead, most simply opted to lock into the high Bretton Woods dollar standard. Of course, some in Latin America and elsewhere had too much domestic inflationary pressure to be able to keep their dollar exchange rates fixed. But, even when any one less-developed country (LDC) experienced a currency crisis with devaluation, the authorities usually avowed to return to the fixed rate dollar standard when able, thus dampening expectations of further inflation.

6.6   LOSING THE ANCHOR, 1968–73: THE ADVENT OF FLOATING EXCHANGE RATES

With hindsight, the old fixed rate dollar standard began to unravel in the late 1960s as WPI inflation in the United States – the center country – began to escalate toward 3 percent per year (Figure 6.1, second panel). Other countries, particularly Germany, became unwilling to maintain their old dollar parity and import even moderate inflationary pressure. The Deutschmark was revalued upward in 1969. More importantly, the United States was then hampered by the Keynesian belief (as encapsulated in the so-called Phillips curve) that disinflation would permanently increase domestic unemployment. So largely for doctrinal reasons, the center country refused to embark on a serious program of disinflation.

Nevertheless, the ongoing inflation reduced America's industrial competitiveness. Worried about America's declining foreign trade position, President Nixon in August 1971 closed the vestigial 'gold window'; he ended America's formal commitment under the old Bretton Woods articles to formally fix the dollar's value in terms of gold. Simultaneously, Nixon imposed an across-the-board tariff of 10 percent on American imports of manufactures, and insisted that the tariff would not be removed until all other industrial countries appreciated their currencies against the dollar. They all appreciated between 10 and 20 percent before re-establishing their new 'Smithsonian' dollar parities in December 1971. However, because the center country continued to inflate, the Smithsonian dollar parities were destined to fail. In February 1973, industrial countries gave up on their dollar parities and moved to no-par floating.

In the 1970s and into the 1980s in the United States, high and variable price inflation coupled with high and volatile nominal interest rates (see the third panel in Figure 6.1) largely eroded the dollar's usefulness as a nominal anchor. In most developing countries, as well as many industrial ones, inflation also increased sharply. Many industrial countries were now quite willing to have their currencies appreciate against the dollar to better insulate themselves from what had become a maelstrom of variable inflation rates worldwide. (Europeans were induced to look for a new center currency as their anchor, and tried to rebuild monetary stability around the Deutschmark. This effort culminated with the successful advent of the euro in the late 1990s.) The collective effect of this worldwide monetary instability on world productivity growth was catastrophic. Without a common anchor for domestic price levels and exchange rates, productivity in the industrial world and its periphery – except for the East Asian 'tigers' – slowed dramatically after 1973 through to the early 1990s.

6.7   PARADISE REGAINED IN THE 1990S?

But from the early 1990s into the new millennium, the last panel in Figure 6.1 shows a return to price stability in the United States, with US interest rates becoming moderate to low, once more. Thus, the dollar has again become attractive as an international anchor currency and as the predominant reserve asset worldwide. After the dollar's decline as a reserve asset in the inflationary 1970s and 1980s, the dollar's share in official foreign exchange reserves has greatly increased over the last decade. Table 6.2 shows the dollar rising from 51.3 percent of official holdings of foreign exchange (of members of the International Monetary Fund) in 1991 to 68.2 percent in 2000. Moreover, if one assumes a pro rata share of 'unspecified currencies' to be dollars, the dollar's current share in international reserves seems well over 75 percent.

Surprisingly, the advent of the euro has not reduced the dollar's predominance in international reserve holdings. Table 6.2 also shows that the share of euros in official foreign exchange reserves in 1999 and 2000 was no greater than was the sum of the old legacy currencies – marks, francs, and guilders – before the advent of the euro on 1 January 1999. Although the euro has been very successful for securing regional monetary integration in Europe, the dollar remains king in international finance worldwide.

Table 6.2   Share of currencies in total holdings of foreign exchange, end-year[1, 2]

(%)	1991	1992	1993	1994	1995	1996	1997	1998	1999	2000
All countries										
US dollar	51.3	55.3	56.7	56.6	57.0	60.3	62.4	65.9	68.4	68.2
Japanese yen	8.5	7.6	7.7	7.9	6.8	6.0	5.2	5.4	5.5	5.3
GB pound	3.3	3.1	3.0	3.3	3.2	3.4	3.7	3.9	4.0	3.9
Swiss franc	1.2	1.0	1.1	0.9	0.8	0.8	0.7	0.7	0.7	0.7
Euro	–	–	–	–	–	–	–	–	12.52	12.72
Deutschemark	15.4	13.3	13.7	14.2	13.7	13.1	12.9	12.2	–	–
French franc	3.0	2.7	2.3	2.4	2.3	1.9	1.4	1.4	–	–
Netherlands guilder	1.1	0.7	0.7	0.5	0.4	0.3	0.4	0.4	–	–
ECUs	10.2	9.7	8.2	7.7	6.8	5.9	5.0	0.8	–	–
Unspecified currencies	6.2	6.6	6.6	6.5	8.9	8.3	8.4	9.3	8.9	9.2
Industrial countries										
US dollar	43.6	48.8	50.2	50.8	51.8	56.1	57.9	66.7	73.5	73.3
Japanese yen	9.7	7.6	7.8	8.2	6.6	5.6	5.8	6.6	6.5	6.5
GB pound	1.8	2.4	2.2	2.3	2.1	2.0	1.9	2.2	2.3	2.0
Swiss franc	0.8	0.4	0.3	0.2	0.1	0.1	0.1	0.2	0.1	0.2
Euro	–	–	–	–	–	–	–	–	10.72	10.22
Deutschmark	18.3	15.1	16.4	16.3	16.4	15.6	15.9	13.4	–	–
French franc	3.1	2.9	2.6	2.4	2.3	1.7	0.9	1.3	–	–
Netherlands guilder	1.1	0.4	0.4	0.3	0.2	0.2	0.2	0.2	–	–
ECUs	16.6	16.7	15.2	14.6	13.4	12.0	10.9	1.9	–	–
Unspecified currencies	4.9	5.7	4.8	5.0	7.0	6.7	6.4	7.4	6.9	7.6
Developing countries										
US dollar	63.3	64.4	64.3	63.0	62.4	64.4	66.2	65.3	64.6	64.3
Japanese yen	6.7	7.7	7.5	7.6	7.0	6.5	4.7	4.5	4.7	4.4
GB pound	5.5	4.1	4.0	4.4	4.4	4.8	5.1	5.2	5.3	5.2
Swiss franc	1.8	1.9	2.0	1.7	1.5	1.4	1.1	1.1	1.1	1.1
Euro[3]	–	–	–	–	–	–	–	–	13.9	14.6
Deutschemark	10.8	10.8	10.5	11.9	11.0	10.6	10.3	11.3	–	–
French franc	2.7	2.3	2.0	2.4	2.3	2.0	1.8	1.5	–	–
Netherlands guilder	1.0	1.0	1.0	0.8	0.6	0.5	0.6	0.5	–	–
ECUs[4]	–	–	–	–	–	–	–	–	–	–
Unspecified currencies[5]	8.2	7.7	8.7	8.1	10.9	9.8	10.1	10.7	10.4	10.4

Notes: Turnover components may not sum to totals because of rounding.
1. Only IMF member countries that report their official holdings of foreign exchange are included in this table.
2. The calculations here rely to a greater extent on IMF staff estimates than do those provided for the group of industrial countries.
3. Not comparable with the combined share of euro legacy currencies in previous years because it excludes the euros received by euro-area members when their previous holdings of other euro-area members' legacy currencies were converted into euros on 1 January 1999.
4. In the calculation of currency shares, the ECU is treated as a separate currency. ECU reserves held by the monetary authorities existed in the form of claims on both the private sector and European Monetary Institute (EMI), which issued official ECUs to European Union central banks through revolving swaps against the contribution of 20 percent of their gross gold holdings and US dollar reserves. On 31 December 1998, the official ECUs were unwound into gold and US dollars; hence, the share of ECUs at the end of 1998 was sharply lower than a year earlier. The remaining ECU holdings reported for 1998 consisted of ECUs issued by the private sector, usually in the form of ECU deposits and bonds. On 1 January 1999, these holdings were automatically converted into euros.
5. The residual amount is equal to the difference between total foreign exchange reserves of IMF member countries and the sum of the reserves held in the currencies listed in the table.

However, in the new millennium, this stronger form of the international dollar standard differs from the High Bretton Woods arrangement of the 1950s and 1960s in at least two important respects: (1) In non-crisis periods, most governments in developing economies stabilize their exchange rates against the dollar, but without declaring official dollar parities. Such informal pegging is also 'soft' in the sense that many other exchange rates drift. (2) Most countries on the periphery of the dollar standard are no longer willing or able to use capital controls. Thus, dollar encroachment on the natural domestic domains of their national monies has become acute. Let us discuss soft pegging and the encroachment problem in turn.

6.8   SOFT PEGGING

In their landmark study of 155 country exchange rate regimes using monthly data, Guillermo Calvo and Carmen Reinhart (1999, 2000) show that the only truly floating exchange rates are the euro, dollar, yen, and possibly the GB pound, against each other. Month-to-month variance in these industrial countries' exchange rates is high – and variance in short-term interest rates is low; short-run shifts in cross-currency portfolio preferences are mainly absorbed by exchange rate changes, while their central banks target short-term interest rates as an instrument of domestic monetary policy.

In contrast, in developing or emerging-market economies, Calvo and Reinhart show that their monetary policies are arranged so that monthly variance in their exchange rates against some key currency – either the dollar or the euro – is low, but that monthly variance in their interest rates is much higher than in the core industrial countries. Except for an Eastern European fringe of countries keying on the euro, the others key on the dollar. The main shock absorber for cross-currency shifts in international asset preferences is changes in their domestic interest rates, except for those developing countries with effective capital controls.

This surprising difference between the core industrial economies at the 'center' and emerging-market economies on the 'periphery', is even more pronounced at higher frequencies of observation. By accepting higher volatility in domestic short-term interest rates, monetary authorities in emerging markets generally succeed in keeping their dollar exchange rates relatively constant on a day-to-day or week-to-week basis. However, at low frequencies, e.g., quarter-to-quarter, these soft pegs sometimes drift; and, in major crises, even short-term exchange rate stabilization may be impossible.

This new regime of informal, i.e., undeclared, dollar pegs for countries on the periphery of the United States differs from High Bretton Woods with its officially fixed dollar parities. In East Asia outside of Japan, for example, all the countries are dollar-peggers to a greater or lesser degree. Only Hong Kong with its currency board admits to an official dollar parity of HK$ 7.8 for one American dollar. The others all claim to be 'independently floating', or a 'managed float', or pegged to a 'currency basket'. Although the Chinese call their regime a 'managed float', the RMB's exchange rate of 8.3 yuan to the dollar has hardly moved since 1994. The others' dollar pegs may drift a bit more when measured at low frequencies, but the variance in their dollar exchange rates is an order of magnitude less than that in the yen/dollar exchange rate.

6.9 NEGLIGENCE OF THE INTERNATIONAL MONETARY FUND

Why this reticence of governments in emerging markets in East Asia and elsewhere to admit to keying on the dollar – or to go further and declare official dollar parities? The reasons are both political and economic.

On the political side, the asymmetry among national monies, with a center and a periphery, is simply too impolitic to admit. Nationalists in any peripheral country would get restless if their government admitted, by declaring an official dollar parity, that it was in thrall to the United States. *De jure*, the original Bretton Woods Agreement appeared to treat all its member countries symmetrically. Under Article IV of the 1945 Agreement, all members were obligated to declare an official parity for their exchange rate against gold or any currency tied to gold. In the event, only the United States adopted a very limited form of a gold peg – whereas all the others chose to peg to the dollar as the Nth currency (as described above). Nevertheless, in the 1950s and 1960s, the Bretton Woods Articles provided an acceptable political fig leaf for disguising what was really a dollar standard. Now, however, the IMF's parity obligation for membership exists no more; it was blown apart by the American inflation of the 1970s.

On the economic side, the modern reluctance of any one government to declare official dollar parity appears too risky precisely because neighboring countries have not done so. If Country A (say, Argentina) declared an official dollar parity, and then its close neighbor Country B (say, Brazil) allowed its currency to depreciate against the dollar, Country A could lose competitiveness and be badly hurt. Better for A not to commit itself formally to a particular dollar exchange rate to begin with, in case it may want to depreciate in response to a surprise depreciation by B. Hence A dare not commit if B, C, D have not committed, and vice versa. In effect, there is a need for collective action, as in 1945, to re-institute a more general system of dollar parities to prevent beggar-thy-neighbor devaluations.

However, the old collective agreement under high Bretton Woods was undermined by the American inflation of the 1970s into the 1980s. With no stable anchor currency, maintenance of the old regime of exchange parities became impossible. Although the American price level has now been quite stable for almost a decade, the IMF has not attempted to orchestrate a collective return to a parity regime. Whence the prevalence of soft dollar pegging where governments, forced to act individually, are unwilling to commit themselves to anything harder.

The IMF's Article VIII, the commitment of member countries to work toward current-account convertibility, i.e., to remove all restrictions on making or receiving payments from importing or exporting or repatriating interest and dividends, was equally important for the success of high Bretton Woods, and retains its crucial importance today.

But, in the 1950s and 1960s, the obligation of member countries to liberalize exchange controls stopped with Article VIII. Because of the bad experience with 'hot' money flows in the 1930s, the peripheral countries around the United States all retained some degree of control over international capital movements, particularly short-term financial flows. The industrial countries of Western Europe retained capital controls well into the 1970s, and Japan into the early 1980s. Indeed, the IMF's articles required any member country receiving funds under a Fund program to impose capital controls if there was any danger of capital flight.

In summary, the IMF's policies today suffer from major sins of omission and commission. On the omission side, it has failed to promote regional exchange rate stabilization (where feasible) by encouraging the restoration of official exchange rate parities, as if the beggar-thy-neighbor exchange rate devaluations of the 1930s had been forgotten. Apart from outright dollarization, the IMF has even leaned on individual developing countries to flex their exchange rates, as if the effect of such changes on neighboring countries did not matter.

For its sin of commission, the IMF has actively encouraged peripheral countries to jettison their capital controls too soon in the process of liberalization, not recognizing the natural asymmetry between a strong center and naturally weaker periphery. (Although within the last year or two, there are signs that the IMF may be repenting.) Consequently, dollar encroachment on the monies of developing countries and emerging markets in domestic uses is more pronounced than need be.

6.10   THE PROBLEM OF DOLLAR ENCROACHMENT

This central role of the dollar in international finance today has a darker side; the potential displacement of national monies for domestic uses – displacement that is particularly marked in the Latin American context. Table 6.3 summarizes how the US dollar might encroach (or has encroached) on the natural domains of national monies as medium of exchange, store of value, unit of account and standard of deferred payment within the country in question. In countries with a history of high and variable price inflation, the dollar encroaches on the national monetary domains in all four dimensions. But outside of this inflationary extreme, encroachment is still a problem.

To be sure, this dollar encroachment is not now a problem in the industrial economies, although it was a potential problem in the aftermath of World War II when European and Japanese currencies suffered from a complete loss of confidence. Most countries in Western Europe, as well as Japan, retained capital controls well into the 1970s – in large part to protect the domains of their domestic currencies. However, systematic European unification, culminating in the late 1990s with the adoption of the euro, ended any lingering problem of dollar encroachment in Europe. This huge new, but highly credible, euro-based regime can operate on a stand-alone basis with perhaps the world's largest market for long-term bonds.

Nevertheless, for countries outside of Europe in the new millennium, let us consider the problem of dollar encroachment in the context of each of the basic domestic functions of money – as laid out in Table 6.3 – in turn.

Table 6.3   Dollar encroachment on national monies in domestic uses

Developing Countries on the Dollar Standard's Periphery	
Medium of exchange	Dollar banknotes or deposits circulate in parallel with domestic money in many Latin American, African, and FSU countries but not generally in Asia.
Safe haven (store of value)	In normal times, domestic currency assets held only at higher real interest rates than those on similar-term dollar assets: the existence of positive country- or currency-risk premiums against the dollar. Private and official liquid dollar assets partially displace holdings of domestic liquid assets.
Unit of account	Money wage and other short-term domestic contracts directly or indirectly linked to dollar exchange rate. Most common in emerging markets with a history of financial volatility – or ones in the throes of an attempted stabilization program. Uncommon in Asia.
Standard of deferred payment	Short-term foreign borrowing – trade credit or interbank borrowing – as well as longer-term sovereign bond issues to foreigners are usually dollar denominated. US Treasuries are the 'risk-free' asset against which risk premiums in interest rates for national dollar bonds are measured. Private long-term bond markets in the domestic currency hardly exist, being dominated by international dollar-bond markets.

As the medium of exchange in Table 6.3, the dollar now circulates widely as hand-to-hand currency throughout Latin America, Africa and many parts of the former Soviet Union. In several Latin American countries, dollar bank accounts (interest-bearing and some checking) have even been legalized. This parallel circulation means that comprehensive capital controls, designed to prevent switching between the domestic money and dollars, are impossible to enforce. (But mild reserve requirements or taxes on foreign borrowing, as in Chile until recently, may still be feasible.)

Why have Latin American monetary authorities and several elsewhere allowed such invasive parallel circulation in dollars, where the demand for the domestic monetary base erodes and becomes quite unstable, to develop?

First, many governments, with short time horizons of their own, want to attract emigrant remittances to the home country. Therefore, they offer domestic dollar deposits to nationals returning money to the country. (Even if Mexico's banking system does not now offer dollar-linked bank accounts, Mexico's long border with the United States with heavy two-way migration makes holding of interest-bearing dollar bank accounts just across the border very easy.)

Second, where records of illegal export earnings do not exist for very important export products, such as narcotics, the national government can neither tax them nor force conversion of dollar export proceeds back into its domestic currency. Better to keep at least some of the dollar proceeds from the coca trade in banks within the country by offering attractive domestic deposit facilities in dollars.

Last, but not least, is the long history in almost all Latin American countries of persistent financial instability; high inflation temporary stabilizations, currency crashes, renewed inflation, and so on. Holders of naked cash balances in the domestic currency have been heavily taxed in the past. Thus, the precautionary motive for holding at least some dollar balances, at home or abroad, is strong. Similar relatively large dollar holdings are commonplace in much of Africa and in the disintegrated fragments of the old Soviet Union – including Russia itself.

Nevertheless, the internal circulation of dollars in parallel to domestic currencies is not a general phenomenon. Virtually all the economies of East Asia provide counter examples. By and large, they did not have the same turbulent history of inflation and currency attacks so common in Latin America in the postwar period. Even in those economies – Indonesia, Korea, Malaysia, Philippines and Thailand – whose currencies were attacked in the great crisis of 1997–98, the internal circulation of US dollars was negligible before the attacks began (with the possible exception of Indonesia), and is negligible today. These crisis economies, as well as the non-crisis ones of China, Hong Kong, Singapore and Taiwan, all had what looked like sustainable, if informal, fixes for their dollar exchange rates before 1997 and after 1998.

However, as a store of value as per Table 6.3, interest-bearing dollar assets dominate domestic assets of the same term to maturity in Asia as well as in Latin America and other developing countries – unless protected by effective capital controls (as in China). A political or economic crisis in any one of the developing countries on this periphery of the dollar standard generates pressure from domestic nationals to fly into interest-bearing dollar assets as a safe haven.

Even in East Asia (except for Japan), firms and households will only willingly hold domestic bonds or interest-bearing deposits if they bear a real rate of return higher than those on dollar bonds at an equivalent term to maturity. In effect, a substantial risk premium must be paid on term deposits (or bonds) in domestic currency compared to term deposits (or bonds) denominated in dollars – and this risk premium is typically much greater at long-term than at short-term. Indeed, the risk premium on long-term bonds denominated in domestic currency may be so great that an open market at the long-end of the maturity spectrum usually does not exist.

How to measure this risk premium, i.e., distinguish it from the expected annualized depreciation (or appreciation) of the domestic currency, is a tricky econometric problem. Moreover, within developing economies, interest rates are highly variable, both in time series and across countries. Before the 1997 currency attacks began in Thailand, the relevant risk premiums on three-month deposits in the East Asian debtor economies averaged about 4 percentage points, whereas in Latin America they averaged closer to 5 to 6 percentage points, above those on benchmark dollar assets.

In the financial markets, the unit of account and standard of deferred payment in Table 6.3 are closely related concepts, and refer to money's role as a *numéraire* in domestic contracts; the former is more of short-term concept, whereas the latter is longer term. For longer-term private debt contracts within Latin American countries, the dollar is commonly used as the standard of deferred payment even when the domestic currency is used as the means of settlement. The presumption is that the dollar keeps its real purchasing value through time better, and that one can get instantaneous exchange rate quotes on the value of the dollar in domestic currency when the contract matures. Correspondingly, private debt contracts are seldom linked to domestic price indexes, such as the WPI or CPI, in part because of doubts over the statistical reliability of such indexes and because of lags in collecting price data.

Even with the dollar as *numéraire* for domestic private as well as many sovereign bond issues, such bond issues are usually short-term, or have a floating interest rate set by the yield on short-term (30-day) assets. Dollar predominance in international long-term bond markets, where US Treasuries are considered the world's 'risk-free' asset, provides a competing asset that inhibits the issue of long-term bonds, particularly those issued by the private sector in developing countries. The absence of a firm long-term exchange rate parity that keeps the purchasing power of domestic bonds fairly constant in terms of the world's risk free asset, i.e., US Treasuries, significantly hinders markets for domestic long-term bonds in the peripheral countries.

The upshot is what Ricardo Hausmann calls 'original sin' in emerging-market economies. Finance remains very short-term, and the (large) international component of borrowing and lending is denominated in someone else's currency, i.e., dollars. Without a domestic bond market, financial systems in the peripheral countries are more accident prone, which in turn reinforces the inherent asymmetry between weak currencies on the periphery and the strong currency at the center. Both the domestic financial instability that he emphasized, and the international competition from dollar assets that is emphasized here, combine to make redemption from original sin very difficult.

6.11   THE EAST ASIAN EXCHANGE RATE DILEMMA

With this view of how the world dollar standard works in the modern era, what are its implications for East Asia? The East Asian economies including Japan now trade as much with each other as they do with the rest of the world. Because this economic integration continues, a common monetary standard is becoming more necessary. Interest rates must be better aligned and exchange rates made more stable.

Otherwise, in the face of great interest rate disparities and uncertain exchange rates, 'hot' money flows – i.e., cycles of over-borrowing followed by capital flight and currency crashes as in Indonesia, Korea, Malaysia, the Philippines and Thailand, in 1997–98 – will recur. When exchange rates change, the spillover effects from one country to another can generate waves of regional inflation or deflation. Thus much of the potential economic benefit from the ongoing integration in goods and capital flows in East Asia could be lost, as the countries of the European Union (EU) learned to their discomfort before the advent of the euro in January 1999.

On the positive side, East Asian countries collectively have the fiscal potential for securing regional monetary stability. Each, with the possible major exception of Indonesia, has sufficient taxing capability, or a large enough domestic banking system, to support its government's finances without inflating. True, their governments can fail to properly regulate their banks and control their money supplies. Nevertheless, unlike most countries in Latin America and Africa, countries in East Asia need not resort to the inflation tax and ongoing currency depreciation out of fiscal necessity. Thus, East Asian governments could collectively decide on regional monetary harmonization with stable domestic moneys. 'Could' is not the same as 'will', of course. But, unless the economic pros and cons are spelled out, the political will is always going to be lacking.

Short of introducing an 'Asian euro' (and certainly none is in prospect), what monetary impasse inhibits collective progress toward regional exchange rate stability? This 'East Asian dilemma' has three interrelated facets.

First, all the East Asian countries except Japan have more or less pegged their currencies to the US dollar, both before and since the 1997–98 crisis. In the absence of major crises, dollar pegging had served before 1997, and does serve now, as a nominal anchor for their domestic price levels while reducing risks in international flows of short-term capital. However, the continued use of an 'outside' currency as the monetary basis for securing economic integration seems anomalous and remains controversial.

Second, Japan's position with respect to the United States is peculiarly unbalanced. Although Japan is the region's and world's largest creditor country, most of its accumulated claims on foreigners are denominated in a foreign currency, i.e., dollars. When the yen appreciates, Japanese financial institutions suffer balance-sheet losses (measured in yen). Moreover, since 1945, Japan has been vulnerable to American pressure to change this or that domestic policy. Sometimes this pressure is warranted, as when the Americans push for greater liberalization of the Japanese economy. On the negative side, however, episodic American pressure on Japan to appreciate the yen from 1971 into 1995, ostensibly to reduce Japan's trade surpluses, imparted the deflationary momentum to Japan's economy, which continues today. Since the late 1970s, this expectation of an ever higher yen and ongoing deflation has helped drive nominal interest rates on yen assets about 4 percentage points below those on dollar assets.

Since 1995, however, the yen has not appreciated on net balance, although it continues to fluctuate widely against the dollar. Nevertheless, the interest differential between yen and dollar assets at all tenors remains as wide as ever, some 3 to 5 percentage points. Part of the differential could be explained by the market's fear that American mercantile pressure on Japan to appreciate the yen might return, particularly if the American economy turns down. A second part of the differential arises from the risk that Japanese financial institutions now see from holding large stocks of dollar assets that have been accumulating over the past 20 years of Japan's current account surpluses. Because the yen value of these dollar assets fluctuates with the exchange rate, a negative risk premium reduces interest rates on yen compared to those on dollar assets. Otherwise, private Japanese financial institutions would have insufficient incentive to hold the 'surplus' dollar assets.

These two sources of upward pressure on the yen, i.e., the fear of American mercantile pressure and the huge stocks of dollar assets now owned by Japanese financial institutions, force Japanese nominal interest rates below American when the yen/dollar rate is untethered. As long as American nominal interest rates were high as in the 1970s and 1980s, having interest rates lower in Japan was relatively harmless. However, when American interest rates themselves fell to lower levels (on average) from the mid-1990s through to 2001, short-and long-term nominal interest rates on yen assets became trapped near zero. In this 'externally imposed' liquidity trap, the Bank of Japan remains helpless to deal with the country's deflationary slump.

Third, the financial interaction between Japan and the East Asian dollar bloc has been a major source of instability caused by unpredictable changes in the untethered yen/dollar exchange rate when other East Asian countries are tethered to the dollar. These fluctuations in the yen/dollar rate aggravate fluctuations in income and employment. When the yen is overvalued against the dollar, it is also overvalued against all its East Asian trading partners. This induces an inverse business cycle; other things being equal, when the yen is high, the other smaller economies boom while Japan's is depressed, and vice versa.

In addition, the discrepancy between very low interest rates in Japan and the normally higher interest rates in the dollar bloc of East Asian trading partners exacerbates 'hot' money flows in the region. For both banks and non-financial corporations in East Asian emerging markets, the margin of temptation to borrow unhedged in foreign exchange can be overwhelming when interest rate differentials are large.

The so-called yen carry trade is a case in point. Before the 1997–98 crisis, banks in some of the East Asian debtor economies would accept low-interest dollar, or even lower-interest yen, deposits; then they would lend on at the much higher yields available on domestic currency loans. This risky currency mismatch was not confined to financial institutions in the debtor economies themselves. With a low-cost deposit base in yen, Japanese banks acquired higher yield assets in dollars, baht, won, rupiah and elsewhere. Last but not least were (and are) the highly speculative so-called hedge funds that would borrow in Tokyo and lend in Seoul, Bangkok, Jakarta and so on. These hedge funds move funds immediately with any whiff of a possible exchange rate change…very hot money indeed!

Such hot money flows were the genesis of the 1997–98 crises. In the debtor economies of Indonesia, Korea, Malaysia, Philippines and Thailand, corporations and banks had built up huge uncovered dollar and yen liabilities. When their currencies were attacked, these short-term foreign currency liabilities could not be rolled over. This sudden switch from capital inflows to capital outflows left them helpless to prevent their currencies from depreciating. The depreciations made repaying their foreign currency debts from earnings denominated in their domestic currencies impossible.

A less well-known consequence of the crisis was severe deflation in the dollar prices of all goods entering East Asian trade. As the demand for imports by the crisis economies collapsed, and their exports were artificially stimulated by the deep devaluations of their currencies against the dollar, the American nominal anchor could not hold. That is, commodity arbitrage with the center country was insufficient to prevent the dollar prices of goods and services in East Asia from dipping substantially below those prevailing in the United States. Thus, those East Asian economies that were not forced to devalue, i.e., China and Hong Kong, have maintained their pre-crisis dollar exchange rates to the present day, and hence have suffered severe internal deflations, i.e., price declines measured in terms of their domestic currencies. But, their exchange rate steadfastness in the face of falling domestic price levels saved East Asian economies from the much greater calamity that would have ensued if China and Hong Kong had depreciated as well.

Clearly, the East Asian monetary system remains unbalanced and accident-prone. The post-crash 'honeymoon' of 1999 until the present, where short-term interest rates in the crisis economies have fallen to unusually low levels, and financially chastened corporations, banks and regulators have turned ultra cautious, will not persist indefinitely. The unusually low interest rates on baht, won and ringgit bank deposits reflect overshooting (over-devaluation) of their currencies, leading to some net expectation of mild appreciation. Once equilibrium real exchange rates are restored, interest rates in these peripheral economies will increase, and the interest differential with the US and Japan (the margin of temptation to over borrow) will widen once more – particularly with Japan stuck in a deflationary slump where its short–term interest rates remain close to zero.

6.12   REFORM OBJECTIVES

To overcome this financial fragility and lessen incentives for hot money flows, what should be the key objectives of a reformed East Asian dollar standard? A reformed regime should aim for:

1.   greater long-run exchange rate security among all the East Asian economies, not only among the current dollar bloc countries, but with Japan itself;
2.   a common and highly credible monetary anchor against:
     (i)   the risk and fear of inflation in the debtor economies, and
     (ii) the risk and fear of deflation in Japan; and,
3.   mutual understanding of more appropriate policies for regulating banks and international capital flows.

One incidental consequence would be a better interest rate alignment, smaller interest differentials between debtor and creditor. Speculative hedge funds would no longer be attracted to the yen carry trade. The need for draconian regulation of banks and other financial institutions to prevent undue foreign exchange exposure and overborrowing would be lessened. However, for some emerging-market countries, capital controls (as in China) to prevent undue financial risk-taking would still be necessary.

A second consequence would be the dampening, or elimination, of the intra-East Asian business cycle generated from fluctuations in the yen/dollar rate. However, even a reformed East Asian dollar standard would remain vulnerable to worldwide disturbances, including those associated with the United States itself.

A third consequence would be help in overcoming Japan's prolonged economic slump. The expectation of ongoing deflation in Japan is now so ingrained that a major international program for ending the threat of yen appreciation and ongoing internal deflation must be seriously considered.

6.13   THE EAST ASIAN DOLLAR STANDARD

For more than a decade, the Japanese government has lobbied for the formation of a yen zone in East Asia. Fluctuations in the yen/dollar exchange rate have been all the more disruptive in Japan itself because other East Asian nations – ever more important trading partners – have been pegged *de facto* to the dollar. Thus prominent economists in Japan and elsewhere advocate weaning Japan's East Asian trading partners away from their fixation with the dollar and toward pegging to a trade-weighted currency composite. In such a 'basket peg', the yen would have a heavy weight reflecting Japan's role as the largest East Asian trading country. Then, with each of the other East Asian countries pegged to such a basket, changes in their real exchange rates and Japan's would be dampened as the yen/dollar rate fluctuated.

Although smoothing regional fluctuations is all well and good, this basket-peg approach misses the main motivation of why the smaller East Asian economies choose to peg, however loosely and unofficially, to the dollar. The world is on a dollar standard and trade flows in East Asia are overwhelmingly dollar invoiced. Concomitantly, international flows of finance, including huge flows of short-term payments, are also largely dollar denominated. Thus, in non-crisis periods, monetary authorities in emerging markets in East Asia have a dual motivation for trying to keep their exchange rates from moving much against the dollar. Those motivations are:

1.   Each central bank seeks an external nominal anchor as a target or instrument, or both, for securing its national price level when its domestic capital market is underdeveloped. To anchor the domestic price level effectively, a country's dollar exchange rate cannot be allowed to move too much on a low frequency basis, i.e., measured monthly or quarterly, although a few East Asian countries have allowed some drift either up or down at these frequencies.

2. Because finance is so short-term in emerging markets, generally, and in East Asia, in particular, monetary policy is organized so as to keep dollar exchange rates very stable at high frequency levels, i.e., measured on a weekly, or even daily basis. Foreign payment risk is reduced under high frequency dollar pegging.

Therefore, if East Asian emerging markets change their policies and opt to peg – both at low and high frequencies – against a composite currency basket, dollar exchange rates will necessarily fluctuate more widely. Hence, a country's nominal anchor for domestic prices would become less secure and domestic financial risks would increase, possibly leading to a higher risk premium in its domestic interest rates.

Why not go to the opposite extreme and have all emerging markets in East Asia peg to the yen? The problem is that the yen is not an international currency. Official yen pegs – certainly at high frequencies – would increase the risks of making high-frequency dollar payments. Nor would a peg to the yen on a monthly or quarterly basis be a satisfactory nominal anchor for prices and interest rates in other East Asian countries. For over a decade, Japan has been unable to shake its ongoing price deflation and economic slump. Thus, other East Asian countries would not want to import that deflation by pegging to the yen, and still less would they want interest rates near zero, as in Japan. In contrast, US monetary policy in the 1990s up until now presents a better choice for a common East Asian monetary anchor. But, unlike diamonds, nothing is forever.

East Asia still does not have the degree of economic integration of countries in the European Union. Nor is it anywhere close to having the necessary political cohesion to impose the fiscal conditions on member countries necessary, as in the mode of the Maastricht Treaty, for introducing an independent regional currency similar to the euro. Thus, to resolve the exchange rate dilemma, the East Asian dollar standard needs to be rationalized, rather than jettisoned.

6.14   NEW RULES FOR THE DOLLAR STANDARD GAME: A RETURN TO FIXED EXCHANGE RATE PARITIES?

One way of creating a zone of greater exchange rate stability around Japan would be to require the other East Asian countries to peg more to the yen. But then, the ten emerging markets in East Asia would collectively (and against what they correctly perceive to be their own best interests) have to change their existing exchange rate practices of keying on the dollar. Instead, the political economy of the situation suggests an alternative route. To build an East Asian zone of monetary and exchange rate stability around Japan, Japan itself should join the dollar bloc; 'if you can't beat 'em, join 'em'.

Could fixing the yen to the dollar within a narrow range in the medium term, with no upward drift in the longer term, ever be done credibly? Yes, only if there is an explicit agreement with the United States. Beginning in 1971, episodes of American pressure to get the yen up in the face of high and rising Japanese trade surpluses set in train, by the 1990s, much of the deflationary pressure and near-zero interest rates we see in Japan today. Thus, quashing the expectation of an ever-higher yen and ongoing deflation requires a pact between the US and Japan with two main provisions:

1. a commercial accord, perhaps in the form of a bilateral free trade agreement, for mediating trade disputes without resorting to, or advocating, changes in the yen/dollar exchange rate; and,
2. a monetary agreement establishing a long-term parity or benchmark value for the nominal yen/dollar rate close to its purchasing power parity (PPP), i.e., that rate which approximately equalizes producer costs in the two countries on the day that the agreement is signed.

To maintain this new parity, say 120 yen/dollar, the two governments would then stand ready in the short term to intervene jointly, but only if the market rate began to diverge sharply from 120. Without committing themselves to a narrow band with hard margins, they would stand ready to keep nudging any errant market rate back toward 120. As long as these interventions were done jointly and in a determined fashion, the signaling effect to the markets would be sufficiently strong that little if any immediate monetary adjustment would be required in either country.

However, to maintain the constant rate in the medium and longer terms, monetary adjustment would be necessary. The main responsibility for adjusting would be with the Bank of Japan, rather than with the US Federal Reserve Bank. As nominal interest rates on yen assets rose toward those on dollar assets (Japan escapes from the liquidity trap), the Bank of Japan would stand ready to withdraw or inject domestic base money into the system to maintain the yen/dollar benchmark parity.

In contrast, the Federal Reserve would not adjust the American monetary base to fluctuations in the yen/dollar rate, or in any other exchange rate. Instead, as befits the center country, the Fed would focus, as it does now, on managing the US money supply to stabilize the American price level. Under the dollar standard, the American price level becomes the anchor to which other countries adjust.

Once the 'loose cannon', i.e., the yen/dollar rate, is properly secured over the long term, other East Asian countries could more easily convert from informal dollar pegging with drift, to fixed dollar parities with no long-term drift. However, why should they even bother converting to more formal long-term exchange parities? The answer is threefold:

1. A currency attack on any one country becomes less likely, and less damaging if it does occur. If the long-term parity is credible, then any sudden crisis where the government has to float the currency and let it depreciate sets up the regressive expectation that the domestic currency must eventually appreciate back to its long-term parity level. Regressive exchange rate expectations limit the extent of any immediate crisis-induced devaluation while reducing the increase in short-term interest rates necessary to defend the currency.
2. Contagion through (inadvertent) beggar-thy-neighbor devaluations is better contained. If markets know that an unexpected devaluation by any one country is only temporary, then the mercantile pressure on neighboring East Asian countries to let their currencies depreciate will be less. To complete the virtuous circle, any one East Asian country would find it much easier to maintain the credibility of its long-term dollar parity if neighboring countries, which are also mercantile competitors, were on the same exchange rate regime.
3. Developing a long-term domestic bond market, while reducing risk premiums at all tenors becomes easier. Under a world dollar standard, US Treasury bonds are the 'risk free' or safe haven assets in international capital markets. For a smallish and financially open emerging market economy, domestic long-term bond issues will never be attractive unless their payouts at maturity have the same (rough) purchasing power as US Treasuries.

So, the payoffs from formalizing the East Asian part of a world dollar standard could be substantial. More secure exchange rate commitments by the smaller, crisis-prone debtor economies, and by Japan as the big creditor, would mutually reinforce the common nominal anchor. A fixed yen/dollar exchange rate is a more powerful anchor against ongoing deflation in Japan, if Japan's East Asian neighbors also have secure long-term dollar parities. Vice versa is also true. Emerging markets like Korea would find that long-term dollar pegging is much more attractive when the yen/dollar rate is finally tethered.

Because of China's rapid economic growth and now huge GNP, its ongoing commitment to a longer-term dollar parity is (would be) particularly beneficial for the East Asian economic system, as a whole. Indeed, China's maintaining a fixed exchange rate of 8.3 yuan to the dollar during the great crisis of 1997–98 prevented contagious devaluations from becoming much worse.

China now has an additional reason for formalizing its exchange rate commitment at 8.3 yuan per dollar. Because of the recent large influx of Chinese exports into Japan, Japanese businesspersons and farmers are lobbying with some success for tariff and quota protection against Chinese goods. They also want the Chinese government to appreciate the renminbi! Of course, appreciation of the RMB would force more deflation on China, just as the lobbying by American businesses to get the yen up in the 1970s through 1995 forced deflation on Japan! Better to secure the East Asian economy by formalizing long-term parity commitments so that governments cannot be credibly accused of manipulating their exchange rates for commercial advantage. A common monetary standard in East Asia should be neutral, and seen to be impartial, to the ebb and flow of mercantile competition.

REFERENCES

Calvo, Guillermo and Reinhart, Carmen (1999), 'Capital Flow Reversals. The Exchange Rate Debate and Dollarization', *Finance and Development*, **36**(3), pp. 13–15.
Calvo, Guillermo and Reinhart, Carmen (2000), 'Fear of Floating', University of Maryland, Working Paper, September.
Kenen, Peter B. (1983), 'International Monetary Arrangements', International Monetary Fund Staff Papers, **30**(3), pp. 656–61.

PART TWO

East Asia's Currency Crisis and Monetary
Responses

7. Causes of the currency crisis: Indonesia, Korea, Malaysia, the Philippines and Thailand

Chayodom Sabhasri, June Charoenseang and Pornkamol Manakit

7.1 THE CAUSES OF EAST ASIA'S CRISIS[1]

The causes of Asia's problems are complex. Economists have developed models of currency crises that fall into two broad categories: 'first generation' and 'second generation' models. The 'first generation' models explain crises as the result of fundamental inconsistencies in domestic policies. Therefore, the 'first generation' models predict that a deterioration in the fundamentals is indicated by overvalued real exchange rates, large current account and trade deficits, a high depletion rate of international reserves, growing budget deficits, high rates of monetary growth, high inflation, and rising domestic interest rates.

'First generation' models of speculative attacks emphasize that the acceleration in domestic credit expansion related to the monetization of fiscal deficits is the key factor that explains the loss of reserves that leads to a currency crisis. In other words, a currency crisis in a country with a fixed exchange rate is caused by an excessive budget deficit. To finance this deficit, the government prints money whereas its central bank must commit to defending the exchange rate. Such defense is possible only if it has a sufficient stock of foreign exchange reserves. However, as the government continues printing money, reserves will fall, as the private sector would rather hold other currencies and thus exchange local currencies for foreign currency.

By contrast, the interaction in expectations directly influences macroeconomic policy decisions in 'second generation' models of currency crises. These models provide a generic feature of theoretical macroeconomic policy models with rational expectations, in which market expectations directly influence macroeconomic policy decisions. These 'second generation' models thus emphasize that a currency crisis can still occur even if macroeconomic policies are consistent with a fixed exchange rate policy. In other words, a spontaneous speculative attack on a currency can cause a crisis, even when fiscal and monetary policies are well conducted. In such models, governments rationally choose – on the basis of cost and benefit assessments in terms of social welfare – whether or not to maintain a fixed exchange rate regime by adopting the adequate macroeconomic policies.

Self-fulfilling expectations play a pivotal role in these models. If the public does not believe that its government will maintain its fixed exchange rate, it would then believe that its currency will soon devalue. As a result, domestic bondholders will demand higher interest rates to compensate for exchange rate risk. Furthermore, if investors anticipate a speculative run, they will try to exchange their claims on financial institutions for foreign currencies. As a result of this, banks need to liquidate their investments. If, unfortunately, most of their banks' investments are in the form of long-term investments, they can be liquidated only at highly discounted rates. Eventually, banks become insolvent, which validates the initial expectation of a run. That run could spread to the entire banking and financial system and eventually lead to a substantial loss of international reserves. This would raise the government's cost of maintaining a fixed exchange rate, thus encouraging the government to leave the fixed exchange rate regime. Consequently, devaluation would become a self-fulfilling phenomenon. Nonetheless, 'second generation' models do not imply that speculative attacks will lead a country to a crisis. If a country's fundamentals are strong, a crisis will not occur. Countries are vulnerable only if their economic fundamentals are weak and if the loss of confidence is strong.

Prior to the Asian crisis, regional economies had different economic conditions, which resulted in uneven adjustment processes. Nonetheless, there were some common trends in these adjustment processes, and all of these economies started their recovery programs using tightened policies, but later shifted to expansionary policy stances. Furthermore, recovery signs in all of these countries started in the later part of 1998, since their public debts had risen steadily and heavily over time.

The purpose of this chapter is to explore the role of macroeconomic policies adopted in the adjustment processes in the five countries referred to above during 1997–2000.

7.2   INDONESIA

Indonesia was one of those most affected in the financial turmoil. GDP growth for 1997 declined by 3.7 percent, compared to GDP growth of 5.5 percent in

1996. The drastic decline in the rupiah's exchange rate substantially affected its inflation rate. Its consumer price index rose 11.6 percent year-on-year by December. The growth rate of broad money (M2) moved from 27.2 percent in 1996 to 25.5 in 1997. Moreover, its prime lending rate rose substantially from 20 percent to 30 percent.

At the end of October 1997, Indonesia reached an agreement with the IMF. The program provided an economic assistance package of $23 billion. By adopting this three-year adjustment program, Indonesia had to maintain both fiscal and monetary discipline. Key reforms included a restructuring of its banking sector and trade barriers.

However, the implementation of the IMF program was not quite successful, since there was mismanagement of monetary policy that resulted in high inflation. In order to prevent bank runs, the Bank of Indonesia injected large liquidity support into troubled financial institutions. Therefore, the growth rate of money supply rose to 63.5 percent in 1998, compared to 25.2 percent in 1997. This uncontrolled monetary expansion together with low progress in structural reform not only led the economy to very high inflation, but it also caused a sharp depreciation in domestic currency. Consequently, the Indonesian economy ended up with a 13.1 percent contraction in its GDP.

After nearly two years of economic turmoil, the economy started to recover when GDP growth became 0.3 percent in 1999. An increase in public spending was a significant factor that led to this recovery. A budget deficit was then recorded at 2.3 percent, whereas private investment continued to contract as a result of slow progress in corporate debt restructuring.

Despite signs of recovery, unemployment still increased from 5.5 percent in 1998 to 6.4 percent in 1999. Its consumer price index decreased from 58.5 percent in 1998 to 20.7 percent in 1999. A steady build up of reserves and a tightened monetary policy were key factors in greater stability of the exchange rate. A lower inflation rate, lower interest rates and greater exchange rate stability led to an improvement in share prices. However, export performance remained weak because of the problems of corporate indebtedness and lack of access to credit. The current account surplus of $4.9 billion in 1999 was mainly attributed to a decline in imports.

Economic growth reached 4.8 percent in 2000. This increase in GDP growth was largely attributed to export performance. The substantial depreciation of the rupiah against other major currencies provided greater incentive for other countries to import from Indonesia. Nonetheless, foreign direct investment was only about two-thirds of the pre-crisis level, even though foreign direct investment increased by 60 percent over that of the previous year.

A major consequence of the crisis recovery program has been a sharp increase in public debt. The budget deficit in fiscal year (FY) 2000 was 4.8 percent of the GDP, compared to that of 2.3 percent in FY 1999 and 3.7 percent in FY 1998.

The largest public expenditure component was interest payments on domestic debt that amounted to 4.2 percent of GDP, or approximately one-fifth of total expenditures.

Monetary policy was also put off track as monetary aggregates rose faster than the targeted rate, while inflation was also higher than the targeted rate. This growth in monetary aggregates was largely attributed to demand for currency and more liquid bank deposits. Interest rates rose over the year. For example, the one-month certificate rate increased from 12.5 percent at the end of 1999 to 14.5 percent in the same period of the following year, whereas one-month treasury bill rates moved above three-month rates. These rates reflected not only the lack of confidence in the short-term prospects of the rupiah but also a lack of confidence in the banking system.

7.3   REPUBLIC OF KOREA

Prior to the economic crisis, the Republic of Korea (henceforth referred to as Korea) had grown steadily from the beginning of the 1990s. Its economic growth reached its peak of 8.9 percent in 1995, and then started to decline steadily. The growth rate dropped to 6.8 percent in 1996 and 5.0 percent in 1997. The slowdown was first caused by weak external demand, lower prices for semiconductors, and sluggish capital investment.

However, the declining economic growth did not raise any serious concerns until the third quarter of 1997. A series of insolvencies at large business conglomerates, together with instability in international financial markets caused by the East Asia currency crisis, led to a loss of confidence in the Korean financial market. Consequently, the government asked for help from the IMF in the form of a US$57 billion bailout package. In exchange for this arrangement, Korea was not only required to undergo extreme contraction in both its fiscal and monetary stances, but was also required to strengthen its economy. For example, the package called for the restructuring of financial institutions to create a better financial industry. The IMF also required the government to set a timetable for trade liberalization in line with its WTO commitments.

The monetary policy goal was to maintain inflation at 9 percent, within 1998, and to limit downward pressure on the won. As a result, the targeted money supply was broadened to M3 in 1998. Furthermore, the targeted money supply indicator was projected to increase by only 13 percent, compared with 16.5 percent in 1997.

The initial tight monetary policy by the IMF was aimed at preventing the substantial currency depreciation with an initial depreciation–inflation spiral. However, this tight monetary policy resulted in high interest rates, which caused a profound credit crunch and some corporate bankruptcies.

The Korean won had been depreciated by 121 percent during 1997. This substantial depreciation led to inflationary pressures, which co-existed with an increase in import prices. As a result, market participants widely expected that the inflation rate would increase. It was limited to 9 percent in the first half of 1998. Furthermore, higher inflation and the tight monetary policy caused nominal interest rates to rise significantly as well. Benchmark corporate bond yield rates drastically increased to above 30 percent, compared with an average of 20 percent before the crisis.

However, the severity of the economic downturn led the government to begin relaxing both its monetary and fiscal discipline in the second half of 1998. Nonetheless, the effectiveness of its monetary policy was constrained by the credit crunch, even as an inflation targeting system was introduced in September 1998, under the provisions of a fully revised Bank of Korea Act of 1997. As a result, the primary objective of Korea's monetary policy would be to maintain price stability.

The adoption of inflation targeting implies that policymakers believed that monetary policy could not permanently influence real economic outcomes. In the second half of 1998, the inflation rate was very well contained and became lower than that of pre-crisis levels. High nominal interest rates also decreased significantly. Moreover, the yield spread on government global bonds was decreased substantially in the second half of 1998, implying lower sovereign risk.

Thus, in this period of accommodative policy, fiscal policy had to play a pivotal role. In fact, the Korean government had maintained a balanced budget for a long time prior to the crisis. To help recover the economy, the government provided funds for financial restructuring and recapitalization, which helped boost the economy. Consequently, stability in the financial system was restored and the economy recovered significantly. The Korean economy started to stabilize in the second half of 1998, where over half of the initial exchange rate depreciation had been reversed by the end of the year. The stock price index in Korea rose by 49 percent as foreign investor confidence had improved and foreign private capital inflows resumed.

Nonetheless, the cost of the above intervention was a sharp increase in government debt. The pre-crisis government debt was less than W50 trillion, which was approximately 11 percent of its GDP, however, a budget deficit of two consecutive years led to public sector debt of around W94 trillion by the end of 1999.

The inflation target for 1999 was set at 3±1.0 percent. The GDP growth rate reached 10.7 percent. On the production side, the manufacturing sector was the leading sector. Although the Korean government had pursued an expansionary stance, prices were extremely stable. The consumer price index decreased drastically from 7.5 in 1998 to 0.8 in 1999.

In 2000, the Bank of Korea set an inflation target of 2.5±1.0 percent. In 2001, the bank also introduced a mid-term inflation target of 2.5 percent to maintain consistency in monetary policy and suppress inflationary expectations. Despite GDP growth of 8.8 percent in 2000, the annual core inflation remained within its target range of 2.5±1.0 percent.

7.4   MALAYSIA

Prior to the financial turmoil, the Malaysian economy enjoyed the strongest macroeconomic performance among the five East Asian countries. Its GDP growth rate was 10.0 percent in 1996, and inflation was maintained at around 3.5 percent. The economy also enjoyed full employment.

The East Asian economic meltdown reduced its GDP growth rate to 7.3 in 1997 and –7.4 in 1998. Lower confidence in markets, together with the loss of purchasing power, propelled the economy to a fall in aggregate demand. The inflation rate increased by 4 percent due to strong credit growth before the crisis hit the economy. Despite a lower economic growth, the unemployment rate was relatively low, at the rate of 2.5 percent.

Merchandise exports increased by 6 percent, whereas merchandise imports increased by 7 percent as a result of depreciation of the ringgit. This significant increase in imports, together with the deficit in income and service accounts exacerbated a widening current account deficit of 4.7 percent of GDP.

Malaysia financed its development expenditures by using public savings rather than borrowing. As a result, the Malaysian government successfully maintained a fiscal surplus of 2.4 percent of its GDP. However, after the crisis, its monetary stance was quite tentative, because Malaysia had tried to stop the ringgit from further depreciation and prevent a collapse of the Malaysian stock market. Foreign exchange controls were first adopted in August 1997. These controls actually caused a capital outflow, resulting in significant weakening of the ringgit. Consequently, the government abandoned these controls. The government eventually tightened monetary policy, there was a control over credit expansion, and the benchmark interest rate was raised. In other words, the standard IMF package was thus implemented without being officially constrained by IMF conditions.

The Malaysian economy started a strong recovery in 1999 as GDP growth rate was rebound to 6.1 percent. Most of the growth was generated by greater external demand for manufactured goods and greater consumer confidence. Inflation rate also decreased to an average of 2.7 percent due to an excess capacity, a slower increase in food prices, and greater exchange rate stability.

Despite an increase in the services and transfer deficit, the balance of payments was improving as a result of the trade surplus coupled with higher net long-term capital inflows. In 1999, some of the capital control measures were relaxed, which made Malaysia more attractive than during the period of strict capital controls.

7.5 THE PHILIPPINES

Despite the currency crisis, the Philippine economic performance was satisfactory in 1997. GNP and GDP recorded relatively high growth rates of 5.8 and 5.1 percent, respectively. The difference between GNP and GDP was mainly explained by the remitted earnings of overseas Filipino workers. Broad money (M2) grew about 23.1 percent in 1997, and the inflation rate was at 5.9 percent. The trade deficit was at $11.4 billion as a result of the appreciation of the real effective exchange rate, whereas the current account deficit was at 5.3 percent. As foreign investment and capital inflows dropped substantially, the capital account surplus could not cover the current account deficit. The overall balance-of-payments deficit was greater than US$3 billion, which put a downward pressure on international reserves. Its reserves decreased to $8.8 billion by the end of 1997. The crisis got stronger in 1998, when GDP growth declined substantially to –0.6 percent. Export growth dropped from 22.8 percent in 1997 to 16.9 percent in 1998, while the growth of imports also declined from 22.9 percent in 1997 to 10.8 percent in 1998. The balanced budget shifted to a deficit of 1.9 percent of GDP. Monetary policy has shown slight contraction over the post-crisis era, and the growth rate of broad money has dropped sharply from 23.1 percent in 1997 to 8.6 percent. The inflation rate increased from 8.0 percent in 1997 to 9.8 percent mainly due to deficient supplies of agricultural products as a result of the El Niño drought. The current account balance improved and registered 2.4 percent.

In 1999, the economy experienced GDP growth of 3.3 percent, as the agricultural sector recovered strongly from the El Niño phenomenon in 1998, also resulting in a reduction of the inflation rate to 6.6 percent. Inflation dropped to 6.7 percent. However, efforts to stimulate domestic demand resulted in a substantial fiscal deficit that increased to about –3.7 percent or nearly double the 1998 rate. The trade balance improved and thus achieved a surplus of 14.7 percent. Although short-term private capital continued to flow out, a variety of official inflows such as two-year standby facilities from the IMF caused a current account surplus at 9.1 percent, leading to a significant increase in international reserves to almost US$15 billion.

7.6 THAILAND

The East Asian financial crisis started in Thailand in July 1997 and pushed

Thailand – once one of the most vibrant economies – into a deep recession. The GDP growth rate decreased significantly to –1.8 percent in 1997 from 5.5 percent growth in 1996. Speculative attacks on the baht and the closing of finance companies caused a substantial depreciation of the baht. Inflation increased during the second half of 1997 as the cost of imports skyrocketed. Nonetheless, at the end of December 1997, the year-on-year inflation rate dropped from 5.9 percent in 1996 to 5.6 percent because of the contraction of the economy, the cut in salaries and annual bonuses, and the sell off of inventories.

In August 1997, Thailand received a US$17 billion line of credit with the IMF in exchange for implementing an austerity program. Adopting the program implied tightened macro policy. Thailand had to maintain an inflation rate at 9.5 percent in 1997 and 5 percent in the following year. Thailand had to implement a budget surplus of 1 percent of GDP in 1998.

After six months, the economy showed hardly any sign of recovery. The fiscal and monetary targets of the adjustment program of 1997 and early 1998 pushed the country to a greater recession. GDP growth fell to –10.8 percent in 1998, whereas unemployment hit its historical high at 6.1 percent of the total labor force. Policymakers started questioning the appropriateness of the IMF program. Consequently, the Thai government policies shifted towards an expansionary stance in the latter part of 1998. The following year, the GDP grew by 4.2 percent as a result of several government stimulus packages in the previous year. These packages included reducing the value-added tax rate from 10 to 7 percent and cutting taxes on petroleum products. The government continued to relax its public sector deficit target in 1998; it further launched two economic stimulus packages, with expenditures of Bt53 billion and Bt100 billion, together with tax and tariff reductions.

Despite an expansionary monetary stance, the inflation rate was well contained and became lower than the pre-crisis level. Inflation decreased significantly from 8.1 percent in 1998 to a historically low rate of 0.3 percent in 1999. Meanwhile, the growth rate of money supply remained low at 2.1 percent in 1999, compared to 8.1 percent in 1998. Interest rates dropped substantially to very low levels. For instance, the interbank rate was at 1.23 percent and deposit rates were at 4.00–4.25 percent in December 1999. The exchange rate also remained stable. The current account surplus moved from 12.7 percent of GDP in 1998 to 9.1 percent in 1999 because of higher import growth. Nonetheless, net capital movements were still at a deficit of US$6.1 billion due to large private economic outflows to reimburse external debts. External debt fell from $86.2 billion in 1998 to $75.6 billion in 1999.

GDP growth of 4.2 percent in 2000 was largely attributed to strong export performance, the effects of earlier fiscal stimulus packages, and accommodative monetary policy. However, fiscal policy became less accommodative in 2000. The fiscal deficit dropped to 2.2 percent of GDP from 2.8 percent in the previous year. Nonetheless, total public debt was Bt2.8 trillion, which was more than triple that of the pre-crisis level.

NOTE

1.   Asian Development Bank, *Asian Development Outlook*, various issues, Manila.

BIBLIOGRAPHY

Eichengreen, Barry, Andrew Rose and Charles Wyplosz (1996), 'Contagious Currency Crises', *NBER Working Papers*, 5681.

Flood, Robert P. and Peter M. Garber (1986), 'Collapsing Exchange-Rate Regimes: Some Linear Examples', *Journal of International Economics*, **17**(1), pp. 1–13.

Krugman, Paul (1979), 'A Model of Balance-of-Payments Crises', *Journal of Money, Credit and Banking*, **11**(3), pp. 311–25.

Masson, Paul (1998), 'Contagion: Monsoonal Effects, Spillovers, and Jumps Between Multiple Equilibria', *IMF Working Papers*, 142.

Obstfeld, Maurice (1996), 'Models of Currency Crises with Self-Fulfilling Features', *European Economic Review*, **40**, pp. 1007–47.

Yung C. Park and Jong-Wha Lee (2001) 'Recovery and Sustainability in East Asia', *NBER Working Papers*, 8373.

8. Exchange rate policy and the Asian crisis: Thailand, Indonesia and Korea[1]

Peter Warr

8.1 INTRODUCTION

Since the early 1960s, it has been well understood that a pegged exchange rate cannot be maintained simultaneously with both open capital accounts and domestic monetary independence (Mundell, 1962). This combination of policies is now known as the 'impossible trinity'. However, during the decade leading up to the Asian crisis of 1997, this basic point was disregarded. In the presence of greatly increased international mobility of financial capital, controls on capital movements were steadily dismantled in those countries where they had previously existed, but exchange rates continued to be pegged to the US dollar. At the same time, central banks attempted to use monetary policy to 'sterilize' the domestic effects of capital inflows. The result was the steady development of vulnerability to a currency crisis. This chapter demonstrates the process through which this occurred.

The chapter focuses on the three most prominent crisis countries: Thailand, Indonesia and Korea. Each of these countries was an outstanding economic performer prior to the financial crisis of 1997, measured in terms of sustained economic growth, moderate inflation and stable policy. Each was maintaining a pegged exchange rate, using the US dollar as its reference currency, and regarded this exchange rate policy as the cornerstone of its macroeconomic stability. By 1998, each was in deep recession, having abandoned its fixed exchange rate policy prior to the crisis in favor of a floating exchange rate, but with a very much depreciated currency thereafter, compared to the pre-crisis situation. Moreover, having previously been considered examples of competent macroeconomic management that other developing countries might emulate, all three were now subject to stringent and humiliating IMF supervision.[2] What went wrong?

The Asian crisis had three components:

1. A currency crisis, with rapid outflow of financial capital in anticipation of a possible currency depreciation, inducing depletion of reserves, and forcing radical changes of policy – in this case abandonment of fixed exchange rates in favor of floating rates during a period of loss of confidence;
2. A financial crisis, with collapse of domestic financial institutions induced by currency depreciation and high domestic interest rates that resulted from the currency floats; and,
3. An economic crisis, with contraction of output causing a loss of government revenue, loss of employment and consequent loss of household incomes, producing serious hardship for large numbers of people.

The currency crisis occurred first. The financial crisis resulted directly from it and the economic crisis arose from the combined effects of both. In the absence of the currency crisis, the other two would not have occurred. Accordingly, explaining the currency crisis is the focus of this chapter.

The literature provides two rival depictions of the causes of the currency crisis. The most common is the contagion theory. According to this description, Thailand experienced a financial panic, due to such factors as corrupt government and corporate practices, inadequately supervised banks and venal currency speculators. Confidence in the currency and banking system collapsed, capital flight resulted, provoking a float of the Thai currency and a drastic decline in its market value. Investors who had not gotten out in time were ruined. These events led to a loss of confidence in the prospects of other East Asian countries. International investors and fund managers lumped all of the various East Asian countries into a common conceptual category, such that neighboring countries, with otherwise perfectly healthy economies, suffered the same loss of confidence that had just devastated Thailand.

The 'contagion' theory draws an analogy with a viral infection, which spreads through the air unpredictably. There is no defense, except through restrictive measures like capital controls. The implication is that unless the Thai crisis could have been anticipated, there was no way to predict the crises that other countries would suffer. It was only the contagion that came from elsewhere, in this case Thailand, which caused their problems. That is, the crises in countries other than Thailand were not predicted because they were inherently non-predictable in terms of the economic fundamentals of these countries.

Many leading economists hold views close to this. For instance, Bhagwati (1998) writes that 'none of the Asian economies that were hit [by the crisis] had any serious fundamental problems that justified the panic that set in to reverse huge capital inflows [and] ... the only explanation that accounts for the massive net [capital] outflows is panic and herd behavior'. Similarly, according to Tobin (1998, p. 353), the recent Asian example shows that 'countries can suffer liquidity crises through no fault of their own'. Radelet and Sachs (1998) state that, 'the crisis was triggered by dramatic swings in creditors' expectations about the behavior of other creditors, thereby creating a self-fulfilling [sequence of events] although [individual] rational financial panic [may have played a part]' (p.43). Economists belonging to the 'statist' school of thought on East Asian development have also been attracted to the panic theory in their attempts to justify state-engineered 'guided lending' in some countries (particularly in Korea) during the period leading up to the crisis (see for instance, Wade, 1998 and Chang et al., 1998).

A defect in this theory is that it attempts to explain how Thailand's crisis was exported to others – through 'contagion' – but it does not provide a coherent explanation of why Thailand's crisis occurred. Such factors as corruption, poor bank supervision and so forth, have been features of the Thai economy for decades. Why they should have produced a crisis in 1997 and not earlier is left unexplained by the 'contagion' account. In any case, the implication is that Thailand's crisis was caused by Thai-specific factors quite separate from the 'contagion' that transmitted it to neighboring countries. A second defect is that it is not apparent why investors would be so ignorant as to assume that all countries of a particular region were similar. In fact, not all East Asian economies suffered crises, and the presence or absence of capital controls did not seem a complete explanation for the differences. Taiwan, China, Singapore and India, while very different, did not experience the same financial panics as Thailand, Indonesia, Korea, Malaysia and the Philippines. If the contagion theory was correct, why did some of Thailand's neighbors succumb to the contagion while others did not? At best, the 'contagion' theory seems incomplete.

An alternative is the vulnerability theory. According to this hypothesis, some economies were vulnerable to a crisis because of fundamental economic features that predisposed them to severe crises if they were subject to shocks that initiated the expectation of an exchange rate devaluation. The concept of vulnerability does not mean that a crisis will occur, only that if something happens to undermine confidence, the result may be severe. The analogy of a tightrope walker may be helpful. If the rope is a few inches above the ground, then a slight loss of balance due, say, to an unexpectedly strong gust of wind, is easily accommodated. But if the rope is high above the ground – a state of vulnerability – then any loss of balance could be disastrous.

There is a large difference between the two extreme forms of the contagion and vulnerability interpretations. The vulnerability account implies that observable features of economies may leave them more or less susceptible to crises. The most extreme versions would say that if high levels of vulnerability develop, then a crisis is inevitable and any random event could actually provoke it. Extreme forms of the contagion theory deny, or at least dismiss, the importance of observable signs of vulnerability. But, intermediate variants are possible and in general these seem more reasonable than either extreme.

Intermediate explanations for the crisis that are closest to the contagion end of the spectrum generally place principal emphasis on international speculators, irrational behavior of hedge fund managers, unstable international capital markets, and so forth. The intermediate variants closer to the vulnerability end of the spectrum relegate the contagion story to the role of one possible form of trigger, but only one possible form. While a trigger may be required to provoke a crisis, the vulnerability perspective focuses primary attention on the economic conditions that may turn such a trigger into a crisis in one type of economy, but not in another.

But what if all crises were different, with vulnerability taking different and unpredictable forms each time? If so, the 'vulnerability' account may not be particularly useful; there may be no way to know in advance which forms of vulnerability to look for. The sources of vulnerability could only be discovered *ex post*. It is therefore important to determine whether the sources of vulnerability to a currency crisis are relatively stable over time.

The degree to which the vulnerability argument can be sustained has considerable policy relevance. If clear evidence can be established of increasing vulnerability prior to the crisis itself, using information that was in principle available at the time, this will mean that the signs of growing danger were available but insufficiently noticed. This will, in turn, mean that had these signs been properly heeded, policy actions, which may have averted the worse effects of the crisis, could have been taken but were not. To the extent that this is true, the immense social cost of the crisis is in part attributable to an analytical failure, a failure on the part of government officials, international institutions and independent researchers like academics, to draw proper attention to the signs of growing vulnerability and the danger that they represented. That is what this chapter will argue.

The second section of the chapter draws on economic theory to clarify the conditions likely to produce vulnerability to a currency crisis. Three such indicators of vulnerability are identified. The third section explains the empirical procedures adopted in the chapter in applying the analysis derived from this discussion to the three countries studied. The fourth section uses this empirical framework to ask whether the vulnerability account fits with the experience of Thailand, Indonesia and Korea. In particular, it asks whether it might have been possible to identify the conditions of vulnerability in these three economies prior to the crisis itself. The answer is yes. The fifth section concludes the chapter.

8.2   THEORY

A currency crisis occurs when market participants lose confidence in the currency of a particular country and seek to escape assets denominated in that currency. Because investors try to avoid short-term capital losses, they exit from countries where they expect that a large nominal exchange rate depreciation will soon take place. Thus, the fundamental concerns governing their action are the likelihood that the currency will depreciate should capital inflows reverse, and the possible magnitude of that depreciation. Under what conditions might asset owners make a radical upward revision in their assessment of the probability of a large currency depreciation?[3]

8.2.1   Vulnerability vs. Trigger

Vulnerability means susceptibility to a currency crisis. The concept must be understood in relation to the concept of a trigger. As Dornbusch (1997, p. 21) noted, '[V]ulnerability means that if something goes wrong, then suddenly a lot goes wrong'. A state of vulnerability by itself does not give rise to a currency crisis. There needs to be a certain disturbance (a trigger) that will push a vulnerable situation into an actual collapse. Some likely disturbances are policy errors such as a minor devaluation in the context of a significant and persistent overvaluation of the real exchange rate, failure to implement a promised crucial policy reform, or simply a contagion – investor panic spreading from events in a neighboring crisis country. Since an actual currency crisis requires both vulnerability and a trigger, analysis of vulnerability alone could not be expected to enable one to predict the timing of a currency crisis.

The central focus of the concept of vulnerability is that owners of assets wish, on the one hand, to obtain high returns from these assets and, on the other hand, to avoid the risk of capital losses. A central danger, in terms of possible capital loss, is a large exchange rate depreciation in the country where the assets are located and where the assets are priced in terms of the local currency. Owners of internationally mobile assets are constantly revising their assessments of the probabilities of large exchange rate movements that may affect the capital values of their assets. Vulnerability to capital flight arises when there is an increase in the probability that owners of internationally mobile assets will form the expectation of a large nominal depreciation. Under what conditions might relatively small external shocks cause asset owners to make a radical upward revision in their assessment of the probability of a large devaluation?

We identify three such determinants of a possible large revision of expectations. The analysis builds on the discussion of the Mexican crisis of 1994 and its aftermath provided in Sachs, Tornell and Velasco (1996), subsequently Sachs et al. These authors point out that some Latin American economies – notably Brazil and Argentina – apparently suffered from significant contagion effects resulting from Mexico's crisis, whereas others, notably Colombia and Chile, did not. Drawing in part on earlier work of Krugman (1979 and 1996), Sachs et al. identified three variables which, according to them, help explain the differences in these country experiences.

Suppose that a country is maintaining a pegged exchange rate and that a substantial and unexpected outflow of capital suddenly occurs – due to some trigger causing a loss of confidence in the capacity of the central bank to maintain the exchange rate. Can the peg be defended? First, we note the accounting identity:

$$\Delta R = K + C \tag{8.1}$$

The change in the level of reserves (a flow) is equal to the net balance on capital accounts, K, plus C, the net balance on current account (both flows). Suppose, for simplicity, that the current account was initially in deficit, the capital account was initially in surplus and that the two magnitudes were approximately equal, implying that the net change in the level of reserves was zero. Starting from this position, a capital outflow now implies a lower level of the net balance on capital account. If nothing else changes, the level of reserves must fall.

8.2.2 Three Possible Responses

Three policy responses are now possible. First, the authorities could defend the currency and permit the level of reserves to decline until confidence is restored. Whether this is possible depends on the adequacy of the level of reserves in relation to the possible size of the capital outflow. In particular, the smaller the reserves (a stock) relative to the volume of short-term foreign liabilities (also a stock), the lower the credibility of this policy response. If reserves are inadequate to meet a sudden outflow caused by investor panic and the government still wishes to maintain the exchange rate peg, then it is necessary to ameliorate the loss of reserves by containing the right-hand side of the above identity – the negative value of the net balance on capital account plus the net balance on current account.

The second possible response is an increase in the interest rate. This may be expected to ameliorate the downward pressure on the level of reserves in two ways. First, it helps maintain relative expected returns to investment in the given country by compensating for the potential loss of return due to (the expected) exchange rate depreciation. This reduces, and possibly reverses, the net deficit on the capital account, which resulted from investor panic. Second, it may bring about a reduction in domestic absorption (private consumption and investment), which reduces the negative value of the net balance on current account.

But the feasibility of using interest rate policy in the event of a speculative outflow depends on the health of the domestic financial institutions. If these institutions have been operating with unsound (fragile) asset portfolios characterized by high non-performing loans, low levels of capital adequacy and other related weaknesses, an interest rate increase is likely to engineer a domestic credit squeeze, bank failure and business bankruptcies leading to economic collapse. Therefore, the more fragile the banking system, the less scope exists for the government to use interest rate policy to defend the currency and the less credible is the policy option of raising interest rates to defend the currency.

If the solution of increasing interest rates cannot be adopted, then the required adjustment has to come through the third possible response – a depreciation of the real exchange rate, by which we mean an increase in the domestic prices of tradables relative to non-tradables. Real exchange rate depreciation facilitates a domestic expenditure switch against tradables and towards non-tradables, and thus accommodates a reduction in the current account deficit. Maintaining the existing exchange rate peg means that the nominal prices of tradables will remain roughly constant. A real depreciation therefore requires a decline in the nominal prices of non-tradables and this will require a monetary and/or fiscal contraction, and presumably a recession, depending on the downward flexibility of non-tradable prices. The required degree of real depreciation and thus the required magnitude of this recession will be greater the more appreciated the real exchange rate is relative to the level compatible with lower capital inflows.

It is important to emphasize that a steady, systematic appreciation of the real exchange rate that occurs in line with changes in underlying economic circumstances is not problematic. If a country borrows to invest and/or attracts significant foreign direct investment, the resulting capital inflow naturally strengthens the real exchange rate – which is the expected effect of an inward transfer. An appreciation can also be a reflection of deep reforms that open up large and lasting opportunities for economic expansion. The 'Balassa-Samuelson' effect – long-term improvement in productivity that normally has a greater price-lowering effect on tradables than on non-tradables – can be another factor. Provided these events are permanent rather than temporary, real appreciation arising from them should not cause concern about the macroeconomic health of the economy.

A persistent, excessive appreciation (exchange rate misalignment), that is, an appreciation caused by temporary, reversible events, is what bothers investors and may induce a run on the currency. Such an appreciation implies that the authorities may be unable to defend the currency successfully in case of a speculative capital outflow, because the required real depreciation consistent with lower capital inflows may be too large. In summary, the relevant question is not the actual level of the real exchange rate, but its sustainability. There is no unique benchmark against which to judge the current level of the real exchange rate. On the other hand, a real exchange rate that is far higher than ever before and which continues to appreciate is suspicious, even when past major reforms and access to capital markets have justified some real appreciation.

The discussion so far points to three key indicators that may help in assessing a country's vulnerability to a currency crisis:

1. inadequacy of reserves relative to the stock of volatile (mobile) capital;
2. financial sector fragility; and,
3. real exchange rate misalignment.

A state of vulnerability – a situation where there is reason to doubt the ability of the country to defend the currency in the event of a sudden loss of confidence on the part of the holders of internationally mobile financial assets – can be created by one or a combination of these factors. Does this way of looking at things help explain the crises in Thailand, Indonesia and Korea? Yes.

8.3 EMPIRICAL MEASURES FOR CRISIS VULNERABILITY

There is no unique way of implementing the above concepts empirically. Further discussion is thus needed on the empirical procedures adopted in this study.

8.3.1 Adequacy of Reserves

What surprised observers of the Asian crisis, as well as most of its participants, was the rate at which very large volumes of funds could be presented at central banks for conversion into foreign exchange and thereby the rapidity with which seemingly adequate reserves could be placed under unexpected pressure. The standard measures of 'reserve adequacy', which focus on the capacity of reserves to finance imports has nothing to do with this concept. What presumably requires attention is the stock of funds that can be presented at short notice against reserves, that is, the volume of volatile capital.

Returning to the balance of payments identity given by equation (8.1) above, the capital account balance reflects the following components:

foreign direct investment (F);
equity consisting of stock market purchases (S);
debt instruments (D) such as bonds;

bank credit, long-term (B_L) and short-term (B_s);
non-resident bank accounts (N);
other unrecorded items (U);

As normally conceived, the elements of the above list that are 'non-volatile' in the short run consist of F, B_L and possibly some components of U. The other components are considered more volatile, but these assignments are ultimately empirical matters. Suppose we divide K in equation (8.1) into two components: volatile and non-volatile. For reasons that will become apparent we use the notation:

$$K = \Delta K^* + \Delta K^0 \qquad (8.2)$$

where ΔK^* and ΔK^0 denote the changes in the stocks of volatile and non-volatile foreign capital, respectively. Rearranging equation (8.1), we get:

$$C + \Delta K^0 = \Delta R - \Delta K^* \qquad (8.3)$$

The right side of this equation may be conceived as the change in the vulnerability of reserves to capital flight. It is apparent that the right side may be negative although reserves are rising. For example, let there be a current account deficit of 80 ($C = -80$), and a capital inflow of 100. Then $\Delta R = 20$. Now suppose this capital inflow is equally divided between volatile and non-volatile components. Then $\Delta R - \Delta K^* = -30$, and reserves have become more vulnerable to attack motivated by capital flight.

Large current account deficits are not necessarily required for vulnerability to increase. Looking at the left-hand side of equation (8.3), the focus is the size of the current account deficit in relation to the volume of non-volatile capital inflow. When the former exceeds the latter, vulnerability increases. If this situation continues for long enough, the accumulated stock of volatile capital may become large relative to the stock of international reserves, making reserves vulnerable to capital outflows. To obtain measures of vulnerability based on this line of reasoning what is required are calculations of the accumulated stock of volatile capital, which may then be compared to the volume of reserves.

Except for reserves, where data on stocks is published, the stocks described above must be assembled by the researcher. Balance of payments data for each country are used for this purpose. The exercise is commenced a decade before the first data point shown. The magnitude of capital stocks in this initial year is assumed to be zero and net flow data are used to assemble the stocks shown, using the inventory method. Figures 8.1 through 8.3 show the results of applying these concepts to the balance of payments data of Thailand, Indonesia and Korea.

8.3.2 Financial Sector Fragility

Building upon the theoretical discussion of vulnerability above, two measures of financial sector fragility are used in this study. First, the ratio of total loans outstanding from the banking system to GDP considered as a measure of exposure of the banking system to increased interest rates. As the loan/GDP ratio rises, the average quality of loans may be expected to fall. An increase in interest rates will bankrupt weaker borrowers leaving them unable to service their loans. If the average quality of loans has deteriorated, as through a prolonged credit boom, this will leave the banking system exposed to higher interest rates because large numbers of bankrupt borrowers may make the banks themselves insolvent. Second, the ratio of foreign liabilities to total loans is used as a measure of exchange rate exposure of the banking system. As this ratio increases, so does the exposure of the banking system to exchange rate depreciation, because such depreciation will raise the costs of servicing foreign loans relative to bank revenues. All of the data used comes from central bank sources of the respective countries. See Figures 8.4 to 8.6.

8.3.3 Real Exchange Rates

The literature talks about two types of measures of the real exchange rate: (1) measures of the relative prices of traded to non-traded goods within the country; and (2) measures of the prices at which that country's traded goods can be exchanged internationally, compared to the traded goods of other countries. They are not the same. These two measures relate to two different concepts of 'competitiveness'. Measure (1) relates to the capacity of industries producing (internationally) traded commodities within Thailand to compete for resources with Thai industries that produce goods that are non-traded. It is therefore about domestic competitiveness, the capacity of one type of Thai industry to compete for resources against other types of Thai industries. Measure (2) is about the capacity of traded goods produced within Thailand to compete for sales against imperfect substitutes for them that are produced by traded goods producers within other countries. It is therefore about international competitiveness.

Traded/non-traded goods relative prices

The Australian model of the balance of payments rests upon the distinction between traded and non-traded goods and services, and on the different manner in which their prices are determined. Exponents of this model have demonstrated its analytical value, but empirical applications are rare. The problems are, first, that assembling indices of the prices of actual traded and non-traded goods and services is laborious and costly, and second, that the concepts of traded and non-traded goods and services – also referred to as tradables and non-tradables, respectively – are abstractions.

For an index of tradable commodity prices, we turn to wholesale price data using commodities that correspond approximately to the analytical category of traded commodities – those that enter into international trade and whose domestic prices are determined by exchange rates, international prices and any domestic taxes that may apply to them. The index is formed by using the weights applying to these commodities in the construction of a wholesale price index. 'Non-tradables' prices are assembled similarly using consumer price series and aggregating the resulting price data using the weights applying to these commodities in the construction of the consumer price index. It must be recognized that assigning actual commodities to each of these categories always involves a degree of arbitrariness. The results are presented in the series labeled 'Relative Price' in Figures 8.7 through 8.9.

Competitiveness indices
We shall also present data on other measures of real exchange rates, also commonly called measures of 'competitiveness'. All three are based, not on domestic relative prices, but on nominal exchange rates adjusted by foreign and domestic price levels. The general form of these measures is:

$$E^R = EP^*/P \tag{8.4}$$

where E denotes the nominal exchange rate, measured in units of domestic currency per unit of foreign currency, P^* is a measure of foreign prices, measured in foreign currency, and P is a measure of domestic prices, measured in domestic currency. The measures chosen for P vary. Some studies use foreign wholesale prices, while others use foreign consumer prices and the foreign country weights used to aggregate them also vary, including domestic export shares to these countries, import shares and even 'trade' shares, the sum of exports and imports. The measures used for P^* also vary, some measures using consumer prices, others wholesale prices.

The two most commonly used in the literature are labeled the 'IMF/World Bank Index', the export share weighted sum of trading partner consumer price indices, each multiplied by the bilateral exchange rate, divided by the domestic consumer price index; the 'Morgan-Guaranty Index', where the two consumer price indices described above are replaced by foreign and domestic wholesale price indices, respectively.

Finally, the series labeled 'Preferred Index' replaces foreign consumer prices in the numerator of the 'IMF/World Bank RER Index' with foreign wholesale prices, but it retains the domestic wholesale price index in the numerator. This index is preferable to either of the other two as a proxy for traded goods prices relative to non-traded goods prices. The reason is that the share of traded goods in wholesale price indices is thought to be higher than its share in consumer price indices. Thus, the numerator of this index, the export share weighted sum of foreign wholesale price indices, each multiplied by the bilateral exchange rate, may be taken as a (very rough) proxy for domestic traded goods prices and the denominator, the domestic consumer price index, may be taken as a (very rough) index of domestic non-traded goods prices. For the reasons demonstrated by Warr (1986), all three of these exchange rate based measures, but especially the first two, may be expected to understate the magnitude of a real appreciation, compared with changes in the domestic relative prices of traded goods to non-traded goods.

8.4   EVIDENCE

8.4.1   Adequacy of Reserves

The data for Thailand (Figures 8.1a and 8.1b) show that the short-term capital increased relative to reserves throughout the boom decade preceding the crisis but especially after 1993.[4] By 1994 the total stock exceeded the volume of Thailand's international reserves and by 1997 was roughly double the level of reserves. These facts are by now relatively uncontroversial. Figures 8.2a and 8.2b for Indonesia and 8.3a and 8.3b for Korea show that virtually the same circumstances applied to these two countries. The crisis was preceded by a large increase in the volume of short-term capital relative to reserves. The adequacy of reserves declined markedly in the years preceding the crisis in each of these countries.

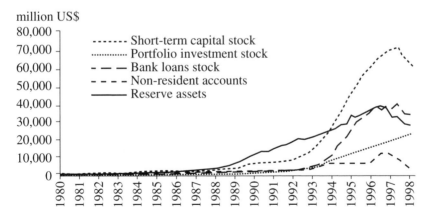

Figure 8.1a   Thailand: stocks of long-term and short-term capital and international reserves, 1980–98

million US$

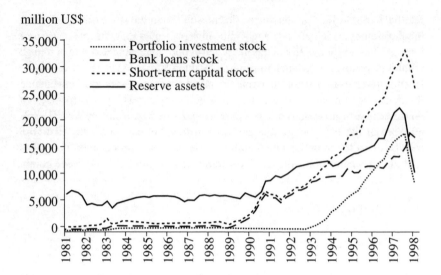

Figure 8.1b   Thailand: components of short-term capital stocks and international reserves, 1980–98

million US$

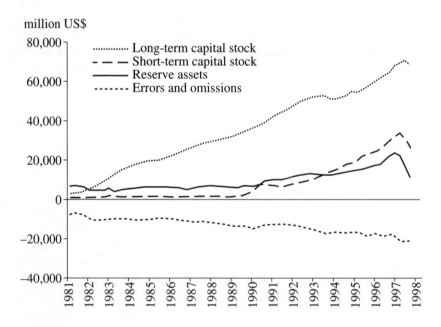

Figure 8.2a   Indonesia: stocks of long-term and short-term capital and international reserves, 1981–98

million US$

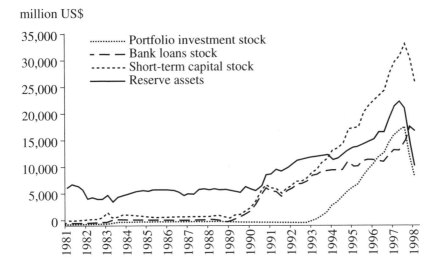

Figure 8.2b Indonesia: components of short-term capital stocks and international reserves, 1981–98

million US$

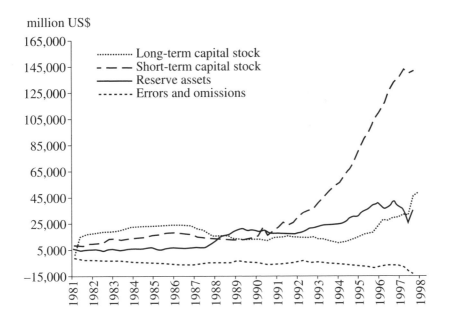

Figure 8.3a Korea: stocks of long-term and short-term capital and international reserves, 1981–98

million US$

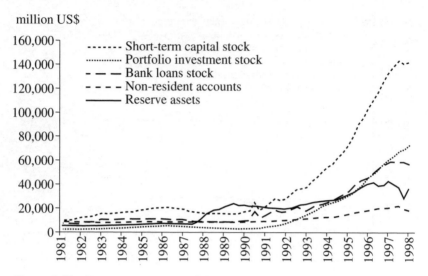

Figure 8.3b   Korea: components of short-term capital stocks and international reserves, 1981–98

8.4.2   Financial Sector Fragility

Figures 8.4 to 8.6 show that the crisis in each of the crisis-affected countries was preceded by a domestic credit boom. In all but Indonesia, there was a large increase in foreign liabilities relative to total loans. The vulnerability of the banking sectors to interest rate increases had risen markedly.

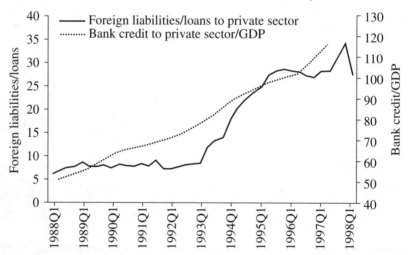

Figure 8.4   Thailand: bank exposure, 1988–98

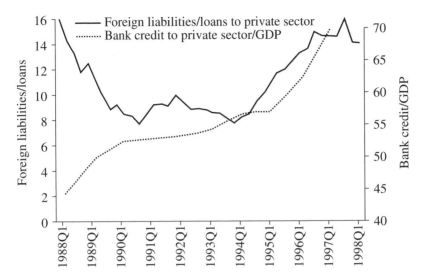

Figure 8.5   Indonesia: bank exposure, 1988–98

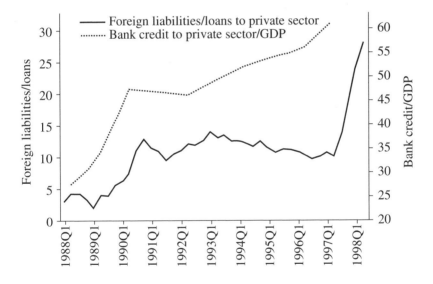

Figure 8.6   Korea: bank exposure, 1988–98

8.4.3   Real Exchange Rates

In each of the crisis-affected countries the real exchange rate, properly measured, appreciated significantly over the boom period preceding the crisis. Do external exchange rate changes explain this outcome? The question arises because it is now well understood that the depreciation since 1995 of the Japanese yen and other currencies relative to the US dollar meant that any currency pegged to the dollar would suffer a real appreciation and each of the crisis-affected countries was indeed pegging to the dollar. But the answer is no.

The real appreciation within Thailand, Indonesia and Korea demonstrated in Figures 8.7 to 8.9 was not only confined to the period since 1995, when the US dollar was appreciating. A large real appreciation within Thailand can also be seen in the first 5 years of the 1990s when the dollar was depreciating relative to the yen and other currencies. Much of the real appreciation from 1990 to mid-1997 was already evident by mid-1994, well before the appreciation of the US dollar began. External exchange rate changes were clearly relevant, but they were not the main causal factor.

The principal cause of the real appreciation indicated resided in forces operating within the Thai, Indonesian and Korean economies – not external exchange rate adjustments. A principal source was the demand effects of very large foreign capital inflows, only partially sterilized. The effect of the real appreciation was that it undermined the competitiveness of traded goods industries in these countries, meaning their capacity to attract resources within the domestic economy in competition with non-traded goods sectors.

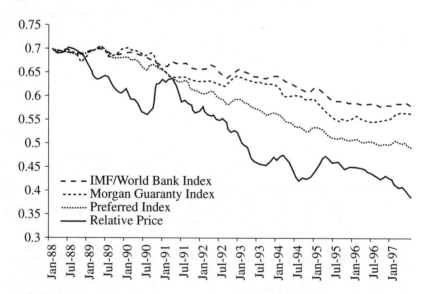

Figure 8.7   Real exchange rate indices: Thailand, 1988–97

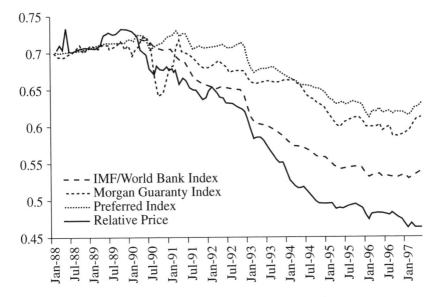

Figure 8.8   Real exchange rate indices: Indonesia, 1988–97

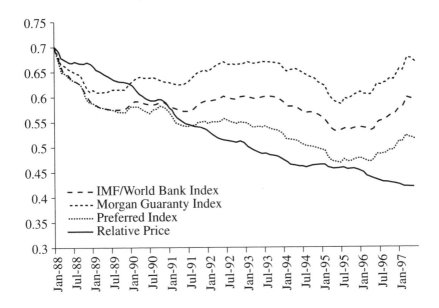

Figure 8.9   Real exchange rate indices: Korea, 1988–97

8.5   CONCLUSIONS

During the boom decade preceding 1997, all of the countries that subsequently succumbed to the crisis were growing rapidly and were enjoying large inflows of foreign direct investment (FDI). However, some basic lessons of economics were ignored. Most important was the 'impossible trinity' demonstrated by Mundell more than three decades earlier. During the pre-crisis decade, all of the crisis-affected economies were:

1. pegging their exchange rates to the US dollar;
2. opening their capital markets, where they were not already fully open; and,
3. attempting to use domestic monetary policy to 'sterilize' the domestic monetary effects of inflows of FDI.

Mundell's Nobel Prize-winning contribution to economics was in showing that these three policies cannot be implemented at the same time.

The fact that it was possible to raise domestic interest rates above foreign rates at all reveals that capital mobility was incomplete and, more importantly, that domestic debt was an imperfect substitute for foreign debt. However, the effect of the attempted sterilization in the presence of a high degree of capital market openness was to encourage the inflow of short-term capital from abroad. This took the form of bank loans, as a substitute for more expensive domestic borrowing, portfolio investment from abroad and foreign holding of domestic bank accounts, in response to the high domestic interest rates.

As this chapter has demonstrated, the principal source of increased vulnerability to a currency crisis was precisely the accumulation of this stock of mobile foreign-owned capital. Eventually, its size dominated the level of the country's international reserves, leaving it vulnerable to a currency crisis. The two other sources of vulnerability identified in this chapter are also attributable to the excessive inflow of short-term capital: over-exposure of the domestic banking system, and a 'Dutch disease' appreciation of the real exchange rate that undermined the profitability of traded goods industries.

Ignoring the 'impossible trinity' directly laid the foundations for the crisis. In 1962 Mundell showed that under a pegged exchange rate with an open capital market the effects of domestic monetary contractions or expansions will be undone by the international movement of short-term capital. This is indeed what happened. In these circumstances, monetary policy is ineffective in cooling a boom. In recognition of the impossible trinity, the over-heating that characterized the boom decade preceding the crisis could only have been controlled by implementing some combination of:

1. fiscal contraction;

2. capital controls; and
3. floating exchange rates.

Fiscal contraction alone may not have been enough by itself, because the booms in East Asia were extremely large. Therefore, the central contradiction was between the opening of the capital account and the maintenance of pegged exchange rates. These conclusions have implications for current proposals to reduce the volatility of flexible exchange rates by re-establishing pegged exchange rates, abandoned in the post-crisis chaos. Any such proposal must address the problems of vulnerability that culminated in the crisis of 1997. If pegged exchange rages are to be resumed, ways must be found to avoid the development of vulnerability to the kinds of currency crises that caused so much pain in the late 1990s.

NOTES

1. Helpful discussions with Premachandra Athukorala, Bhanupong Nidhiprabha and David Vines are gratefully acknowledged. The author is responsible for all defects.
2. Another East Asian country, the Philippines, was also under IMF supervision in 1998, but its experience is significantly different from the three countries discussed in this chapter. The Philippines had been a poor economic performer and under a continuous close relationship with the IMF for many years prior to 1997.
3. Throughout the following discussion we assume that the country under consideration is in an adjustable (quasi) peg exchange rate regime – a characterization that is valid, during the period leading up to the crisis, for all countries covered in this study.
4. Warr (1999) provides an explanation for the rapid increase from 1993 onwards.

BIBLIOGRAPHY

Athukorala, P. (1998), 'Malaysia', in Ross H. McLeod and Ross Garnaut (eds), *East Asia in Crisis*, London: Routledge, pp. 85–91.

Backstrom, U. (1997), 'What Lessons can be Learned from Recent Financial Crises? The Swedish Experience', in Federal Reserve Bank of Kansas City, *Maintaining Financial Stability in a Global Economy*, Wyoming: Jackson Hole, pp. 55–96.

Bhagwati, J. (1998), 'Asian Financial Crisis Debate: Why? How Severe?', paper presented at the international conference *Managing the Asian Financial Crisis: Lessons and Challenges*, Asian Strategic Leadership Institute and Rating Agency Malaysia, 2–3 November 1998 (Kuala Lumpur).

Bhagwati, J. (2001), 'The Asian Economic Crisis: What Do We Know Now?', in his *The Winds of the Hundred Days: How Washington Mismanaged Globalization*, Cambridge, Mass: MIT Press, Chapter 5, pp. 51–60.

Calvo, G.A. (1995), 'Varieties of Capital-market Crises', *Center for International Economics Working Paper*, **15**, College Park, MD: University of Maryland.

Chang, H-J., H.J. Park and C.G. Yoo (1998), 'Interpreting the Korean Crisis: Financial Liberalisation, Industrial Policy and Corporate Governance', *Cambridge Journal of Economics*, **22**(4), pp. 735–46.

Cooper, R.N. (1996), 'Comments on Sachs, Tornell and Velasco', *Brookings Papers on Economic Activity*, **1**, pp. 203–8.

Cooper, R.N. (1999), 'The Asian Crisis: Causes and Consequences', in Alison Hardwood, Robert E. Litan and Michael Pomerleano (eds), *Financial Markets & Development: The Crisis in Emerging Markets*, Washington, DC: Brookings Institution Press, pp. 17–28.

Corden, W.M. (1999), *The Asian Crisis: Is There a Way Out?*, Singapore: Institute of Southeast Asian Studies.

Corsetti, G. (1998), 'Interpreting the Asian Financial Crisis: Open Issues in Theory and Policy', *Asian Development Review*, **16**(2), pp. 1–45.

Corsetti, G., P. Pesenti and N. Roubini (1999), 'What Caused the Asian Currency and Financial Crisis?', *Japan and the World Economy*, **11**(2), pp. 305–73.

Dornbusch, R. (1997), 'A Thai-Mexico Primer: Lessons for Outmaneuvering a Financial Meltdown', *The International Economy*, **55**, September/October, pp. 20–23.

Edwards, Sebastian (1989), *Real Exchange Rates, Devaluation and Adjustment: Exchange Rate Policies in Developing Countries*, Cambridge, Mass: MIT Press.

Eichengreen, B. (1999), *Towards a New International Financial Architecture*, Washington, DC: Institute for International Economics.

Federal Reserve Bank of Kansas City (1997), *Maintaining Financial Stability in a Global Economy: A Symposium*, Kansas City: Federal Reserve Bank of Kansas City.

Fischer, S. (1998), 'Lessons from a Crisis', *The Economist*, **3**, October, pp. 19–23.

Furman, J. and J. Stiglitz (1998), 'Economic Crises: Evidence and Insights from East Asia', *Brookings Papers on Economic Activity*, **2**, pp. 1–136.

Garnaut, R. (1998), 'The Financial Crisis: A Watershed in Economic Thought about East Asia', *Asian Pacific Economic Literature*, **12**, pp. 1–11.

Goldstein, M. (1998), *The Asian Financial Crisis: Causes, Cures, and Systemic Implications*, Washington, DC: Institute for International Economics.

Goldstein, M. and C. Reinhart (1998), *Forecasting Financial Crises: Early Warning Signals for Emerging Markets*, Washington, DC: Institute for International Economics.

Huhne, C. (1998), 'How the Rating Agencies Blew it on Korea: An Industry Insider's Honest Admission', *International Economy*, May/June, pp. 46–9.

IMF (International Monetary Fund) (1997), *Exchange Rate Arrangements and Exchange Rate Restrictions – Annual Report*, Washington, DC: IMF.

Kaminski, G., S. Lizondo and C.M. Reinhart (1997), 'Leading Indicators of Currency Crises', *IMF Working Paper*, **WP/97/79**, Washington, DC: IMF.

Keynes, J.M. (1925) [1963], 'The Economic Consequences of Mr. Churchill', in his *Essays in Persuasion*, New York: W.W. Norton, pp. 244–70.

Kindleberger, C.P. (1996), *Manias, Panics, and Crashes: A History of Financial Crises*, 3rd Edition, New York: John Wiley & Sons.

Kregal, J.A. (1998), 'East Asia is not Mexico: The Difference between Balance of Payments Crises and Debt Deflation', in K.S. Jomo (ed.), *Tigers in Trouble: Financial Governance, Liberalization, and Crisis in East Asia*, London: Zed Books, pp. 44–62.

Krueger, A.O. (1984), 'Problems of Liberalization', in A.C. Harberger (ed.), *World Economic Growth*, San Francisco, CA: ICS Press.

Krugman, P. (1979), 'A Model of Balance-of-Payments Crises', *Journal of Money, Credit and Banking*, **11**, August, 311–25.

Krugman, P. (1991), 'International Aspects of Financial Crises', in M. Feldstein (ed.), *The Risk of Economic Crisis*, Chicago: University of Chicago Press, pp. 85–109.

Krugman, P. (1996), 'Are Currency Crises Self-Fulfilling?', *NBER Macroeconomics Annual*, MIT Press, 345–406.

Krugman, P. (ed.) (2000), *Currency Crises*, Chicago: University of Chicago Press.

McKinnon, R.I. (1998), 'Exchange Rate Coordination for Surmounting the East Asian Crisis', *Asian Economic Journal*, **12**, pp. 317–29.

Michaely, M., D. Papageorgiou and A.M. Choksi (1991), *Liberalizing Foreign Trade: Lessons of Experience in the Developing World*, Oxford: Basil Blackwell.

Miller, M. (1998), 'Asian Financial Crisis', *Japan and the World Economy*, **10**, pp. 355–8.

Mishkin, F.S. (1996), 'Understanding Financial Crises: A Developing Country Perspective', *Annual World Bank Conference on Development Economics*, pp. 29–61.

Mundell, R.A. (1962), 'The Appropriate Use of Monetary and Fiscal Policy for Internal and External Stability', *IMF Staff Papers*, **9**, pp. 70–79.

Nidhiprabha, B. (1999), 'Economic Crises and the Debt Deflation Episode in Thailand', *ASEAN Economic Bulletin*, **15**, pp. 309–18.

Norland, M., L-G. Liu, S. Robinson and Z. Wang (1998), *Global Economic Effects of the Asian Currency Devaluation*, Washington, DC: Institute of International Economics.

Radelet, S. and J. Sachs (1998), 'The East Asian Financial Crisis: Diagnosis, Remedies, Prospects', *Brookings Papers on Economic Activity*, **2**, pp. 1–89.

Sachs, J.D., A. Tornell and A. Velasco (1996), 'Financial Crises in Emerging Markets: The Lessons from 1995', *Brookings Papers on Economic Activity*, **1**, pp. 147–215.

Tobin, J. (1998), 'Asian Financial Crisis', *Japan and the World Economy*, **10**, pp. 351–3.

Wade, R. (1998), 'From "Miracle" to Cronyism: Explaining the Great Asian Slump', *Cambridge Journal of Economics*, **22**(4), pp. 693–706.

Warr, P.G. (1986), 'Indonesia's other Dutch Disease: Economic Effects of the Petroleum Boom', in J.P. Neary and S. van Wijnbergen (eds), *Natural Resources and the Macroeconomy*, Oxford: Basil Blackwell, pp. 288–320.

Warr, P.G. (1999), 'What Happened to Thailand?', *The World Economy*, **22**(7), pp. 631–50.

Warr, P.G. (2000), 'Macroeconomic Origins of the Korean Crisis', in H. Smith (ed.), *Looking Forward: Korea after the Economic Crisis*, Asia Pacific Press, Canberra: pp. 23–40.

Williamson, J. (1999), 'Development of the Financial System in Post-Crisis Asia', paper presented at the High-Level Dialogue on Development Paradigms, 10 December, Tokyo: Asian Development Bank Institute.

9. Inflation targeting after the currency crisis: the case of Thailand

Chayodom Sabhasri, June Charoenseang and Pornkamol Manakit

9.1 INTRODUCTION

This study is divided into several sections. First, the chapter briefly reviews the changes in the choice of monetary framework of East Asian countries. The advantages of inflation targeting over its alternatives, as well as the challenges to its implementation, are also discussed.

In the following section, the relationship between exchange rate volatility and inflation targeting has been explored, to evaluate an open economy with an inflation targeting framework. The experiences of the developed and developing countries are summarized in the next section. In particular, the economic performance of the Korean economy is briefly presented in order to observe its performance after the implementation of inflation targeting methods. Later, the study discusses how the interdependence of monetary policy and fiscal policy affects the rate of inflation, and how government budget deficits can influence inflationary pressures. Finally, inflation targeting in Thailand is analyzed as a new macroeconomic management policy. The outcome of this policy could be undesirable and inappropriate if it leads to a public debt crisis or high inflation rates. A fiscal stimulus package is needed to boost the economy, but the risk of taking on an excessively high government budget deficit does not always result in higher returns, and yet could yield devastatingly long-lasting outcomes.

9.2 THE INFLATION TARGETING ALTERNATIVE

During the initial stages of financial liberalization, the real appreciation of pegged currencies (baht, peso, rupiah, ringgit, won) that fixed their currencies to the

US dollar had provoked an unsustainable external disequilibrium. The reason for this was that it caused a sharp turnaround in international capital flows – capital flight – and the real overvaluation of domestic currencies deteriorated current accounts. Pegging systems at least provided some support in stabilizing domestic inflation. However, their implicit guarantee of exchange rate stability resulted in risk-taking behavior among domestic as well as international investors to take advantage of opportunities in international arbitrage.

Leaving the exchange rate pegs that their currencies had had with the US dollar was the first attempt to regain export competitiveness when the crisis occurred in 1997. Some of the five East Asian countries immediately embarked upon the process of reshaping their economies in the aftermath of the 1997 debacle.

Together with central banking law reform, Korea and Indonesia altered their monetary policy frameworks toward inflation targeting methods. Korean central banking law was reformed in December 1998 after the introduction of inflation targeting policies in September 1998, whereas Indonesia had its laws reformed in May 1999 before launching inflation targeting policy in January 2000.[1] The new central bank laws of Korea shifted monetary policy decision-making from its Ministry of Finance and Economy to the Financial and Monetary Committee chaired by the central bank governor.

Thailand implemented inflation targeting policies in May 2000, before the draft of the new Bank of Thailand Act was finalized. The Philippines has also worked towards an explicit inflation targeting framework since 2001.

Inflation targeting involves several elements. In one step, public announcements need to be made concerning the numerical indicators to be used – which could signify a range, a point, or ceiling. An institutional commitment is needed on the primary and long-term goals of monetary policy in price stability and in the achievement of targets. An information inclusion strategy should be implemented. Ongoing communication with the public should be maintained for more transparency in monetary policy and the objectives of monetary policymakers. Higher accountability by the central bank is needed to achieve inflation targets. Key factors to success are the independence of the central bank, the exercising of fiscal discipline and accuracy in forecasting future rates of inflation.

9.3   THE ADVANTAGES OF INFLATION TARGETING

Mishkin (1999) compared international experience in four types of monetary policy regimes: exchange rate targeting, monetary targeting, inflation targeting and monetary policy with an implicit – but not explicit – nominal anchor. To reach the desirable long-term outcome, choices in discretionary monetary policy depend on transparency and accountability. They, in turn, hinge upon the individual country's history, as well as on political, cultural and economic institutions. Many countries have discarded monetary targeting because the linkages and causality between monetary growth and various goal variables are unstable. Speculative attacks on their currencies have also threatened countries employing exchange rate targeting. These attacks have resulted in costly interest rate adjustments and output instability.

The advantages of inflation targeting are significant. It allows monetary policy to be an independent element that can respond to shocks in the domestic economy and does not rely on a relationship between money and inflation, i.e., stability of velocity is irrelevant. The target can be transparently communicated to the public. The explicit goal of an inflation target is a numerically targeted inflation rate that leads to greater accountability by the central bank. Consequently, time-inconsistent policies such as overly expansionary monetary policy – to expand output and reduce unemployment – can be totally avoided.

Inflation targeting is more transparent than monetary targeting and it also focuses on the accountability of central banks. It is a forward-looking policy since it sets a goal on future inflation rates. The central bank must be independent from the government and political influence in implementing its monetary policy. Also, the public can easily monitor the results of central bank measures toward inflation to see whether they meet the target or not. The success of the central bank initiatives will lead to greater credibility of the bank, and its long-term standing in maintaining economic stability.

The framework of inflation targeting includes a means of policy communication between monetary authorities and private economic agents. It provides a commitment to the public with policy rules, rather than discretionary measures that are time inconsistent. Private economic agents can then exploit this information and integrate it into their decision-making processes without concern about policy uncertainties. Inflation targeting in Thailand is, however, being implemented within an elastic system, because the monetary policy board is aware of the need for economic recovery. Policy optimization has therefore called for a weighting of 60 percent on the core inflation target and 40 percent on economic growth targets. This implies that policy decisions will take into account economic activity when monetary authorities make recommendations toward inflation targets.

Inflation targeting serves as a medium-term strategy for monetary policy that is an anchor for the value of money. Inflation targeting, as compared to strict monetary or exchange rate targeting, could be a better policy in dealing with cyclical adjustments of an economy. This is because inflation targeting is a monetary framework rather than a rule, as stated by Mishkin and Posen (1997), that leaves room for discretion in conducting monetary policy with some flexibility toward counter-cyclical supply or demand shocks. Jonsson (1999) states that a rigid target, such as an exchange rate or monetary aggregate, might not be compatible with stabilization of supply and demand shocks that themselves imply volatile output and inflation development.

Under inflation targeting, an increase in aggregate demand, as a shock, will put inflationary pressure on an economy, and that tightening monetary policy will help contain both inflationary pressure and increases in the output gap. It can be concluded that inflation targeting allows for more flexibility than monetary growth with nominal exchange rate targets, and it is also not as risky as a fully discretionary policy that could lead to inefficient output stabilization.

After the crisis, signs of low inflationary pressure in EastAsia became obvious due to the lack of local demand. Inflation targeting thus received timely introduction, as monetary authorities required less effort to introduce a new policy framework under such circumstances.

9.4   CHALLENGES IN IMPLEMENTATION

One of the major concerns in implementing inflation targeting is output instability. Usually, inflation targeting countries will choose a slow-adjustment approach in choosing their target inflation rate in order to prevent a reduction in output. However, after the economic crisis, output and employment declined sharply, and along with limited domestic demand, this resulted in low rates of inflation. The opportunity to launch inflation targeting in East Asian countries came when the cost of economic adjustment was at its minimum. A similar experience occurred in European countries after the 1990s EMS crisis. The impacts of inflation targeting are often misunderstood, and this leads to low and unstable output growth and employment. On the contrary, once the public believes in the credibility of the central bank to maintain its inflation target, consumers and investors will optimize their behavior without perceived uncertainties in inflationary policy, which in turn promotes real economic growth, while also controlling the inflation rate. Empirically, New Zealand is a good example of this argument.

Inflation targeting may take some time to become effective and there will be a cost to output stability during the transition period. Within that period, it may take time for the central bank to achieve recognition for its commitment to the inflation target, if without the explicit support of the government toward non-intervention. The short-term cost in terms of output stability may be substantial as long as private economic agents are not convinced of the credibility of the inflation target. When the public develops trust in the targeting, expectations toward inflation will lead the economy to the targeted zone. The success of the inflation target depends on the use of discretion in an appropriate setting of monetary policy. The effectiveness of such policy is dependent upon a decent inflation-forecasting model and policy instruments that accurately affect the inflation forecast. Besides this, the monetary transmission mechanism must be able to carry out adjustments to policy instruments to eventually yield the ultimate target.

As Mishkin (1999) summarized, the interpretation of inflation targeting as a rule is incorrect, and stems from a confusion that has been created by the rules-versus-discretion debate. He pointed out that the recommended strategies are rule-like, or can be said to be a form of constrained discretion with the involvement of forward-looking behavior. This prevents policy-makers from systematically implementing unwanted long-term outcomes.

Mishkin (2000) mentioned that the disadvantage of inflation targeting emanates from the long lags experienced between monetary policy implementation to the resultant inflation outcomes. Inflation targeting also cannot prevent fiscal dominance or the exchange rate flexibility required by inflation targeting, which might cause financial instability. These disadvantages often apply to emerging markets. In such markets, if the inflation target is applied to bring excessively high inflation down, the inflation forecast tends to be large. Credibility of the central bank in emerging countries is then difficult to achieve. Only in cases where inflation targeting is implemented when inflationary pressure is not severe, can that credibility be convincingly gained.

Fiscal discipline is the key element for efficiency in inflation targeting. If a government insists on pursuing fiscal deficits, the inflation target may be lost. Fiscal deficits will eventually have to be monetized. As with Sargent and Wallace (1981), if the fiscal authority's deficits cannot be financed solely by new bond sales, then monetary authorities will be forced to create money and accept the consequences of inflationary pressure. Also, fiscal deficits can bring about exchange rate depreciation, with inflation following.

A fully functional financial market is potentially another element to support the success of inflation targeting. A crippled system cannot transmit monetary policy signals or even monetary policy adjustments to the market. Besides this, monetary intervention under inflation targeting works itself out from adjustments in short-term rates of interest, such as through repurchase rates that influence the cost of financing.

9.5   HOW TO CONTROL EXCHANGE RATE VOLATILITY UNDER INFLATION TARGETING

Inflation targeting requires nominal exchange rate flexibility in line with relative purchasing power parity. Eichengreen (2001) argues that inflation targeting will become less attractive the more open an economy is, as it allows for exchange rate variability and this variability is costly to economic performance. That is to say, exchange rate fluctuations are unavoidable in this framework. Among the sacrifices to inflation targeting are protracted suffering from deterioration in external accounts, and higher risk exposure to financial crisis if a country is a net lender in foreign-denominated debt. Emerging countries are mostly net borrowers that raise funding from overseas, in particular through external debts that are either US dollar- or yen-denominated, depending on the relationship with the particular lender. In Asia, yen-denominated debt is very common, especially in the case of Thailand. Kumhof, Li and Yan (2000) analyzed open economies where fiscal deficits are incompatible with inflation targets, ultimately leading to speculative attacks. Monitoring to detect signs of exchange rate volatility is crucial, as such volatility or depreciation directly affects the external debt profile. However, exchange rate stability is second, or subordinate, to the inflation objective. That is to say, there must not be an explicit commitment by the central bank to intervene in the foreign exchange market.

In dealing with variability in exchange rates, Mishkin (2000) suggested that inflation targeting central banks in emerging market countries should adopt a transparent policy of smoothing short-term exchange rate fluctuations to help mitigate potential destabilization and abrupt changes in exchange rates. At the same time, it must communicate to the public that exchange rates will be allowed to change and reach a market-determined level in the end. Eichengreen (2001) also noted that openness could expose an economy to external shocks through international financial and trade transactions. The adjustment of a central bank's monetary policy will directly influence output, and indirectly the exchange rate, via interest rate parity. Therefore, to implement monetary policy adjustments, monetary authorities must take into account the lagging effect of the policy in an open economy model, carefully weighing the mixture and relationship of inflation and output. Flexible inflation targeting can be very useful in this application. In an open economy, exchange rate adjustments will partly eliminate deviation in inflation given the influence of foreign inflation on relative purchasing power parity. Therefore, the use of discretionary monetary policy can be minimized.

9.6   EXPERIENCES OF OTHER COUNTRIES

New Zealand was the first country to employ inflation targeting, in March 1990. Canada (in February 1991) and Australia (in April 1993) went to inflation targeting because the relationship between their money supply and inflation rates was no longer stable after the development of their new financial markets. The UK (October 1992) and Sweden (January 1993) used to link their currencies with a basket of European currencies, but they left that system after the currency crisis in 1992 and turned to floating exchange rates with inflation targeting. Spain implemented its targeting in the summer of 1994.

For developed countries, Mishkin and Posen (1997) concluded that inflation targeting has been highly successful in assisting countries such as New Zealand, Canada and the UK to maintain low inflation rates that were not the case in the past. For those countries, inflation targeting also helps to keep the performance of economic outcomes – such as the levels of exchange rates and economic growth – manageable in order to achieve low inflation rates. This new monetary framework has also assisted in improvements in economic growth. In terms of monetary policy strategy, it increases transparency and communication, accountability and institutional commitment to lower inflation.

Jonsson (1999) illustrated developments in inflation and output in such inflation targeting economies as New Zealand, Finland, Canada, Australia, Sweden, Spain and the United Kingdom, as well as in several industrial economies – including some 11 major EU members – plus Japan, the United States and Switzerland between 1985 to 1998. He found that all the inflation targeting countries he reviewed had lower inflation rates, on average. However, it is notable that the global rate of inflation was falling, in general, at that time. One must consider the real variables. Average GDP growth rates and their patterns are not affected by whether or when inflation targeting is implemented. Unemployment rates evidently do not increase due to switching to inflation targeting. No empirical evidence was found that reductions in inflation volatility after the introduction of inflation targeting are accompanied by higher output volatility. Debelle (1997) examined the performance of several developed countries that have elected to use inflation targeting and found that their frameworks of inflation targeting appeared to be successful. New Zealand, Canada, the UK and Sweden successfully maintained inflation within the target band, and Australia, Finland and Spain managed to keep their inflation rates close to the target rate. However, Debelle found that lower rates of inflation are generally accompanied by a rise in unemployment rates, except in the case of New Zealand, where the unemployment rate was declining.

We might consider further the inflation targeting frameworks used by emerging market countries. Masson, Savastano and Sharma (1997) provided an analytical basis for understanding how inflation targeting has been applied in industrialized countries and used this to evaluate the framework's applicability to developing countries. There were two major prerequisites for adopting such a framework: (1) a degree of independence in monetary policy – especially from fiscal dominance, and (2) the absence of commitment to other nominal anchor variables such as nominal exchange rates or nominal wages. These conditions are hardly met in developing countries. Only five countries, Chile, Colombia, Indonesia, Mexico and the Philippines are likely to adopt inflation targeting successfully. However, with the high degree of capital mobility present resulting from financial liberalization and instability of demand for money, alternative nominal anchors to inflation targeting may be less desirable.

Mishkin (2000) also briefly discussed the experiences of emerging market countries and developing countries in using inflation targeting. Chile is a successful case of implementing inflation targeting by launching it with an official inflation projection earlier, prior to deciding on and announcing a hard target. Chile also passed new central bank legislation in 1989 that provided independence for the central bank in order that it can mandate price stability as its primary objective.

After the introduction of inflation targeting in 1990, inflation rates have fallen from over 20 percent to slightly over 3 percent in ten years. Economic growth rates were over 8 percent until the financial crisis in East Asia that contagiously reduced the Chilean growth rate to below zero. One reason that this sharply reduced the growth rate in Chile was that it tightened monetary policy so as to prevent inflation and to maintain exchange rates from the effects of depreciation. Chile has proven that an attempt to undershoot an inflation target is as costly as overshooting the target. The success story of Chile is also due to its fiscal discipline in having an absence of large fiscal deficits, and its rigorous regulation and supervision of the financial sector.

Brazil adopted inflation targeting after its currency crisis in early 1999. The inflation rate was kept under 10 percent even if there was substantial exchange rate depreciation. Fiscal discipline remains a major problem in Brazil. Eichengreen (2001) also cited several other emerging market countries that are referencing inflation targets. Aside from Brazil, they include Chile, the Czech Republic, Israel, South Africa, Poland, Columbia, Thailand, Mexico, the Philippines and South Korea.

The Korean inflation target was set at 9.0 ±1.0 percent in 1998, but the core inflation rate was then far below the target. The inflation target for 1999 was set at 3.0 ±1.0 percent, whereas the Consumer Price Index was projected at 3.0 percent. The GDP growth rate reached 10.7 percent. On the production side, the manufacturing sector was the leading sector. Although the government pursued an expansionary stance, prices were extremely stable. The country's Consumer Price Index decreased drastically from 7.5, in 1998, to 0.8 in 1999. It actually undershot the target.

In 2000, the Bank of Korea set an inflation target of 2.5 ±1.0 percent. This year, the bank also introduced a mid-term inflation target of 2.5 percent to maintain consistency in monetary policy and suppress inflationary expectations. Despite GDP growth of 8.8 percent in 2000, annual core inflation remained within its target range of 2.5 ±1.0 percent, with a 2.1 percent increase in the Consumer Price Index. Nonetheless, prices have accelerated since the second half of that year as a result of higher international oil prices and public service charges. Current accounts recorded a surplus of US$11 billion. However, stock prices fell sharply from May due to concerns over the liquidity problems of some large companies, together with concerns over structural reform in the corporate and financial sectors. There was stability in the foreign exchange market as a response to the excess supply of foreign currency in 2000. Nonetheless, the Korean won depreciated substantially due to a weakening of other major currencies against the US dollar, coupled with the fear of losing external credit standings because of delays in the restructuring process.

In 2000, the Bank of Korea set an inflation target of 3.0 percent, ±1.0 percent, where the mid-term target was set to remain at 2.5 percent. The Korean government expected that the rate of price increase would be slower after the second half of 2001, and thus was allowed to converge to the mid-term target range in 2002. Certain factors explain this expectation. Among them were the slowdown in world economic growth and seasonal factors, which were expected to stabilize oil prices, thus costs were expected to be quite stable. Increased flexibility in their labor market, as a result of corporate and financial restructuring efforts, would not cause a substantial increase in wages. However, public service charges were expected to continue to rise in 2002, and thus exert inflationary pressure.

The target in Korea was rather wide. The inflation target for the Korean case was adjustable from one year to the next. In 1999, the inflation rate undershot the target but it returned to the targeted range a year later. After three years of inflation targeting, the inflation rate declined from that over the period just after the crisis. The economic growth also strengthened.

One of the major difficulties experienced by emerging market countries is that the main source of the government budgets depends on seignorage revenue, along with a weak tax base system. In addition, governments implicitly guarantee contingent bailout liabilities for weak financial systems, or overspend when economic performance shows signs of recession. Effective inflation targeting requires no fiscal dominance. To have a government commit to the target, the government – not the central bank – must announce the targets, as in Chile and Poland, or a joint effort between the government and its central bank to announce the target should be used, as in Brazil and Israel. This will enhance the credibility of the target.

9.7   MONETARY AND FISCAL POLICY INTERDEPENDENCE

The uses of monetary policy always link to the fiscal stance. The classic work by Sargent and Wallace (1981) argues that there is a strong relationship between monetary and fiscal policies, as government budget deficits can be inflationary. This case occurs when fiscal authorities do not have a credible commitment to a sufficient sequence of taxes to finance its spending in present value, and there is some limit to the debt-to-GDP ratio, i.e., a debt ceiling. Monetary authorities can only control the money supply when the debt ceiling is reached, and they will then have to accommodate government spending through seignorage revenues. This phenomenon is commonly experienced in emerging market countries.

With the introduction of inflation targeting, fiscal dominance is one of the most debatable issues for efficiency in this methodology. The arguments by Sargent and Wallace, as well as Dahan (1998) also examine the budgetary implications of monetary policy measures. Tight monetary policy may cause a short-term decrease in government debt because of an increase in the budget deficit.

The consequence of a higher budget deficit is higher rates of interest, resulting in a lower market value for government debt, thereby meaning that debt servicing of existing public debt may become more expensive. The net outcome depends on whether the stock effect or the flow effect will dominate.

Moreover, Beddies (1999) using a stochastic model, concludes that unrestricted central bank independence may not be 'optimal' from a social welfare standpoint, regardless of the central bank's objectives vis-à-vis inflation, or about both inflation and output. Optimal inflation targeting for an independent central bank will see output as the most desirable solution.

Consider the strategic interaction between fiscal and monetary implementation. Dahan suggests, with some probability, that policymakers will be able to alter the degree of the independence of their central bank. With the inherent loss of credibility, tight monetary policy with high public debt, large budgetary deficits, and a large share of short-term bonds, will lead to an environment of higher inflation rather than lower inflation.

The 'political economy games' between governments and their central banks determine the degree of credibility and the size of budgetary cost. Additionally, Leitemo (2000) formally proves that the strategic interaction between fiscal and monetary authorities when monetary policymakers pursue inflation targeting can lead to different results, depending largely on the game theoretical setting. The Stackleberg equilibrium is preferred to the Nash equilibrium because the fiscal policymaker can reduce strong movements in interest rates as well as exchange rates. Given that the public understands the implementation and strategies of inflation targeting, the fiscal policymaker will not pursue over-ambitious employment targets that conflict with the inflation targeting framework. There are two requirements in Leitemo's model. They are a long enough commitment for the fiscal stance, and for transparent monetary policy reactions to take place. Fiscal policymakers may act as the leader and improve the policy mix, resulting in lower real interest rates and lower exchange rate volatility.

9.8   PUBLIC DEBT PROBLEMS AND THE ROLE OF MONEY CREATION IN FINANCING BUDGET DEFICITS

One of the legacies of the Asian economic crisis has been that it left heavy debt. It has put fiscal pressures on the governments of the hardest-hit countries. The balanced budgets of five East Asian countries – Korea, Malaysia, Philippines, Thailand and Indonesia – fell to deficit. The crisis increased budget deficits because, first, overall tax revenues decreased as a result of lower income and reduced imports. Meanwhile, government spending could not adjust instantaneously. Furthermore, the depreciation of their currencies also raised interest payments on foreign debt. Many governments strongly intervened into their financial systems, and public debt – as a share of GDP – rose sharply.

Moral hazards were another major factor causing the 'Asian Meltdown'. With economic warnings of over-investment, excessive external borrowing, and current account deficits, foreign creditors still seemed willing to extend loans to domestic economic agents because of foreseen future bail-outs by their governments (Corsetti, Pesenti and Roubini, 1998). With these government external liabilities, governments undertook domestic fiscal reforms that possibly involved recourse to seignorage revenues through money creation. However, inflationary financing will lead to collapse of a currency and financial crisis.

Empirically, Burnside, Eichenbaum and Rebelo (2001) explored the different means of financing fiscal costs of twin banking and currency crises as a result of inflation and depreciation rates. The major costs are due to the restructuring and recapitalizing of failing financial systems. They found that the Mexican government dealt with the crisis in 1994 by financing most of the fiscal cost of its crisis through the printing of money, whereas the Korean government is likely to finance the cost of its 1997 crisis with a mixture of future implicit and explicit fiscal reforms.

Those reforms include an increase in tax revenue, as a percentage of GDP, and a very slow increase in won values of expenditure resulting from the depreciation of the won. As a result, the Mexican inflation rates increased substantially, while the Korean government accumulated an enormous amount of new debt – roughly 17.3 percent of GDP – to finance its crisis in the short term. Money creation can lead to undesirable inflationary pressure that could last for a long time.

Public sector debt is now approximately 90 percent of the GDP in Indonesia, approximately 70 percent in the Philippines, and in the range of 35–50 percent in Korea, Malaysia and Thailand. Room for further fiscal expansion is narrowing in Indonesia, the Philippines and, to a lesser extent, Thailand. Large deficits and growing public sector debt have greatly reduced the scope of offsetting future negative demand shocks through government budget deficits. Therefore, a fiscal expansion stance should be viewed with caution because of the high levels of non-performing loans in these countries.

In order to resolve the non-performing loan problem and recapitalize banks, substantial amounts of public funding will be required, which will then put more pressure on public spending and thus public debt. If fiscal positions deteriorate further, increasing interest rates arising from rising public debt could deteriorate investment, which could lead to another recession.

9.9 INFLATION TARGETING AND MACROECONOMIC POLICY MANAGEMENT IN THAILAND

So far, several publications have argued that inflation targeting has been beneficial to both developing and developed countries. The advantages of inflation targeting are also discussed in its preference to both monetary aggregate targets and interest rate targeting. In Thailand prior to the 1997 crisis, the nominal exchange rate was implicitly the main focus of monetary policy. During the period of IMF assistance, monetary policy relied on monetary supply targeting and high short-term interest rates to maintain the value of the Thai baht. Three years later, after the economic crisis in May 2000, the Bank of Thailand adopted inflation targeting with the target band range from 0 to 3.5 percent between the years 2000 and 2002.

Santiprabhob (2001) has briefly reviewed the performance of the Thai economy after the introduction of the economic crisis. He concluded that core inflation has been kept within the target range. However, he argued that the target range might not be appropriate since it did not take into account the expected inflation. In practical terms, the range was set based on historical performance. Core inflation rates have moved in the lower half of the range, between the mid-point of the band and the floor at zero percent. Between the second quarter of 2000 and the first quarter of 2001, yield curves shifted downward. However, bond yields rose sharply between February and April of 2001 due to a supply of new bond issues, as well as central bank intervention. Nevertheless, the change in yield curves may not have been caused only by inflation expectations, as there may have been some other factors – in particular, the bond market, which is rather new and thin. In dealing with external shocks, monetary policy seems to be a rather passive choice as it is no threat to the inflation rate.

Since inflation targeting has only just been implemented in Thailand, much cannot yet be said about its success. However, no country, whether developed or developing, has abandoned inflation targeting after having implemented it. Even though the period of time in place in Thailand has been very short, it can be evaluated that this framework has shown no sign of harming economic performance. In particular, the framework seems to be transparent and easily disclosed compared to implicit exchange rate targeting, which in the past was uncertain and left room for speculators to be active, while the monetary aggregate target was hard to understand.

Our study has attempted to perform a simple empirical test (not shown here) on the causal relationship between the short-term interest rates and real variables. The interbank rates represent short-term rates. The test indicates that an interbank rate affects the monetary aggregate, core inflation exchange rate and the manufacturing production index. Moreover, a monetary aggregate operand influences inflation and exchange rate. Thus, a central bank may place its emphasis on short-term interest rates such as an interbank rate. That is, the study suggests that an interbank rate may be adopted as an operating target since it significantly links to the real sector and inflation rate. Using a co-integration test, the result shows that when an interbank rate is adopted as an operating target, it causes variations in the real and financial sectors, and these effects are significant in the end. There is no apparent relationship between volatility in exchange rates and the inflation rate. Concerning the relationship between inflation stability and exchange rate volatility, the controlling of volatility in an inflation rate does not guarantee stability in an exchange rate. These findings may be due to the short period of observation in the test. Actually, adjustment of repurchase rates is a monetary policy tool for inflation targeting, but changes in repurchase rates also affect the interbank rate. So, from this, we can approximate certain findings.

In the matter of this policy implementation in Thailand, and its impact on economic recovery, monetary policy is not likely to be very effective. Several reasons support this argument. There is considerable excess liquidity in the market and there is an environment of historically low interest rates. However, the credit growth rate remains negative. One reason explaining this situation is the ill-functioning condition of financial markets due to the slow process of private debt restructuring. A monetary policy of expansion will not be appropriate until the liquidity trap is solved. Besides this, financial intermediaries have not been proactive in extending loans to investors so as to boost the economy. The role of monetary policy is thus rather limited.

The high percentage of public debt seems threatening to the overall economy. However, if we use the same standards as the convergence criteria in the Maastricht Treaty – where a public debt ceiling may be permitted up to 60 percent of GDP, the debt profile for Thailand (Table 9.1) is not as serious as it seems to be. However, the potential for economic growth is rather low because domestic demand is limited due to the low confidence of consumers and investors toward economic performance. Also, international trade competitiveness is a major concern as export performance in 2001 was, as expected, way off target. Export demand, under such circumstances, is not a reliable source of foreign income.

Table 9.1   Public debt profile for Thailand (fiscal year)

	1997	1998	1999	2000	2001 (until March)
Public debt**	4.5	9.9	20.9	23.1	23.3
Domestic debt***	15.0	45.0	62.0	65.0	65.0
Foreign debt***	85.0	55.0	38.0	35.0	35.0
State owned enterprises**	11.5	11.5	16.6	18.8	17.9
Domestic debt***	34.0	35.0	38.0	48.0	49.0
Foreign debt***	66.0	65.0	62.0	52.0	51.0
FIDF* debt**	19.0	21.2	16.7	16.2	15.1
Total public debt**	35.0	42.7	53.9	58.1	56.3

Notes: * Financial Institutions Development Fund.
        ** Share of GDP.
        *** Share of total debt.

Source: Bank of Thailand.

Fiscal stimulus may be the last resort in accommodating economic recovery. A government may need to launch a substantial number of fiscal packages to boost the local economy. However, fiscal stimulus is constrained by several factors. In the Thai Budgetary Act, government borrowing to finance the deficit is limited to 20 percent of total fiscal year budget, and not more than 80 percent of the budget is the limitation for the repayment of interest and principal on existing loans. Aside from this, fiscal discipline is likely to be dominated by the inflation targeting.

In an extreme case, the government could, with a majority of the House of Parliament, alter existing legislation for special short-term purposes to accommodate economic recovery. Therefore, fiscal limitations could be partially relaxed for a short time. The government is also able to issue new bonds to finance its budget deficit. New issuances could be sold in the local market that currently has high liquidity, or could be sold externally if the interest rate on them is attractive enough.

On another tack, new issuances of bonds could be financed by the central bank, but that could break down inflation targeting. Most strikingly, unlike the case of Korea and Indonesia that introduced their central bank law reforms prior to the implementation of inflation targeting, the new Bank of Thailand Act is still in the draft process more than 12 months since the start of inflation targeting. The draft law sets as its objective for the central bank to maintain price stability and safeguard the stability of the financial system.

In emergencies, the central bank is allowed to lend to the government only for spending indicated in the annual budget. Hence, with only a draft version of the act in process, central bank independence remains doubtful, and that threatens the benefit of the inflation targeting. Fiscal dominance could damage the credibility of inflation targeting.

9.10   SUMMARY

Several developed and developing countries have turned to inflation targeting as their monetary policy. So far, no country has left this framework. Several countries in Latin America and East Asia have adopted inflation targeting after experiencing economic crises. In this chapter, the advantages of inflation targeting have been discussed and contrasted to its alternatives, while the challenges of inflation targeting are also stated. The management of macroeconomic policy when employing inflation targeting for an open economy can be rather complicated. The experiences of developed and developing countries are briefly summarized. In developed nations, inflation targets seem to work well in maintaining economic stability. Due to the short period of observation, formal empirical tests for East Asian countries using inflation targeting were not performed. However, a test for the case of Thailand's monetary mechanism was done and it shows a relationship between short-term interest rates and real variables that can be adopted as an operating instrument.

The economic crisis has left us with high public debt. Dealing with debt while accommodating economic recovery is not a simple task. While the implementation of inflation targeting in Thailand has been in effect for over a year, doubts about the independence of the central bank remain. One reason, among others, is found in the long period required for deliberation on the draft of the new Bank of Thailand Act. From the experiences of other developing countries, Thailand may greatly benefit from an inflation targeting framework, but adverse fiscal dominance could damage the credibility of the central bank that it has built up over the past 12 months. This is due to the problems of public debt and slow economic recovery, where attempts to use fiscal stimuli can be beneficial only if the policy mix is appropriate. A sharp turnaround of the economy with an excessive fiscal stimulus package and poorly managed monetary policy could degrade the credibility of inflation targeting and lead to undesirable outcomes. A fiscal stimulus package is currently needed to boost the economy above the poor economic performance thus far; however, the high risk of taking on excessive government budget deficits does not always result in high returns, and could produce devastating and long-lasting undesirable consequences.

APPENDIX: THE INTERDEPENDENCE BETWEEN MONEY CREATION AND BUDGET DEFICIT FINANCE

An important part of the Thai public deficit is its FIDF liabilities. It remains unclear how the government will fiscalize these liabilities, as the burden should not be passed on to the central bank. From the experience of several emerging countries, seignorage revenue may be resorted to, and has been so rather commonly and unsurprisingly, to service the government budget deficit. We can use a very simple model to evaluate the impacts of such a policy choice. The interdependence between money creation and budget deficit financing is as follows. If the real government budget deficit $\{D_t\}$ for $t = 0, 1, \dots, \infty$, where G_t is the real value of government expenditures, and T_t is the real value of government revenue in period t (note that the interest payment is not included in D_t):

$$D_t = G_t - T_t, \text{ for } t = 0, 1, \dots, \infty, \tag{9.1}$$

$$D_t = B_t^g - (1 + r)B_{t-1}^g + (M_t - M_{t-1})/P_t. \tag{9.2}$$

The government has some amount of real outstanding government debt at the beginning of each period t, B_t^g, and must pay its creditors a real amount, expressed as $(1 + r)B_{t-1}^g$ in period t. The real money creation for each period t is the amount $(M_t - M_{t-1})/P_t$. The real interest rate on government debt is constant at $r_t = r$. Theoretically, a government never defaults on its debt. It can be said that borrowing demand is on the left-hand side, and the borrowing supply is on the right-hand side:

$$D_t + (1 + r)B_{t-1}^g = B_t^g + (M_t - M_{t-1})/P_t. \tag{9.3}$$

Another way of expressing the statement is that the government's real budget deficit plus the interest payment on the debt must be paid by the net new bonds and/or seignorage, i.e., the real value of net new notes:

$$D_t + rB_{t-1}^g = B_t^g - B_{t-1}^g + (M_t - M_{t-1})/P_t. \tag{9.4}$$

Let the growth rate of money supply and output (GDP) equal as follows, where M_t and Y_t are money supply and GDP at period t. The quantity theory of money is assumed to have a constant velocity of one. The money growth rate is constant at z, and the economic growth rate is constant at g. M_0 and Y_0 are greater than zero:

$$\text{The money growth rate, } M_t = (1 + z)M_{t-1} \tag{9.5}$$

$$\text{Economic growth rate, } Y_t = (1 + g)Y_{t-1} \tag{9.6}$$

$$\text{Quantity theory of money, } M_t/Y_t = P_t. \tag{9.7}$$

The deficit-to-GDP ratio, D_t/Y_t, is denoted as d_t and the debt-to-GDP ratio, B_t^g/Y_t, is denoted as b_t^g. Therefore, the debt financing equation can be rewritten as:

$$(D_t/Y_t) = (B_t^g/Y_t) - [(1 + r)B_{t-1}^g/(1 + g)Y_{t-1}] + [1 - (M_{t-1}/M_t)], \tag{9.8}$$

or

$$d_t = b_t^g - \{[(1 + r)/(1 + g)]b_{t-1}^g\} + [1 - (M_{t-1}/M_t)] \text{ for } t = 1, 2, \ldots, \widetilde{\infty}.$$

Substituting the growth rate of money supply and the economic growth,

$$d_t = b_t^g - \{[(1 + r)/(1 + g)]b_{t-1}^g\} + [z/(z + 1)] \tag{9.9}$$

as $[1 - (M_{t-1}/M_t)] = 1 - [1/(1 + z)] = [z/(1 + z)]$

$$b_t^g = \{d_t - [z/(z + 1)]\} + \{[(1 + r)/(1 + g)]b_{t-1}^g\}. \tag{9.10}$$

The real outstanding government debt is the real deficit less seignorage as a fraction of GDP and the existing real debt indexed by the GDP growth. By recursively substituting the above equation, we can re-express the real outstanding government debt as:

$$b_t^g = \Sigma_{i=1}^t \{[(1 + r)/(1 + g)]^{i-1}[d_t - z/(1 + z)]\} + \{[(1 + r)/(1 + g)]^t b_0^g\}, \text{ and}$$
$$b_0^g > 0 \text{ to reflect the initial public debt.} \tag{9.11}$$

Keep in mind that the model is quite simple without any stochastic process. We are now ready to analyze the relationship between the monetary and fiscal policies. The problem can be analyzed as two separate cases: without money creation and with money creation. When we assume that money creation is not possible, the inflation target may be easily achieved. With zero money creation, the money growth rate is constant at zero. Also, the inflation rate is determined by GDP growth, and deflation is not ruled out in this case. With a zero rate of GDP growth, the inflation rate is zero. The outcome of zero money growth may be undesirable as compared to the 'optimal' choice of monetary policy. Also, inflation may hit the lower bound of the target band.

For simplicity, we also assume that d_t is constant over time. The real public debt is insolvency when its value in the infinite period is non-negative, i.e., $b_\infty^g > 0$.

If money creation is zero, then the real budget deficit at time t is the accumulation of the budget deficit and the initial real outstanding debt:

$$b_t^g = d\Sigma_{i=1}^t [(1+r)/(1+g)]^{i-1} + \{[(1+r)/(1+g)]^t\, b_0^g\}. \qquad (9.12)$$

In an infinite time horizon, the limit of b_t^g is zero if $r < g$. That is to say, that the real rate of interest is lower than the economic growth implies that the economy is performing well. Intuitively, the real outstanding public debt is sustainable if the economy outperforms the cost of fiscal financing. On the other hand, the public debt will not be sustainable if the economy slumps for a long period, i.e., when $r > g$. The policy implication of this result is that government stimulus packages must be wisely and timely spent in the productive sector in order to generate enough growth to cover the future government liabilities.

On the other hand, if money creation is one of the fiscal financing sources, the result and its policy implication will be more interesting. The value of the real outstanding debt is:

$$b_t^g = [d - z/(1+z)]\Sigma_{i=1}^t \{[(1+r)/(1+g)]^{i-1}\} + [(1+r)/(1+g)]^t\, b_0^g$$
$$\text{for } t = 0, 1, \ldots \infty. \qquad (9.13)$$

Let K be defined as $[d - z/(1+z)]$. Then, we can rewrite the real value of public debt at time t as:

$$b_t^g = K\Sigma_{i=1}^t \{[(1+r)/(1+g)]^{i-1}\} + [(1+r)/(1+g)]^t\, b_0^g$$
$$\text{for } t = 0, 1, \ldots \infty. \qquad (9.14)$$

There are two interesting cases depending on whether r is less than, or greater than, g. Let's consider the case that r is less than g ($r < g$). When time approaches the infinite period, the first term is a positive finite number, whereas the last term is zero. Thus, $b_t^g = K[(1+g)/(g-r)]$ as time approaches the infinite period. The sustainability of the real public debt depends on the relative value of budget deficit and the fraction of the money creation to GDP. The values of b_t^g at infinity are shown in the following table:

	$K > 0$	$K = 0$	$K < 0$
$r < g$	$b_\infty^g > 0$	$b_\infty^g = 0$	$b_\infty^g < 0$

Besides the case where $K = 0$, another possibility for sustainable public debt is where $K < 0$. That is to say, when an economy outperforms the cost of fiscal financing, a lower deficit-to-GDP ratio than fraction of money growth is preferred. The inflation rate can be calculated from the quantity theory of money, and is expressed as:

$$\text{inflation rate} = (z - g)/(1 + g) \tag{9.15}$$

If $r < g$ and $K > 0$ together with money growth are higher than GDP growth, the inflation rate is increasing and the public debt is not sustainable. That is to say, if $K > 0$, money creation will not help public debt to achieve solvency. Therefore, if the government has a strong desire to boost the economy with excessive public debt financing through money creation, the outcome could be devastating. The reason for this is that chronic deficit-to-GDP ratio will occur in the long run. Inflation targeting will certainly be broken down due to the failure of fiscal dominance. The policy implication here is that excessive budget deficits will result in debt insolvency and inflationary pressure in the future.

Another case in point is when the real rate of interest is higher than, or equal to, the economic growth rate. The values of real public debt into infinity are reported in the following table:

	$K > 0$	$K = 0$	$K < 0$
$r > g$	$b^g_\infty = \infty$	$b^g_\infty = \infty$	$b^g_\infty > 0$ [for some K]

The results illustrate that such debt is not sustainable when economic growth is outperformed by the cost of fiscal financing. There exist some cases where the public debt remains sustainable for some values of K less than zero, i.e., the money growth fraction to GDP is greater than the deficit-to-GDP ratio.[2] To have sustainable public debt in the end, when economic growth yields a relatively low rate of return, the only way to have sustainable debt is to earn seignorage revenue by creating money. The outcome will be inflationary. Therefore, when a government stimulates its economy thus but achieves only a poor rate of growth, it unavoidably generates an inflation tax to finance its expenditures. Otherwise, the government might have to resort to a debt moratorium. Fiscal discipline is needed to keep inflation low. It is also apparent that budget deficits must be spent in the productive sector. Hence, when $r > g$ and $K > 0$, i.e., the debt-to-GDP ratio is excessive relative to the inflation tax fraction, and the real interest rate dominates economic growth, we then create an economic crisis with high inflation and public debt crises. A fiscal stimulus package that aims at high return from economic growth could result in unbearably high risk.

One of the most important requirements for an inflation target to be effective is that it be supportive to a fiscal stance. Excessive public debt or a long-term government budget deficit could lead to higher inflation in the future via expected earnings from seignorage revenue. A public debt crisis and a breakdown of inflation targeting could occur if the budget deficit is not wisely spent. The central bank would run into great difficulty in achieving its ultimate goal in inflation targeting, as well as risk its credibility.

NOTES

1. 'Inflation Targeting Booming in Asia', Japan Rating and Investment Information, 14 July 2000.
2. In the infinite period, there exist some values of $b^g_\infty < 0$.
   $K\Sigma^t_{i=1}\{[(1+r)/(1+g)]^{i-1}\} + [(1+r)/(1+g)]^t\, b^g_0 < 0$, which implies
   $K/b^g_0\, [-\{[(1+r)/(1+g)]^t\}/\Sigma^t_{i=1}\{[(1+r)/(1+g)]^{i-1}\}$.
   The left-hand side is a negative value and K is a negative value. Hence, there must be some values of K that satisfy this condition.

REFERENCES

Beddies, Christian H. (1999), 'Monetary Policy and Public Finances: Inflation Targets in a New Perspective', *IMPF Staff Papers*, **46**(3) (September/December).

Burnside, Craig, Martin Eichenbuam and Sergio Rebelo (2001), 'On the Fiscal Implications of Twin Crises', *NBER Working Paper*, **8277**.

Corsetti, Giancarlo, P. Pesenti and N. Roubini (1998), 'Paper Tigers? A Model for the Asian Crisis', *NBER Working Paper*, **6783**.

Dahan, Momi (1998), 'The Fiscal Effects of Monetary Policy', *IMF Working Paper*, **98**(66).

Debelle, Guy (1997), 'Inflation Targeting in Practice', *IMF Working Paper*, **97**(35).

Eichengreen, Barry (2001), *Can Emerging Markets Float? Should They Inflation Target?*, mimeo, University of California, Berkeley.

Jonsson, Gunnar (1999), 'The Relative Merits and Implications of Inflation Targeting for South Africa', *IMF Working Paper*, **99**(16).

Kumhof, Michael, S. Li and I. Yan (2000), *Balance of Payments Crises under Inflation Targeting*, Working Paper, Department of Economics, Stanford University.

Leitemo, Kai (2000), *Strategic Interaction between the Fiscal and Monetary Authorities under Inflation Targeting*, Research Department, Norges Bank, Norway.

Masson, Paul R., Miguel A. Savastano and Sunil Sharma (1997), 'The Scope for Inflation Targeting in Developing Countries', *IMF Working Paper*, **97**(130).

Mishkin, Frederic S. (1999), 'International Experiences with Different Monetary Policy Regimes', *NBER Working Paper*, **7044**.

Mishkin, Frederic S. (2000), 'Inflation Targeting in Emerging Market Countries', *NBER Working Paper*, **7618**.

Mishkin, Frederic S. and Adam S. Posen (1997), 'Inflation Targeting: Lessons for Four Countries', *NBER Working Paper*, **6126**.

Santiprabhob, Veerathai (2001), *Bank of Thailand's Inflation Targeting: Recent Performance and Future Challenges*, Working Paper, Corporate Planning and Information Department, Siam Commercial Bank, PCL.

Sargent, Thomas J. and Neil Wallace (1981), 'Some Unpleasant Monetarist Arithmetic', *Federal Reserve Bank of Minneapolis Quarterly Review*, **5**(3), pp. 1–17.

10.   Rethinking capital controls: the case of Malaysia

Masahiro Kawai[1] and Shinji Takagi[2]

10.1   INTRODUCTION

The 1990s saw a proliferation of capital account crises in emerging market economies. Such crises were characterized by sudden reversals of capital inflows that forced abrupt current account adjustments and major macroeconomic disruptions. It is now well understood that one of the most important factors behind those recent emerging market crises were some stock imbalances, such as high levels of public sector debt (Argentina, Brazil and Turkey) and currency or maturity mismatches in the structure of highly leveraged private sector liabilities (Argentina, Indonesia, Korea and Thailand). Unlike conventional current account crises, flow imbalances played a comparatively small role. However, the precise propagation mechanisms running from those stock imbalances to currency crises differed across countries. Also, the nature of those stock imbalances themselves has complicated the problem of tackling the crises once they broke out.

In the last decade, a number of emerging economies – including those in East Asia – pursued financial market deregulation, capital account liberalization (both for inflows and outflows), and financial sector opening. Deregulation and liberalization have, no doubt, brought economic benefits in the form of greater financial resource mobilization to domestic investment and economic growth. At the same time, this has created new sources of vulnerabilities in the balance sheets of commercial banks, corporations and the public sector. The implication is that emerging economies wishing to integrate themselves with the international financial market must manage the process of such integration in a prudent way to minimize its potential negative impact.

The high frequency of emerging market crises has led policymakers to cast doubt on the virtue of unrestricted capital mobility in an increasingly globalized and potentially volatile world economy. It is not surprising, therefore, that some Latin American countries – notably Chile and Colombia – have recently employed capital inflow controls, and that Malaysia has resorted to capital outflow controls. With capital control measures, these countries have tried to insulate their economies from the vagaries of unstable capital movements. This chapter is an attempt to assess the role of capital controls in the light of recent emerging market experience.

The chapter is organized with Section 2 arguing that, in order to avoid capital account crises and to minimize their negative effects once they occur, emerging market economies should pay sufficient attention to the needs of sound macroeconomic policies, greater resiliency in domestic financial systems, and adequate availability of international liquidity, together with private sector involvement, and regional financial cooperation. Section 3 presents rationales for capital controls, examines the costs and benefits of three types of control regimes (namely, Chilean-style reserve requirements), prudential regulations on short-term capital inflows, and controls on short-term capital outflows. Section 4 takes up the experience of Malaysian capital controls and argues that the controls have had a generally salutary effect, mainly because they were supported by a sound macroeconomic policy framework, accompanied by bank and corporate restructuring, backed by an undervalued currency, implemented with credible supervision, and placed explicitly as a temporary measure. Section 5 concludes the chapter.

10.2   MANAGING FINANCIAL MARKET INTEGRATION

Emerging market crises in recent years have highlighted the explosive combination of open capital accounts, overvalued exchange rates and poorly regulated financial systems. The East Asian currency crisis has been clearly an example of such a combination. To enjoy the substantial benefits of global financial integration, emerging market economies must attempt to minimize the risk of capital account crisis by avoiding exchange rate overvaluation and by strengthening supervisory and regulatory frameworks governing their financial systems. This section focuses on the importance of sound macroeconomic management and information disclosure, the orderly sequencing of capital account liberalization, the availability of international liquidity to calm the currency market, private sector involvement to reduce moral hazard, and regional financial cooperation to contain contagions.[3]

10.2.1   Macroeconomic Management, Exchange Rate Policy and Information Disclosure

The most important policy focus for any emerging economy that is integrated with global finance should be to maintain sound macroeconomic policy and sustainable external debt, so that a currency crisis can be prevented from occurring in the first place. Macroeconomic policies should be aimed at avoiding excessive cycles of domestic boom and bust, an overvaluation of the currency and an unsustainable accumulation of short-term external debt.

With free mobility of capital, choosing an exchange rate regime is not an easy task, particularly for emerging market economies. Authorities must strike an optimum balance among the three objectives of exchange rate stability, free capital mobility and independent monetary policy through an appropriate choice of exchange rate regime. Once an appropriate exchange rate regime is chosen, it must be backed by consistent macroeconomic policies and supported by robust financial systems, so that the regime becomes sustainable and is able to credibly deter speculative attacks. Countries choosing fixed rate regimes must be willing, as necessary, to subordinate monetary policy objectives to fixing the rate.

A sustained real overvaluation of the currency is almost always an important factor behind speculative pressure in the foreign exchange market, and overvalued exchange rates tend to become victims of speculative attacks. Hence, policymakers should avoid currency overvaluation within the constraint of the chosen exchange rate regime.

Much of the over-lending typically found prior to any currency crisis might be avoided if international investors correctly appraised the macroeconomic and structural conditions of the economy. When investors try to undertake due diligence, it is essential that they receive accurate information. Because information is costly to gather, many investors tend not to spend much of their resources collecting valuable information, but instead tend to rely on superficial reviews by third parties, or even become lax and follow the herd. Such behavior may be rational when the economy continues to grow rapidly, thus providing uninformed investors with the ability to claim high upside returns. When prospects become less certain, however, uninformed investors follow others who may move out of the market without paying much attention to fundamentals. This type of herd behavior by uninformed investors may be mitigated by the availability of better information disclosure, which can guide investors to an efficient and productive allocation of financial resources.[4]

There must also be greater transparency on the lenders' side, and the international financial community must coordinate its regulatory frameworks to limit pro-cyclical tendencies and create a more level playing field. Specifically, information disclosure by large international investors, including hedge funds and other highly leveraged institutions, is vital to ensure more prudent decision-making for all. Given the potential impact of large institutional investors on emerging economy capital markets, disclosure should cover, at a minimum, the value of open positions in foreign currency assets, and the country and maturity breakdowns of portfolio investments. To the extent that financial flows are global, an internationally coordinated approach is imperative to better regulate large investors and highly leveraged institutions.

10.2.2 Sequencing of Capital Account Liberalization

Capital account liberalization, which provides emerging market economies with substantial benefits, can set the stage for a build up of vulnerabilities. These include, for example, excessive accumulation of short-term external debt, as well as currency and maturity mismatches. Unrestricted capital mobility may be costly if the macroeconomic and supervisory policy framework is weak and if domestic financial and corporate sectors cannot manage risks prudently, or allocate investment in an efficient manner.

Recent experience with emerging market crises has demonstrated that for the right 'sequencing' of capital account liberalization, the country in question must establish a resilient and robust domestic financial system.[5] Domestic financial institutions need to be sufficiently capitalized with adequate loan loss provisions and must have the capability and expertise to prudently manage assets and liabilities. Authorities should maintain effective regulatory and supervisory frameworks over banks and non-bank financial institutions (NBFIs), coupled with strong disclosure and accounting requirements. With a resilient financial system in place, banks and NBFIs are better able to weather macroeconomic shocks and asset price gyrations. Volatile capital flows will less likely exert adverse systemic impact on domestic financial institutions.

Maintaining a resilient and robust financial sector is the key to reducing the risk of crisis in a world of free capital mobility. Countries with healthy financial sectors will probably suffer less from contagion, as they have greater flexibility to cope with external shocks and to take corrective action, if necessary. It is also important to put in place incentives for sound corporate finance, so as to avoid high leverage and excessive reliance on foreign borrowing. In a world of free access to international capital, a financially disciplined corporate sector is required to maintain a sustainable debt-to-equity ratio and to weather exchange rate and interest rate shocks.

In short, there must be sufficient incentive for sound business finance on the part of corporations, as well as prudent management of loan portfolios on the part of banks. Essentially, banks must monitor their clients' businesses and discipline corporate finance, particularly in the area of external debt financing. Several building blocks are essential for such an incentive framework in sound corporate finance: clear rules of corporate governance, adequate financial disclosure and corporate debt market development are needed. These building blocks must be in place before an economy can fully benefit from free access to international capital markets.

10.2.3   International Liquidity Support with Private Sector Involvement

If a currency crisis results from lack of liquidity and not insolvency, internationally coordinated liquidity support to the crisis country is justifiable. First, it is important to prevent that crisis from growing unnecessarily severe. Availability of international liquidity can help cushion the adjustment process at the time when capital inflows are interrupted and a large current account deficit must be reduced. Second, it is important to limit a contagious spread of problems to neighboring countries.

When liquidity support is provided by international financial institutions (IFIs) in response to a crisis or contagion, it is essential to '*bail in*' private foreign creditors by encouraging them to agree on debt restructuring through such means as the suspension of payments on external debt during a 'standstill' period, the granting of rollovers, extension of maturities and possibly interest or debt reductions. The sharing of the private sector burden is essential, not only because of limits on the availability of official resources, but also because of concerns about moral hazards.[6] Official intervention should not bail them out.

Official standstill provisions in the form of temporary suspension of debt payments may constitute an essential strategic threat needed to limit the moral hazard of investors. In addition, this procedure functions as a floodgate that helps stop sharp decline in currency value and enables the authorities to buy time to put in place a credible adjustment program and to organize creditor debtor negotiations. This arrangement, if accompanied by early debt workout agreements, could result in better outcomes for both the borrower economy, as a whole, and for the creditors.

The role of capital outflow controls can be understood in this context. In cases where official resources are limited relative to the magnitude of the crisis, and private creditors are not amenable to coordination, some involuntary involvement of private investors may be necessary. For example, the authorities of an emerging market economy may want to make an *ex ante* unilateral announcement that, in case of crisis, a forced suspension of debt payments may be imposed in an orderly manner. Such an official provision will serve both as a discouragement to over-investment by the private sector, as well as to introduce rule-based capital controls. In other words, a unilateral control on capital outflows can be considered as an alternative to internationally agreed standstill arrangements that would eventually lead to debt workout. We will return to this possibility in the following section.

10.2.4   Regional Financial Cooperation

Establishing a cooperative framework for regional financial management is logical to cope with currency crises, contagions and economic contraction at the regional level. The reason for this is that a financial crisis may involve – through a contagion – several economies in the same region simultaneously needing coordinated response and financial support. A framework for regional financial coordination would have four aspects:

1. modalities for regional surveillance and monitoring of vulnerabilities;
2. schemes to augment international liquidity;
3. mechanisms to ensure consistent exchange rates within the region;
4. medium-term programs to assist crisis-affected countries to resolve the systemic impact of their crises and accelerate recovery processes.

First, regional economic surveillance and monitoring are instrumental to crisis prevention at the regional level. Through effective surveillance mechanisms, each economy in the region is expected to be under peer pressure to pursue macroeconomic and structural policies that are conducive to stable external accounts and currencies, thereby reducing the risk of crises and contagion. Second, a regional financial facility can play an important role in supplementing global sources of international liquidity. A financing facility that can mobilize large amounts of liquidity rapidly to head off currency crises and contagions is an obvious benefit if these phenomena are the result of herd behavior. Third, choosing appropriate exchange rate arrangements that are mutually consistent for regional economies is also highly desirable when those economies are interdependent. This process may entail coordinated efforts to avoid harmful competitive devaluations, or revaluations, of the regional currencies, or to ensure intra-regional exchange rate stability. Fourth, in the face of a systemic crisis affecting real economic activity at large, mobilizing fiscal resources is essential to quickly resolve the crisis. Fiscal resources needed to support aggregate demand, recapitalize weak banks, facilitate corporate debt restructuring, and strengthen social safety nets may be limited by the crisis country's lack of fiscal headroom, or constraints to external financing at market terms. Regionally concerted action to mobilize such resources, particularly from the core countries in the region, would contribute greatly to crisis resolution.

10.3 CAPITAL CONTROLS AS A FINANCIAL SAFEGUARD

10.3.1 The Effectiveness and Types of Capital Controls

10.3.1.1 Rationales for capital controls

The preceding section has argued that the best protection against currency and banking crises in emerging market economies is to reform the international financial system, as well as domestic policy and institutional framework, complemented by stronger regional financial cooperation. Such efforts provide economies with the capacity to reap the full benefits of global financial integration. In most cases, however, these efforts will take a long time to be effective, rendering financial markets and banking sectors vulnerable to external shocks and liquidity crises until these improvements become effective. Therefore, controls on short-term capital flows may be useful as a financial safeguard during the interim period.[7]

There are additional rationales for capital controls. First, capital controls can secure monetary policy autonomy under fixed exchange rates, allowing the authorities to insulate domestic monetary management from the constraints of a nominal peg. This rationale can be important for an economy using a fixed rate regime if it wishes to sustain stabilization and structural reform programs in the face of large capital flows. Second, private capital flows can be destabilizing because of the systematic failure of speculators to evaluate the fundamentals. Particularly when capital inflows have a negative externality in terms of putting a strain on the entire financial system or overall macroeconomic management, capital controls may be useful to reduce the wedge between the private and social returns of capital inflows. Third, expectations can become self-fulfilling, leading a country to face herd behavior – independent of fundamentals – by investors. Left alone, such behavior may result in multiple equilibria (Dooley 1996a). In this 'second generation' model, capital controls can curtail rapid outflows and prevent the economy from slipping out of a 'good' equilibrium, or from slipping into a 'bad' equilibrium. In this and other arguments, capital controls are justified only as a second best measure, given some distortions or imperfections in the economy (Dooley, 1996b).

10.3.1.2   Features of capital controls
In discussing capital controls, several important distinctions should be made:

1. between controls on inflows and outflows;
2. between permanent and temporary capital controls;
3. between selective and comprehensive controls;
4. between price-based and administrative controls; and
5. between the imposition and effectiveness of capital controls.

First, while controls on inflows may be intended as a measure of crisis prevention, controls on outflows are often used as a crisis management tool. The conventional wisdom based on a wide range of evidence suggests that outflow controls are less effective – particularly when introduced during a crisis.

Second, temporary controls are more effective than permanent controls because economic agents find ways of evading controls over time. This possibility of evasion implies that, if capital controls are effective at all, they tend to be more effective in the short run than in the long run. The scope of evasion and circumvention with capital controls can threaten monetary policy autonomy (Edwards, 1999).

Third, selective controls that allow exemptions are less effective than comprehensive controls that cover all transactions. In a highly open economy with a commitment to transparency and accountability, however, there is a limit to the coverage of capital controls and the rigor with which they can be enforced (Neely, 1999). Some transactions in some sectors are inevitably exempted from the application of controls. For most of the industrial and emerging market economies that are increasingly integrated with global finance, therefore, it is becoming hard to install comprehensive capital controls that cover all possible transactions. The controls, if ever introduced in these economies, are usually selective.

Fourth, the imposition of capital controls does not mean that they are effective in achieving the intended objectives. According to Dooley (1996b), both industrial and developing countries have been successful in driving wedges between domestic and international interest rates, in generating revenue for governments, and in limiting debt-service payments on domestic government debt, through the imposition of capital controls. However, empirical literature does not generally support the 'power of capital control programs to affect other important economic variables, such as the volume or composition of private capital flows, changes in international reserves, or the level of exchange rates'. Nor have capital controls been effective in preventing 'successful speculative attacks on fixed exchange rate systems' (Dooley, 1996b, p. 641).[8]

Finally, price-based capital controls are less distortionary and abrasive than administrative controls. As a result, there is a presumption that if capital controls are to be introduced, they should be price-based so as to ensure greater benefits to the imposing country of access to international capital markets. A typical example of a price-based capital control regime is the well-known Tobin tax (Tobin, 1978), or the system of 'throwing sand in the wheels of international finance' (Eichengreen, Tobin and Wyplosz, 1995; Eichengreen, 2000). The Tobin tax is a small tax on foreign exchange transactions, which is intended to raise the cost of short-term capital movements relative to long-term capital flows. Its technical feasibility and effectiveness is seriously doubted, however, given the need for a complex transnational apparatus of tax collection and allocation – to avoid evasion – and the availability of various derivative instruments to transfer funds without the appearance of foreign exchange transactions (Garber and Taylor, 1995).

In the remainder of this section, we will consider three types of capital control regimes that have recently been either used or proposed for emerging market economies:

1.   Chilean-style reserve requirements on short-term capital inflows;
2.   prudential regulations on the short-term external liabilities of banks and corporations; and
3.   restrictions on short-term capital outflows.

The advantages and disadvantages of each of these regimes are summarized in Table 10.1.

Table 10.1   Advantages/disadvantages of short-term capital control regimes

Factor	Chilean-style Reserve Requirements	Prudential Regulations on Capital Inflows	Restrictions on Short-term Capital Inflows
Costs and their incidence	Raise domestic interest rates, but government gets revenue and liquidity	Raise interest costs to domestic borrowers, as supply of funds is restricted	Lower interest costs but raise administrative costs
Ease of implementation	Complex: requires comprehensive coverage of all inflows to be effective	Complex: requires careful monitoring to ensure compliance	Most complex: incentives to evade are strong, especially if controls are permanent
Effectiveness	May increase maturity of outstanding debt but does not insulate economy from large international price and interest rate shocks	Directly reduce exposure to short-term debt and hence to the vulnerability on account of currency mismatches	Have typically been proven ineffective, though recent outcomes in Malaysia are consistent with goals

10.3.2   Chilean-style Reserve Requirements

Once large-scale capital inflows begin to lead to a rapid build up of short-term external debt, appropriate macroeconomic policy responses are necessary. These may include non-sterilized intervention in the foreign exchange market, the tightening of macroeconomic policy, or the use of exchange rate flexibility. However, non-sterilized intervention and the consequent increase in the money supply may be undesirable, when the economy is overheating. On the other hand, a tight monetary policy may also be undesirable, because higher interest rates can attract more capital inflows. Fiscal policy may not be mobilized in a flexible manner in many countries. Greater exchange rate flexibility, while reducing capital inflows by raising the exchange risk, may not be desirable[9] for all emerging economies because of the high cost of exchange rate volatility – given, for example, the small size of economies, shallowness of financial markets and large foreign currency debt exposure. In the face of such policy dilemmas, a temporary introduction of controls on short-term capital inflows may be useful in preventing the undesirable accumulation of external debt.

Some countries have adopted restrictions on capital inflows as a way of isolating the domestic economy from the volatility of global financial cycles during at least part of the 1990s (World Bank, 2000b). Of these countries, several Latin American countries – Argentina, Chile, Colombia, Costa Rica, and Mexico – have employed reserve requirements that stipulate that borrowers of short-term foreign funds (usually less than 12 months) must deposit these funds at the central bank as a control device. Chile (introduced in 1991) and Colombia (1993) are the two most noteworthy examples, being the heaviest users of restrictions on capital inflows in Latin America.

10.3.2.1   The case of Chile

In June 1991, against a background of real exchange rate appreciation and weakened monetary control, the Chilean authorities introduced what became known as an unremunerated reserve requirement (URR) on new capital inflows. In the initial phase, a rate of 20 percent was applied to all newly entering portfolio capital for up to one year, with reserves to be held in a non-interest bearing account with the central bank. In May 1992, the rate was raised to 30 percent for foreign currency borrowing except by corporations; in August 1992, the rate was made applicable to all transactions; and in 1992, the holding period was set at one year regardless of the maturity. The rate was then lowered to 10 percent in June 1998 before being zeroed out in September 1998.[10] The effectiveness of these controls seemed to diminish progressively as investors learned of ways to circumvent the legislation, requiring successive efforts to expand the coverage of the control regime. By 1998, almost all forms of capital inflows had been covered, except for 'non-speculative' FDI and trade credits.

Two aspects of the Chilean regime may be noted. One is that, in Chile, the coverage of the URR was selective; excluding some potentially volatile short-term flows such as trade credit. There was thus a scope for substitution between exempted and taxed transactions, limiting the overall effectiveness of the control regime (Nadal-De Simone and Sorsa, 1999). It was also discriminatory, in the sense that large firms were better able to obtain direct trade credit from their foreign counterparts, leaving the smaller exporters to bear the burden of the URR tax (Valdes-Prieto and Soto, 1998). Another point is that, during this period, the URR was implemented under an environment of supportive economic policy, which moderated the appreciation of the real exchange rate (see Table 10.2). The Chilean authorities improved the prudential regulation of the financial system, kept a firm hand on money supply and ran fiscal surpluses. Inflation declined each year the URR was in force (Ulan, 2000).

10.3.2.2   The case of Colombia

Experiencing an unprecedented increase in capital inflows, in September 1993, Colombia also adopted a URR on corporate liabilities in foreign currencies, except trade credit.[11] Initially, the rate was set at 47 percent for one year on all foreign loans with maturities of less than 18 months. In 1994, however, the country was flooded with capital inflows, so the coverage of the URR was extended to loans with maturities of less than 36 months (in March), and to those with maturities of less than five years (in August). This time, moreover, the reserve requirements were made progressively tighter for shorter maturity loans, i.e., 140 percent for loans with a maturity of less than one month, 42.8 percent for loans with a maturity of 59–60 months, and so on. The holding period was set equal to the maturity of the loan. The control measures were partially relaxed in 1996, when the pressure from capital inflows had receded. In February 1996, the URR rates were lowered, and the coverage was reduced to the maximum of four years. In March 1996, the coverage was further reduced to the maximum of three years, and the flat rate of 50 percent was adopted for all loans, regardless of the maturity (Cardenas and Barrera, 1997). After a temporary tightening in early 1997 – when the maximum maturity subject to restrictions was raised to five years – the rate was progressively reduced from May 1997 onward, while the maturity was extended to cover all inflows.

In Colombia, all of these control measures had a large number of exemptions, thereby severely limiting their effectiveness. Moreover, following the imposition of the URR, the Colombian authorities relaxed fiscal and monetary policies (see Table 10.2). Between 1993 and 1998, the fiscal deficit grew from 0.7 percent to 4.9 percent of GDP, bank-reserve requirements were cut by more than half between 1993 and 1996, and financial system credit increased by more than 20 percent per year in real terms (Ulan, 2000). As a result, Colombian inflation averaged over 20 percent during most of this period. Colombia's macroeconomic performance was in sharp contrast to that of Chile in the 1990s.

10.3.2.3   Effectiveness of capital inflow controls

Several empirical studies have emerged to evaluate the effectiveness of the Chilean and Colombian capital controls. There is a general consensus that the Colombian restrictions did not work in creating a persistent wedge between domestic and international interest rates. There is, however, limited evidence to suggest that the URR changed the composition of capital inflows in favor of longer-term maturities, although it did not affect the total volume (Cardenas and Barrera, 1997). The poor administrative performance of the Colombian measure may be explained by the fact that they not only allowed a large number of exemptions, but also were not accompanied by supportive macroeconomic policies. Higher inflation may have induced additional capital flows by appreciating the real exchange rate and raising the nominal interest rate. More importantly, poor macroeconomic management may have led to a loss of market confidence and resulted in a sharp capital flow reversal. At least, in the case of Colombia, the URR was not associated with good macroeconomic performance.

Table 10.2 Major economic indicators in Chile, Colombia and Malaysia, 1991–2000

	1991	1992	1993	1994	1995	1996	1997	1998	1999	2000
Average US dollar exchange rate (in local currency units)										
Chile	349	363	404	420	397	412	419	460	509	535
Colombia	633	759	863	845	913	1,037	1,141	1,426	1,756	2,088
Malaysia	2.75	2.55	2.57	2.62	2.50	2.52	2.81	3.92	3.80	3.80
Average real effective exchange rate (1995=100)										
Chile	84.50	89.50	91.60	94.30	100.00	103.40	113.10	111.10	105.40	106.00
Colombia	75.60	82.30	87.30	98.40	100.00	107.00	119.00	113.50	102.70	95.60
Malaysia	95.90	102.50	103.60	99.70	100.00	104.40	103.30	82.10	84.50	86.60
Annual GDP growth (in percent)										
Chile	8.00	12.30	7.00	5.70	10.60	7.40	7.40	3.90	–1.10	5.40
Colombia	2.00	4.20	5.30	5.90	5.20	2.10	3.40	0.50	–4.10	2.80
Malaysia	9.60	8.90	9.40	9.30	9.80	10.00	7.40	9.30	5.80	8.60
Average annual consumer price inflation (in percent)										
Chile	21.80	15.40	12.80	11.50	8.20	7.40	6.10	5.20	3.30	3.80
Colombia	30.40	26.80	22.80	23.80	20.90	20.20	18.90	20.40	11.20	9.50
Malaysia	4.40	4.80	3.60	3.80	3.40	3.50	2.60	5.30	2.80	1.60
Bank lending rate (in percent)										
Chile	28.60	23.90	24.30	20.30	18.20	17.40	15.70	20.20	12.60	14.80
Colombia	47.10	37.30	35.80	40.50	42.70	42.00	34.20	42.20	25.80	18.80
Malaysia	8.13	9.31	9.05	7.61	7.63	8.89	9.53	10.61	7.29	6.77
Current account (in millions of US dollars)										
Chile	–99	–958	–2,554	–1,585	–1,350	–3,510	–3,728	–4,139	–80	–991
Colombia	2,349	901	–2,102	–3,673	–4,596	–4,760	–5,868	–5,231	98	41
Malaysia	–4,183	–2,167	–2,991	–4,520	–8,644	–4,462	–5,935	9,529	12,606	
Financial account (in millions of US dollars)										
Chile	964	3,132	2,995	5,294	2,357	6,665	7,355	3,181	–829	1,239
Colombia	–777	183	2,701	3,530	4,476	6,738	6,901	3,788	17	1,128
Malaysia	5,621	8,746	10,805	1,288	7,643	9,477	2,198	–2,550	–6,619	

Source: International Monetary Fund, *International Financial Statistics Yearbook*, 2001.

The evidence on Chile is mixed. There is consensus that the Chilean controls created a wedge between domestic and international interest rates, at least in the short run, and generated revenue for the government (Edwards, 2000; De Gregorio, Edward and Valdez, 2000). During 1991–96, the tax revenue from the URR amounted to as much as 0.11 percent of GDP (Valdes-Prieto and Soto, 1998). In this sense, the Chilean controls were more successfully administered than the Colombian controls. This relative administrative success of the Chilean controls may be explained by two factors. First, with a relatively simple system and without a large number of exemptions, the Chilean URR was easy to administer. Second, the country had a central bank with enforcement capacity, a long tradition of compliance with laws, and a relatively low degree of corruption (De Gregorio, Edward and Valdez, 2000; Ulan 2000).

In terms of its impact on other economic variables, however, the effectiveness of the Chilean URR was more modest. For example, there is no evidence to suggest that the URR helped contain the real exchange rate appreciation. There was some substitution for exemption of taxed short-term flows, so that the impact on the volume of short-term inflows was not as substantial – relative to a more comprehensive control regime – and limited the scope for an independent monetary policy. However, as in the case of Colombia, evidence suggests that the Chilean URR changed the composition of capital inflows in favor of longer maturities, without reducing the overall volume of capital inflows.[12]

In summary, these and other empirical studies seem to suggest that the Chilean-style capital control had some effect on changing the composition of capital inflows in favor of longer maturities, but that they did not affect the overall volume of capital inflows.[13] In this sense, the overriding objective of introducing the capital control measures – that of moderating the short-term volatility of capital inflows – seems to have been met. Given the moderate rate of URR, however, there is no pretension that these controls had any ability to contain short-term speculative inflows, while they may well have increased long-term non-speculative inflows.

10.3.3   Prudential Regulations on Short-term Capital Inflows

Controls can take the form of prudential regulations over banks and corporations (Stiglitz and Bhattacharya, 1999). It is an empirical question whether or not prudential regulations are more effective and simpler to administer than outright controls. The answer likely depends on the nature of the problem being addressed and the institutional capacity of the authorities concerned. Practically speaking, prudential regulations are limited to the established banking and corporate sectors, which are more amenable to government supervision and regulation. Often, some otherwise innocuous prudential regulations can have a capital control effect, including reporting or approval requirements, prescribed institutions and limitations on foreign currency exposure. Outright controls may also have a prudential purpose. For these reasons, it may not make much sense to speak of prudential regulations as distinct from capital controls in general.

The rationale for prudential regulations on capital inflows arises when excessive international borrowing, particularly by banks or corporations, can have negative spillover effects on other players in the economy. For example, risky and imprudent borrowing decisions by a few banks and firms may cause a sudden loss of investor confidence about the safety and soundness of the whole domestic banking system, triggering a systemic crisis. When disruptions due to a systemic banking crisis can present a large economic cost and control through market-based incentives is difficult, prudential regulations on cross-border banking activities can be useful.

Several prudential requirements can be considered. Limits on short-term external borrowing may be placed on domestic banks, when market-based approaches such as the Chilean-style reserve requirement may not be fully effective. Limits may also be imposed on the net – as well as overall –foreign exposure of banks. Tighter supervision may be required when banks are believed to employ inadequate risk management techniques, especially with respect to borrowers with significant foreign currency liabilities. High capital adequacy standards above the 8 percent required by the Basle standards may be imposed on banks in emerging market economies to reduce the potential for banking sector insolvency caused by a possible loan default.

Growth of foreign currency debt in the corporate sector may be checked indirectly through proper risk management by domestic banks when acting as corporate creditors. Alternatively, it may be checked directly through placing prudential limits on corporate borrowing. For example, offshore funding may be restricted to corporations deemed to meet a minimum creditworthiness requirement, as reflected in their credit ratings. More intrusive – and controversial – regulations would be to limit corporate external borrowing on the basis of its financial characteristics, such as overall leverage, the ratio of foreign to domestic borrowing, or the size of export earnings.

Calvo and Mendoza (1999) have studied the effectiveness of prudential regulations on capital inflows in limiting foreign borrowing by banks. They show that while prudential regulations are less distortionary and less subject to evasion, they are less comprehensive than explicit control regimes with a wider coverage. As a result, prudential regulations on banks may not prevent the type of direct corporate borrowing that was prevalent in Indonesia before the crisis, but they do wall off the financial sector from becoming the largest contingent risk to the government. Prudential regulations on short-term capital inflows by banks and corporations require both a complex and sophisticated system of administration and careful monitoring, and tend to raise interest cost to domestic borrowers.

10.3.4   Restrictions on Short-term Capital Outflows

Historically, controls on capital outflows have been more pervasive than controls on capital inflows (Johnston and Tamirisa, 1998). If introduced as a tool of crisis management, outflow controls can be controversial. For one thing, outright suspension of convertibility for capital account transactions is particularly onerous because producers are quickly shut off from international sources of working capital finance, hampering export and domestic productive activities. In general, outflow controls to pursue an expansionary monetary policy form a recipe for disaster, and this is particularly so if they are used as a substitute for needed structural reform. Moreover, capital outflow controls may have an adverse signaling effect on future capital inflows. Indeed, controls on capital outflows have been problematic, and failures have outnumbered successes (Dooley, 1996a; World Bank, 2000b). Such controls take the form of prohibitions or withholding arrangements on selected types of capital transactions, often being on capital invested for less than a specified period, and they usually have the objective of keeping domestic interest rates lower than they would otherwise have to be in order to prevent a portfolio shift abroad.

Several studies cast doubt on the effectiveness of outflow controls because they can be easily evaded and tend to lose effectiveness over time as financial agents build surreptitious channels around them.[14] For example, multinational corporations can sell goods and services to overseas parent firms at very low bookkeeping prices, thereby transferring real value out of the country. Foreign investors wanting to circumvent the controls can also swap their funds for the overseas assets of a domestic resident. On the other hand, if designed in the context of a credible economic program, temporary controls on outflows may give some breathing time for governments to put their house in order and may help reduce the real cost of resolving the crisis. Crucial to the success of temporary outflow controls is the commitment to a credible policy program and the timing of exit, which is by no means easy to achieve.

Before discussing the Malaysian controls on capital outflows, it is useful to point out that, in May 1997, Thailand also imposed controls, which were subsequently removed in January 1998. The Thai outflow controls were introduced at the height of the speculative attack on the baht, when there was heavy demand for baht credit. Borrowed baht was converted into US dollars in anticipation of baht devaluation, thereby depleting foreign exchange reserves. The controls were effective in shutting down the swap market, i.e., domestic banking system sources of baht credit, and forcing speculators to incur large losses. The controls were not as tightly enforced as in Malaysia, however, and alternative channels for baht outflows were exploited to arbitrage the gap between onshore and offshore borrowing rates, which widened to 12.9 percent in early June 1997. These outflows continued to drain reserves, eventually causing the central bank to float the baht on 2 July 1997.

By the time the controls were lifted in January 1998, the baht had fallen by more than 50 percent (Figure 10.1). The baht then appreciated by roughly 30 percent over four months and stabilized at that level. The realignment of the baht was critical in defusing the external pressure. The launching of financial and corporate restructuring efforts and other structural reforms were necessary to re-establish sufficient confidence to allow interest rates to decline. One may make the argument that it was the removal of controls in January 1998 that contributed to the build up of this confidence. In essence, Thailand used outflow controls in an attempt to defend a fixed and overvalued exchange rate, but could not, and thus eventually had to give them up. The experience of Thailand demonstrates the inherent difficulty of controls on capital outflows, particularly when the created incentives are incompatible with the underlying economic fundamentals.

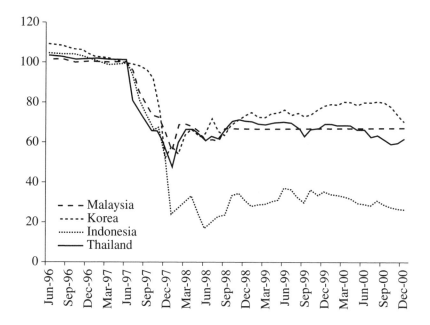

Figure 10.1 Monthly US dollar exchange rates indices for Malaysia, Indonesia, Korea and Thailand, June 1996–December 2000 (June 1997=100)

10.4   MALAYSIAN CAPITAL CONTROLS

10.4.1   The Malaysian Economy in Crisis

With the devaluation of the Thai baht in July 1997, strong pressure began to mount against the Malaysian ringgit. Portfolio positions in the stock market were liquidated, causing stock prices to plunge (Figure 10.2). The authorities intervened in the foreign exchange market to support the ringgit by reducing ringgit liquidity and raising rates on overnight money in the interbank market by as much as 40 percent. Essentially, the authorities attempted to defend the ringgit through interest rate hikes (Figure 10.3). But the persistence of the exchange market pressure and the floating of the Philippine peso indicated that the currency market instability would not dissipate soon, and that a protracted period of high interest rates might be necessary.

The economy began to show signs of weakness in the latter half of 1997 (Figure 10.4). Nonetheless, the government adopted a tight budget in order to generate confidence in the ringgit and the economy. Unfortunately, tight monetary and fiscal policies added contractionary impact to the already weakening economy. Non-performing loans (NPLs) in the financial system began to rise in late 1997 and expanded in 1998 as the economy contracted.

Finance companies' balance sheets began to deteriorate due to their earlier over-extension in real estate and share purchase lending. NPLs continued to

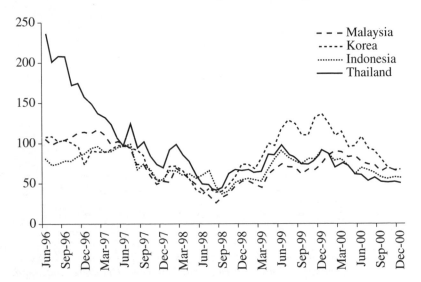

Figure 10.2   Monthly stock prices in Malaysia, Indonesia, Korea and Thailand, June 1996–December 2000 (June 1997=100)

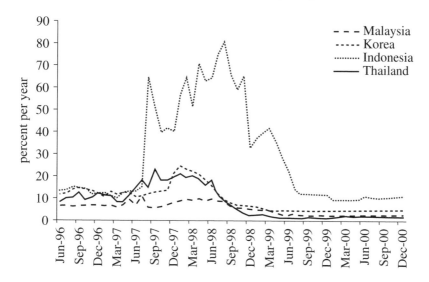

Figure 10.3 Monthly short-term interest rates in Malaysia, Indonesia, Korea and Thailand, June 1996–December 2000

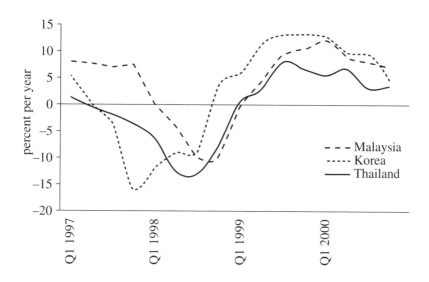

Figure 10.4 Quarterly real GDP growth in Malaysia, Korea and Thailand, 1997–2000

mount and began to affect commercial and merchant banks as well. As financial institutions became more preoccupied with NPLs, loan loss provisions and capital adequacy requirements, the volume of lending began to slow, leading to fears of a credit crunch. The creditworthiness of some borrowers was impaired by high interest rates and demand contraction. For other borrowers, the demand for credit declined in line with their sales. By early 1998, the authorities' main concern was the insufficient credit expansion for economic recovery.

Malaysia had enjoyed net inflows of portfolio capital on an annual basis between 1992 and 1996. On the tide of speculative pressure, however, the capital account registered net outflows of portfolio capital in the first three quarters of 1997. On 4 August 1997, the central bank imposed a $2 million limit on domestic banks' offers of side swaps with non-residents in an effort to stem the speculative attack. This limit created a wedge between domestic and offshore ringgit interest rates, but had only a modest effect in slowing the exodus of portfolio capital.

In response to deepening economic contraction and deteriorating financial sector conditions, the Malaysian authorities adopted a comprehensive program of financial and corporate sector restructuring in June and July 1998 to support economic recovery. This program included the establishment of three new institutions: Danaharta to carve NPLs out from banks; Danamodal to recapitalize weak banks; and the Corporate Debt Restructuring Committee (CDRC) to assist financial and operational restructuring of highly indebted corporations. Bankruptcy laws and courts were modernized, a major corporate governance drive was launched, and an initiative for strengthening banking sector supervision and regulation was begun.[15] In these areas, Malaysia made much greater efforts than many of its neighbors.

At this juncture, however, Russia's debt default caused turmoil in Malaysia's currency and stock markets. By August 1998, interest rates on offshore ringgit deposits had risen to more than 20 percent compared with 11 percent on domestic deposits. After a decline by 4 percentage points in July 1998, the ringgit dropped a further 12 percent in August (Figure 10.1). Fearing an acceleration of capital flight and pressure on domestic interest rates, on 1 September 1998, the authorities imposed a package of capital account regulations. On 2 September, they pegged the exchange rate at 3.8 ringgit per US dollar. While the ringgit had depreciated by 80 percent during the first seven months following the Thai baht crisis, it appreciated by 20 percent from its January 1998 low to September – only then was the exchange rate pegged.

10.4.2   Capital Controls in Malaysia

10.4.2.1   Overview

The Malaysian authorities introduced capital controls in September 1998, aimed at restricting portfolio capital outflows and eliminating offshore ringgit activities.

Portfolio investors were restricted from repatriating funds invested in Malaysia for at least one year, and the trading of the ringgit outside of the country was prohibited. In response, international credit rating agencies immediately downgraded Malaysia's sovereign debt ratings and major international investors removed Malaysia from their investment indices – including the IFC Indices, Dow-Jones Investment Indices and Morgan Stanley Capital Indices (MSCI).

As economic conditions began to stabilize, however, controls on portfolio outflows were eased and eventually removed (Table 10.3).

Table 10.3   Brief summary of major exchange and capital controls

Date	Policy Objectives	Specific Measures
September 1998	Deter speculation on the ringgit and gain monetary policy independence	• Ringgit pegged at 3.80 to the US dollar • Controls on transfers from ringgit-denominated accounts for non-residents not physically present in Malaysia, in effect imposing a 12-month holding period restriction for repatriation of the proceeds from the sale of Malaysian securities, with a retroactive effect • Prohibition on offshore transactions of the ringgit
February 1999	Preempt exodus of capital and re-engage foreign investors	• Easing of some controls, including replacement of the 12-month holding period restriction in repatriation of portfolio capital by a two-tier, price-based graduated exit levy system
September 1999	Provide further relaxation	• Removal of the exit levy on repatriation of principal • The two-tier graduated levy system on repatriation of profits simplified and replaced by a flat 10 percent levy, irrespective of when the profits are repatriated
February 2001	Further easing	• Removal of the 10 percent exit levy on portfolio capital profits repatriated after 12 months
May 2001	Eliminate controls on portfolio investment	• Complete removal of the 10 percent levy

Source: Meesok et al. (2001), pp. 14–15, p. 53.

For example, the 12-month holding period restriction on portfolio capital was replaced by a two-tier, price-based exit system in February 1999, which was further eased and simplified in September 1999 and February 2001, and finally eliminated in May 2001. Only offshore transactions in ringgit remain prohibited. Following the easing of portfolio outflow controls and a strengthening of the economic recovery, Malaysia's sovereign ratings began to be upgraded in the fourth quarter of 1999. Malaysia was also reinstated in the IFC and Dow-Jones Investment Indices in November 1999 and in the MSCI in May 2000.

10.4.2.2   The September 1998 controls

The authorities introduced a set of complex but selective capital controls and a pegged exchange rate regime in September 1998. Basically, they sought to eliminate the opportunity for private investors' taking speculative positions against the ringgit through restrictions of all international financial transactions unrelated to underlying trade and foreign direct investment (FDI). They effectively closed the offshore market, cut off ringgit credit to foreigners and put a 12-month moratorium on the repatriation of portfolio capital. The main elements of the controls can be summarized as follows:[16]

1. imposition of a 12-month holding period restriction on repatriation of the proceeds of sales of Malaysian securities held in external accounts;
2. mandatory repatriation of all ringgit held abroad;
3. restriction on transfers of funds between external accounts;
4. limits on transport of ringgit by travelers;
5. prohibition of resident/non-resident credit arrangements;
6. prohibition of trade settlements in ringgit;
7. prohibition of resident/non-resident offers of side swaps and similar hedge transactions; and
8. the freezing of transactions in Malaysian shares traded at Singapore's Central Limit Order Book (CLOB) over-the-counter market.

Two measures were most notable; the 12-month holding period restriction on principal repatriation of equity investments and the prohibition of ringgit internationalization. It is also important to note that foreign currency transactions for current account purposes – including the provision of up to six months of trade credit for foreigners buying Malaysian goods – and repatriation of profits and dividends from documented FDI were kept free of restriction.

10.4.2.3   A move to an exit levy system and further easing

A concern arose that massive capital outflows might take place at the end of the 12-month holding period – i.e., in September 1999 – which might reduce foreign exchange reserves significantly, thus sending Malaysia into financial difficulties. The authorities decided to ease capital controls well before September 1999 to allow a certain degree of portfolio capital outflows and to reduce the risk of potential difficulties. On 15 February 1999, the 12-month holding period rule for repatriation of portfolio capital was replaced with a two-tier, price-based system of graduated exit levies. The basic arrangement was to distinguish the repatriation of principal from the repatriation of profits – hence two-tier – as well as the investments made before 15 February 1999 from those made after. For investments made prior to 15 February 1999, principal was to be taxed at a declining rate over time; 30 percent if repatriated in less than seven months after entry, 20 percent if repatriated in seven to nine months, and 10 percent if repatriated in nine to twelve months, and would cease to be taxed after one year from the time of entry, or from 1 September 1998, whichever was later. For investments made after 14 February 1999, no tax would be levied on principal, but profits would be taxed at a declining rate in time – 30 percent if repatriated in less than 12 months after the realization of profits, and 10 percent if held for one year or more.

The deadline of 1 September 1999 did not signal the complete end of controls. On 21 September 1999, a further adjustment was made to exempt investments made between 1 September 1998 and 14 February 1999 from the 10 percent exit levy on principal. In addition, the two-tier exit levy system on repatriation of profits was replaced with a flat 10 percent levy, irrespective of when the profits were repatriated. On 1 February 2001, the 10 percent exit levy on repatriation of profits after one year was abolished, with profits repatriated within one year still subject to the 10 percent exit levy. Finally, on 2 May 2001, the 10 percent exit levy on profits repatriated was abolished completely.

10.4.3 Effectiveness of Capital Controls

Together with the pegging of the exchange rate, the capital controls were designed to insulate monetary policy from external volatility through a low interest rate policy and containment of speculative capital movements, thereby facilitating economic recovery and providing breathing space needed to carry out economic adjustment and structural reforms. The authorities announced that the control measures were temporary.

10.4.3.1 Monetary independence

There were immediate effects in September 1998. First, the prohibition on currency trading between external accounts put an immediate and virtually complete stop to offshore ringgit trading. Second, the 12-month holding period curtailed speculative capital outflows. The authorities were careful to identify and close off virtually all other channels for speculative outflows including the freezing of trade in CLOB shares,[17] amendment of the Companies Act to prevent dividend distributions, and withdrawal of large denomination notes from circulation. Third, the controls succeeded immediately in reducing the three-month interbank rate to 7.75 percent, followed by further cuts in April 1999, and by end-1999 the rate was down to 3.15 percent (Figure 10.3). Bank and finance company lending rates fell by 4–5 percent over the second half of 1998. Fourth, the controls allowed statutory reserve requirements to decline in several rounds from 13.5 percent in February 1998 to 4 percent in September, thereby encouraging banks to achieve the minimum target of 8 percent loan growth. Thus, the controls were successful in providing greater monetary independence, protecting the pegged exchange rate, and stemming financial panic, thus facilitating a smaller drop in employment and real wages and paving a way to a faster recovery in real activity (Kaplan and Rodrik, 2001).

10.4.3.2 Capital flows

The tightening of controls on capital outflows and on international transactions in ringgit appears to have had a limited impact on portfolio flows in 1999–2000. They were introduced well into the Asian crisis after a substantial amount of capital – about $10.4 billion – had already left the country during 1997–98, and thus their effects on portfolio outflows were limited. From the beginning it was announced that the controls would be temporary, in part to minimize the negative impact on investor sentiment and the country risk premium. The relaxation of the capital controls in February 1999 was partly a signaling device to reinforce the view that the controls were temporary. Fears that portfolio capital would flow out of the country as the 12-month holding period restriction was replaced with graduated exit levies proved unfounded as only limited outflows were recorded in February and March, and net inflows were recorded in April through July despite the announcement of further reductions in exit levies in April and again in June. The elimination of exit levies on principal in September 1999 resulted in modest outflows, however. Even so, net outflows during the control period as well as the period immediately following were very small, compared to the outflow of RM10 billion in 1997 at the height of the crisis. Foreign exchange reserves moderately rose during this period (Figure 10.4).[18]

Access to short-term financing was negatively affected by the capital controls due to the downgrading of the country's sovereign rating and exclusion of Malaysia from major investment' indices, but only temporarily. With the market sentiment turning bullish in response to monetary easing, the upgrading of Malaysia's outlook and credit ratings, and the improvement in the overall national and regional prospects, however, portfolio inflows rose starting in mid-1999. The inflows increased further in early 2000, as the rising equity market stirred up investor interests.

10.4.3.3 Administrative compliance

The central bank, Bank Negara Malaysia, administered the controls effectively through banks and there is no evidence that they were circumvented on a large scale.[19] Its historically tight control over the banking system with frequent reporting intervals and on-site supervision made it possible to ensure strict compliance. Documentary evidence was required for all international financial transactions to demonstrate the clear linking of the transaction to underlying trade or FDI. Bank Negara Malaysia's reputation as a strict regulator may have also prevented foreign banks from exploring ways to circumvent controls, for fear of losing their local branches. While the complexity of the controls caused some confusion at the outset, the central bank conducted an effective information campaign, placing detailed descriptions of the control measures before the public. Over time it provided updates, clarifications and examples detailing how the controls were to be applied to a variety of transactions.

10.4.3.4   Costs and benefits of Malaysian capital controls

Several benefits of Malaysia's controls on capital outflows may be pointed out. First, they represented a safeguard against further turbulence in international financial markets and ensured greater policy autonomy in lowering interest rates. At the time of the introduction of the capital controls, the Malaysian currency and stock markets were highly volatile, and it was uncertain whether financial instability in the region was likely to intensify or abate. In this sense, the controls, together with the pegging of the ringgit, contained currency speculation and provided a degree of certainty to market participants.

Second, the capital controls provided breathing space to pursue economic adjustment and to accelerate the structural reforms necessary for sustained economic recovery.[20] After experiencing a sharp fall in real GDP growth from 7.3 percent in 1997 to –7.4 percent in 1998, the economy bounced back to 6.1 percent in 1999 and 8.3 percent in 2000 (Figure 10.5). The imposition of controls roughly coincided with the turnaround in Malaysia's economic performance in the third quarter of 1998. It is difficult to identify, however, how much of this should be attributed to the imposition of capital controls alone, but it is clear that banking and corporate sector restructuring and the associated reforms in the regulatory and supervisory framework, which were made possible under the umbrella of capital controls, must have played a major role.

On the negative side there were potential costs to the imposition of controls, to the extent that they created uncertainty for foreign investors and eroded their confidence in the economy. First, international rating agencies, such as Fitch and Moody's, downgraded Malaysia's sovereign risk and credit ratings, immediately and substantially widening the spreads on sovereign debt instruments in September 1998. While the spreads rose for almost all emerging economies following the Russian default in August, the widening of the Malaysian spread was much larger than those for Thailand, Korea and the Philippines, amounting to about 300 basis points. Following the February 1999 shift to a system of exit levies, however, the spread declined significantly, though the decline lagged behind the other countries by about two months.

Hence, the controls had only a transitory adverse effect on Malaysia's access to international capital markets.

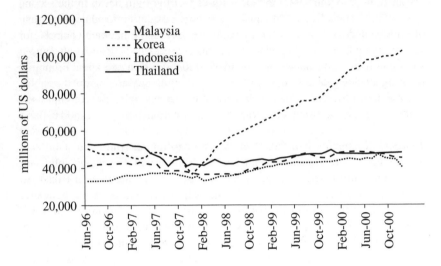

Figure 10.5   Monthly foreign exchange reserves

Second, despite the explicit exemption of foreign direct investment flows from capital controls and a more liberal policy starting in July 1998, foreign direct investment flows declined during 1999–2000 to less than half of pre-crisis levels. Several factors unrelated to capital controls may have contributed to this decline, including the worsening of investor sentiment during the Asian crisis, slower growth in Japan and Taiwan, and the decline in overall investment in Malaysia. Imposition of the selective capital controls may have also led foreign firms to take a cautious approach towards making new direct investments in Malaysia.[21] It is, however, difficult to draw any definitive conclusions regarding the indirect effect of capital controls on foreign direct investment from the limited evidence available.

Third, international investors may view Malaysia's resort to capital controls on portfolio outflows, as a major challenge to its open policy and expect the authorities to repeat this in times of instability. It is too early, however, to conclude whether capital controls will have any long-term negative effect on Malaysia.

10.4.3.5   Cost-benefit analysis
Given these possible benefits and costs of the capital controls, however, it is striking that Malaysia's pattern of recovery was remarkably similar to that in the region's other countries. In all of Malaysia, Korea, Thailand and Indonesia, for example, nominal exchange rates bottomed out in early 1998 and stabilized

by the third quarter, allowing a monetary loosening and interest rate reductions (Figures 10.1 and 10.3). With the application and then expansion of fiscal stimulus in 1998 and 1999, the recovery of GDP growth began in the second quarter of 1998 for Korea and Thailand, in the third quarter for Malaysia, and in the fourth quarter for Indonesia. The similarities in the nature and timing of these developments across different countries make it difficult to attribute a significant and distinct role to the capital controls in bringing about economic recovery in Malaysia.

Kaplan and Rodrik (2001), however, have argued that a simple comparison of the timing in economic recovery in Malaysia with that in Korea and Thailand is misleading. While the recovery was substantially underway in Korea and Thailand in the summer of 1998, with declining interest rates and stabilizing currencies, the situation in Malaysia was far from settled. The ringgit still faced intense pressure, having declined during most of 1998 (Figure 10.1), and offshore ringgit interest rates remained high. According to these authors, there was widespread speculation that Malaysia would be the next country to go to the IMF. To make matters worse, there was also political instability in the summer and fall of 1998. Thus, they argue that, without the imposition of capital controls, the recovery path of Malaysia would have been substantially different. In fact, by carefully comparing the performance of Malaysia from the fall of 1998 – when it would have gone to the IMF in the absence of capital controls – with that of Thailand and Korea from July and October, respectively, of 1997 (when they went to the IMF), they argue that Malaysia had a faster economic recovery, a smaller adjustment in employment, real wages and stock prices, a lower inflation and a greater fall in interest rates.[22]

10.5 ASSESSMENTS

The Malaysian capital controls were put in place at the height of the crisis. At that time, the ongoing economic crisis had been compounded by the negative spillovers from the Russian default in August 1998. The bulk of the portfolio outflows had already occurred and the exchange rate had depreciated sharply. The subsequent turnaround in the stock market, the return to positive GDP growth, the build up of reserves and the relaxation of interest rates were all coincident with the imposition of the controls. However, these improvements were also found in the other crisis-affected countries that did not adopt the same control policies, if not to the same degree.

The controls clearly provided a safeguard against possible further disturbances for a country that opted not to seek an IMF bail-out package. They created a breathing space for pursuing the necessary structural reforms, of which the authorities made good use. The authorities made significant progress in financial and corporate sector restructuring through a consistent framework of Danaharta, Danamodal and the CDRC; they also pushed ahead with the regulatory and supervisory reforms needed for a stronger financial sector and a resilient capital market – an important prerequisite for full capital account liberalization. Essentially, the authorities did not use the capital controls as a substitute for the needed restructuring and reform measures.

The controls were fully effective in achieving the immediate goal of discouraging capital outflows and closing offshore markets. It does not appear that there were any serious attempts to circumvent the controls to magnify damage, if any, to the integrity of the marketplace. The controls and subsequent exit strategy did not result in a lasting flight of portfolio capital, possibly owing to the confidence achieved by the restoration of a pegged exchange rate at what many perceived to be an undervalued level. As a result, a scope for lowering domestic interest rates was created, thereby helping to ease the build up of NPLs in the financial system. Domestic firms were insulated from the potential shocks of further interest rate hikes and exchange rate volatility. No doubt, in all of this, Malaysia has benefited from a competent bureaucracy capable of administering a complex set of regulations with a high degree of compliance, conditions not frequently met in many emerging market economies.

It is clear that the authorities exerted the strongest possible effort to make the capital controls a temporary measure, to disseminate information about the controls and their subsequent revisions, and to clarify misunderstandings. A clear signal of what was to be expected was provided to market participants by the announcement, made well ahead of time, to make a shift in the control regime to a system of exit levies and to terminate much of the controls.[23] In this manner, market confidence was maintained in the long-term commitment of the Malaysian authorities to a fundamentally liberal capital account regime. In a sense, the Malaysian case can be thought of as a type of unilateral 'standstill' arrangement, whereby the authority of a country with basically sound fundamentals forced international investors who held private assets in Malaysia to accept the involuntary extension of repayment.

On balance, the Malaysian controls on capital outflows appear to have had a generally salutary effect, mainly because there was a supporting framework consisting of strong macroeconomic policy, bank and corporate restructuring, an undervalued currency, and a competent regulatory bureaucracy. The favorable initial conditions – a sturdier banking sector and low short-term external debt – also helped capital controls to be effective. The perception, made credible by government actions, that the controls were temporary, also helped maintain market confidence, thus preventing large capital outflows from taking place. To be sure, not all of the subsequent recovery of the Malaysian economy can be attributed to the capital control regime. No doubt, favorable external environments, such as a rise in the global demand for ICT-related products, were helpful. However, the Malaysian experience does suggest that the use of controls should not be rejected categorically. Rather, the probability of success should be evaluated against potential risk under the circumstances specific to the country in question and within its proposed policy framework. In the case of Malaysia, it appears that the controls had only a modest cost, which was kept at a minimum by a careful and comprehensive design and execution, although the benefits may not have been all that large, either.[24]

10.6   CONCLUDING REMARKS

The waves of capital account crises in emerging market economies in the past several years have attracted considerable attention, particularly regarding their policy implications in terms of crisis prevention and management. Much focus has been placed on proposals for the reforms of the international financial system at the global level and domestic improvements in policy and institutional frameworks at the national level. The former include: enhanced information disclosure; the augmentation of international liquidity provisioning; and private sector involvement. The latter include: sound macroeconomic management; the adoption of appropriate exchange rate arrangements; financial system stability through enhanced regulatory and supervisory frameworks; and the adoption of international standards in banking, accounting, disclosure and insolvency procedures. In addition, regional financial cooperation can also complement these global and national efforts.

These efforts are highly commendable, but they will take a long time to be effective. Simply maintaining good macroeconomic policies and a sound financial sector may not suffice to prevent self-fulfilling crises. It may be necessary to go even further and adopt financial safeguards to limit the short-term external debt of banks and corporations.

In some instances, a case can be made for limiting short-term capital inflows through reserve requirements or taxes on capital imports, prudential regulations on inflows, or similar measures. The experiences of Chile and Colombia in the 1990s present some evidence that price-based controls can reduce the vulnerability of capital inflows by lengthening their maturity composition, without affecting the overall volume of capital inflows and the real exchange rate.

In other instances, restrictions on short-term capital outflows may be used to prevent investors' herd behavior from exerting negative influence on financial and real economic activity in emerging market economies with good fundamentals. The Malaysian decision to close short-term capital accounts during its currency crisis provides an important insight. In September 1998, repatriation of non-resident investments in ringgit-denominated financial assets was initially suspended for a 12-month period and ringgit trading in offshore markets – Singapore in particular – was prohibited. Administrative controls on portfolio outflows were replaced by a two-tier, price-based exit system in February 1999, which was further eased and simplified in September 1999 and February 2001, and finally eliminated in May 2001. Currently, only offshore transactions in ringgit remain prohibited.

The primary objectives of these controls, together with the pegging of the exchange rate, were to enhance monetary independence, thereby facilitating economic recovery and providing breathing space for the implementation of structural reforms. By de-linking monetary policy from exchange rate movements, the authorities allowed interest rates to decline without inducing further capital flight and a sharp decline in the ringgit. They maintained that the controls would be removed once stability returned to financial markets and an appropriate global regulatory framework governing international capital flows was in place. Along with the aggressive fiscal thrust, the authorities were able to pursue bank and corporate sector restructuring and the needed reforms, and achieve strong economic recovery in 1999 and 2000.

Of the many episodes of capital outflow controls, the outcomes in Malaysia come closest to meeting the stated objectives of lowering interest rates, stabilizing exchange rates and ensuring greater policy autonomy (Edison and Reinhart, 1999). Although the Malaysian case cannot be generalized without qualification, it is evident that some earlier predictions of massive costs associated with outflow controls were not borne out. As long as the capital outflows represent speculative flight, and controls are temporary and do not substitute for the needed domestic restructuring efforts, capital controls provided breathing space for strengthening the domestic policy and institutional frameworks.

NOTES

1. Deputy Vice Minister for International Affairs, Japanese Ministry of Finance, 3-1-1 Kasumigaseki, Chiyoda-ku, Tokyo 100-8940, Japan.
2. Adviser, Independent Evaluation Office, International Monetary Fund, Washington, DC 20431, USA. The findings, interpretations and conclusions expressed in the chapter are those of the authors alone and do not necessarily represent the views of the Japanese government or the International Monetary Fund.
3. This section draws heavily from Kawai, Newfarmer and Schmukler (2001).
4. As a step in this direction, the International Monetary Fund (IMF) has established a Special Data Dissemination Standard (SDDS) for countries having or seeking access to international capital markets.
5. See McKinnon (1991) and Eichengreen (2000).
6. As long as official financial intervention is required in times of crisis or contagion, private creditors should bear as fully as possible the consequences of the risks that they have voluntarily assumed. In bailing out the private sector, the cases of bank loans and bonds require separate considerations. In the case of commercial bank loans, coordination between foreign creditor banks and domestic debtor banks is relatively easy because the number of participants is

limited. In the case of emerging market bonds, however, such coordination is very hard because a large number of bondholders are involved. For sovereign bonds, the international community is considering a contractual approach – using collective action clauses and a statutory approach based on the sovereign debt restructuring mechanism – in order to obligate bondholders to accept majority rules in proceeding with standstills, rollovers and debt restructuring in case of emergency.

7. See World Bank (2000a), Chapter 5.
8. In this context, Johnston and Ryan (1994) have shown, from the sample of 52 countries over 1985–92, that capital controls are generally more effective for industrial countries than for developing countries, reflecting the difference in the competence of bureaucratic systems.
9. Introducing greater exchange rate flexibility in Thailand in 1995–96, for example, would have allowed the baht to appreciate and reduce capital inflows by raising the exchange risk.
10. See Ariyoshi et al. (2000).
11. At the same time, a withholding tax was introduced in April 1991 on foreign exchange receipts from services rendered abroad and on other transfers, as they could be used to disguise capital transactions. The tax rate was initially set at 3 percent, raised to 10 percent in July 1992, and was reduced back to 3 percent in January 1996 (Cardenas and Barrera, 1997).
12. This result is by no means settled. However, Laurens and Cardoso (1998) show that the controls had no permanent effect on the composition of capital inflows, as the negative impact on short-term capital inflows disappeared after two quarters.
13. This may be a more general result associated with administratively successful capital inflow controls. Montiel and Reinhart (1999) have shown on the basis of a panel of 15 countries – including Argentina, Brazil, Chile, Colombia, Mexico, Indonesia, Malaysia and Thailand – that, during 1990–96, capital inflow controls changed the composition of capital inflows in favor of longer-term portfolio and FDI flows, but did not reduce the overall volume.
14. See Khan and Reinhart (1994), Edwards (1999) and Edison and Reinhart (1999).
15. The World Bank's adjustment loan, the 'Economic Recovery and Social Sector Protection Loan', provided in June 1998, was clearly instrumental to inducing the Malaysian authority to establish a comprehensive framework of bank and corporate restructuring. Notable is the fact that Malaysia hired international private institutions as advisers to Danaharta (JP Morgan and Arthur Andersen), Danamodal (Salomon Brothers and Goldman Sachs) and CDRC (Buchanan).
16. See Hood (2000).
17. Singapore investors were unable to dispose of an estimated 4.9 billion dollars worth of CLOB shares. This remained a source of irritation until it was resolved in February 2000, when the Singapore and Kuala Lumpur exchanges came to agreement on registration and phased release of shares through the Malaysian Central Depository.
18. There were other positive factors preventing massive capital outflows. Conditions in the global financial market had begun to improve following the Long Term Capital Management turmoil. Regional currency and stock markets had begun to broadly stabilize, export growth had begun to recover and capital outflows in the region had abated by early 1999.
19. Neither the non-deliverable forward market nor a black market emerged.
20. Given the lack of a counter-factual, it is difficult to determine how quickly and thoroughly these reforms would have been made in the absence of capital controls. Nonetheless, the controls arguably provided a margin of safety by insulating the economy from further potential shocks and allowed these critical programs to be launched with greater confidence.
21. However, the excessive rate of investment in the pre-crisis period and the emergence and continuing presence of excess capacity throughout the region make it premature to tell whether the controls have had (or will have) an independent, depressing effect on FDI inflows to Malaysia.
22. Though Malaysia did not go to the IMF for financial assistance, it obtained financial assistance from the World Bank, the ADB and Japan during the crisis period, which undoubtedly eased the country's liquidity shortage.
23. The current under-valuation of the ringgit argues for an early move towards greater exchange rate flexibility, which would be helpful in smoothing the process of capital account liberalization. This, however, needs to be coordinated with progress in financial market supervision and regulation.
24. See Hood (2000) for similar assessments.

BIBLIOGRAPHY

Ariyoshi, Akira, Karl Habermeier, Bernard Laurens, Inci Okter-Robe, Jorge Ivan Canales-Kriljenko and Andrei Kirilenko (2000), 'Capital Controls: Country Experiences with their Use and Liberalization', *Occasional Paper*, **190**, Washington, DC: International Monetary Fund.

Athukorala, Prema-Chandra (2000), 'Capital Account Regimes, Crisis and Adjustment in Malaysia', *Asian Development Review*, **18**, pp. 17–48.

Athukorala, Prema-Chandra (2001), 'The Malaysian Experiment', Peter Drysdale (ed.), *Reform and Recovery in East Asia: The Role of the State and Economic Enterprise*, London and New York: Routledge, pp. 169–90.

Bhagwatti, Jagdish (1998), 'The Capital Myth: The Difference between Trade in Widgets and Dollars', *Foreign Affairs*, **77** (3), pp. 7–12.

Calvo, Guillermo and Enrique Mendoza (1999), *Rational Contagion and the Globalization of Securities Markets*, mimeographed, Washington, DC: University of Maryland.

Cardenas, Mauricio and Felipe Barrera (1997), 'On the Effectiveness of Capital Controls: The Experience of Colombia during the 1990s', *Journal of Development Economics*, **54**, pp. 27–57.

De Gregorio, Jose, Sebastian Edwards and Rodrigo O. Valdes (2000), 'Controls on Capital Inflows: Do They Work?', *NBER Working Paper*, **7645**, Cambridge: National Bureau of Economic Research.

Dooley, Michael P. (1996a), 'Capital Controls and Emerging Markets', *International Journal of Finance and Economics*, **1**, pp. 197–205.

Dooley, Michael P. (1996b), 'A Survey of Literature on Controls over International Capital Transactions', *IMF Staff Papers*, **43**, pp. 639–87.

Dornbusch, Rudi (2001), 'Malaysia: Was It Different?', *NBER Working Paper*, **8325**, Cambridge: National Bureau of Economic Research.

Edison, Hali and Carmen Reinhart (1999), 'Stopping Hot Money', mimeographed, Washington, DC: University of Maryland.

Edwards, Sebastian (1999), 'How Effective Are Capital Controls?', *Journal of Economic Perspectives*, **13**, pp. 65–84.

Edwards, Sebastian (2000), 'Interest Rates, Contagion and Capital Controls', *NBER Working Paper*, **7801**, Cambridge: National Bureau of Economic Research.

Eichengreen, Barry (2000), 'Taming Capital Flows', *World Development*, **28**, pp. 1105–16.

Eichengreen, Barry, James Tobin and Charles Wyplosz (1995), 'Two Cases for Sand in the Wheels of International Finance', *Economic Journal*, **105**, pp. 162–72.

Fischer, Stanley (1997), 'Capital Account Liberalization and the Role of the IMF', a paper presented at the seminar, *'Asia and the IMF'*, Hong Kong, Washington, DC: International Monetary Fund.

Garber, Peter and Mark P. Taylor (1995), 'Sand in the Wheels of Foreign Exchange Market: A Skeptical Note', *Economic Journal*, **105**, pp. 173–80.

Gosh, Atish, Timothy Lane, Marianne Schulze-Ghattas, Ales Bulir, Javier Hamann and Alex Mournouras (2002), 'IMF-Supported Programs in Capital Account Crises', *Occasional Paper*, **210**, Washington, DC: International Monetary Fund.

Grilli, Vittorio and Gian Maria Milesi-Ferretti (1995), 'Economic Effects and Structural Determinants of Capital Controls', *IMF Staff Papers*, **42**.

Hood, Ron (2000), 'Malaysian Capital Controls', mimeographed, *East Asia and the Pacific Region*, Washington, DC: World Bank.

Johnston, R. Barry and Chris Ryan (1994), 'The Impact of Controls on Capital Movements on the Private Capital Accounts of Countries' Balance of Payments: Empirical Estimates and Policy Implications', *Working Paper*, **94** (78), Washington, DC: International Monetary Fund.

Johnston, R. Barry and Natalia T. Tamirisa (1997), 'Why Do Countries Use Capital Controls?', *Working Paper*, **98** (181), Washington, DC: International Monetary Fund.

Johnston, R. Barry, Salim M. Darbar and Claudia Echeverria (1997), 'Sequencing Capital Account Liberalization: Lessons from the Experiences in Chile, Indonesia, Korea and Thailand', *Working Paper*, **97** (157), Washington, DC: International Monetary Fund.

Johnston, Simon and Todd Mitton (2001), 'Cronyism and Capital Controls: Evidence from Malaysia', *NBER Working Paper*, **8521**, Cambridge: National Bureau of Economic Research.

Kaplan, Ethan and Dani Rodrik (2001), 'Did the Malaysian Capital Controls Work?', *NBER Working Paper*, **8142**, Cambridge: National Bureau of Economic Research.

Kawai, Masahiro and Shigeru Akiyama (2000), 'Implications of Currency Crisis for Exchange Rate Arrangements in Emerging East Asia', *Policy Research Working Paper*, **2502**, Washington, DC: World Bank.

Kawai, Masahiro and Kentaro Iwatsubo (1998), 'The Thai Financial System and the Baht Crisis: Processes, Causes, and Lessons', *Asia Pacific Journal of Finance*, **1**, pp. 235–61.

Kawai, Masahiro and Shinji Takagi (2000), 'Proposed Strategy for a Regional Exchange Rate Arrangement in Post-Crisis East Asia', *Policy Research Working Paper*, **2502**, Washington, DC: World Bank.

Kawai, Masahiro, Richard Newfarmer and Sergio Schmukler (2001), 'Crisis and Contagion in East Asia: Nine Lessons', *Policy Research Working Paper*, **2610**, Washington, DC: World Bank.

Khan, Mohsin S. and Carmen M. Reinhart (1994), 'Macroeconomic Management in Maturing Economies: The Response to Capital Inflows', *IMF Issues Paper*, Washington, DC: International Monetary Fund.

Krugman, Paul (1998), 'Saving Asia: It's Time to Get Radical', *Fortune*, **138** (5), pp. 74–80.

Lane, Timothy, Atish Ghosh, Javier Hamann, Steven Phillips, Marianne Schulze-Ghattas and Tsidi Tsikata (1999), 'IMF-Supported Programs in Indonesia, Korea, and Thailand: A Preliminary Assessment', *Occasional Paper*, **178**, Washington, DC: International Monetary Fund.

Laurens, Bernard and Jaime Cardoso (1998), 'Managing Capital Flows: Lessons from the Experience of Chile', *Working Paper*, **98** (168), Washington, DC: International Monetary Fund.

McKinnon, Ronald I. (1991), *The Order of Economic Liberalization*, Baltimore: Johns Hopkins University Press.

Meesok, Kanitta, Il Houng Lee, Olin Liu, Yougesh Khatri, Natalia Tamirisa, Michael Moor and Mark H. Krysl (2001), 'Malaysia: From Crisis to Recovery', *Occasional Paper*, **207**, Washington, DC: International Monetary Fund.

Montiel, Peter and Carmen M. Reinhart (1999), 'Do Capital Controls and Macroeconomic Policies Influence the Volume and Composition of Capital Flows? Evidence from the 1990s', *Journal of International Money and Finance*, **18**, pp. 619–35.

Nadal-De Simone, Francisco and Piritta Sorsa (1999), 'A Review of Capital Account Restrictions in Chile in the 1990s', *Working Paper*, **99** (52), Washington, DC: International Monetary Fund.

Neely, Christopher J. (1999), 'An Introduction to Capital Controls', *Review of the Federal Reserve Bank of St. Louis*, pp. 13–30.

Stiglitz, Joseph E. (2000), 'Capital Market Liberalization, Economic Growth, and Instability', *World Development*, **28**, pp. 1075–86.

Stiglitz, Joseph E. and Amarendra Bhattacharya (1999), 'Underpinnings for a Stable and Equitable Global Financial System: From Old Debates to a New Paradigm', *Annual Bank Conference on Development Economics*, Washington, DC: World Bank, pp. 91–130.

Takagi, Shinji (1999), 'The Yen and Its East Asian Neighbors, 1980–1995: Cooperation or Competition?', Takatoshi Ito and Anne O. Krueger (eds), *Changes in Exchange Rates in Rapidly Developing Countries: Theory, Practice, and Policy Issues*, Chicago and London: University of Chicago Press, pp. 185–207.

Takagi, Shinji and Taro Esaka (2001a), 'Sterilization and the Capital Inflow Problem in East Asia, 1987–97', Takatoshi Ito and Anne O. Krueger (eds), *Regional and Global Capital Flows: Macroeconomic Causes and Consequences*, Chicago and London: University of Chicago Press, pp. 197–226.

Takagi, Shinji and Taro Esaka (2001b), 'Risk Premiums and Exchange Rate Expectations: A Reassessment of the So-Called Dollar Peg Policies of Crisis East Asian Countries, 1994–97', *Discussion Paper*, 3 (June), Tokyo: Economic and Social Research Institute, Cabinet Office, Government of Japan.

Tobin, James (1978), 'A Proposal for International Monetary Reform', *Eastern Economic Journal*, **4**, pp. 153–9.

Ulan, Michael K. (2000), 'Review Essay: Is a Chilean-Style Tax on Short-term Capital Inflows Stabilizing?', *Open Economy Review*, **11** (April), pp. 149–77.

Valdes-Prieto, Salvador and Marcelo Soto (1998), 'The Effectiveness of Capital Controls: Theory and Evidence from Chile', *Empirica*, **25**, pp. 133–64.

World Bank (1998), *East Asia: The Road to Recovery*, Washington, DC: World Bank.

World Bank (2000a), *East Asia: Recovery and Beyond*, Washington, DC: World Bank.

World Bank (2000b), *Global Development Finance 2000*, Washington, DC: World Bank.

11. Singapore and Brunei: lessons for monetary clusters within East Asia

Ngiam Kee Jin

11.1 EAST ASIA'S MONETARY COOPERATION

East Asia's currencies and economies have just recovered from the Asian financial crisis that began in Thailand in July 1997. The immediate and important tasks ahead for many of them are to make themselves more resilient and more able to respond quickly and effectively when financial crises strike again. They have begun work at two levels (national and regional) to deal with future financial crises.

At the national level, East Asian countries, especially those badly affected by the crisis, have undertaken painful but necessary corporate restructuring and financial reforms. In addition, many have moved from a largely US dollar peg prior to the crisis to a more flexible exchange rate system, making them less vulnerable to currency attacks.

At the regional level, East Asian countries have made excellent progress with regional financing facilities. Their two boldest moves thus far were the ASEAN Swap Arrangement (ASA) and the Chiang Mai Initiatives (CMI).

In March 1997, the original five ASEAN member countries – Indonesia, Malaysia, the Philippines, Singapore and Thailand – set up the ASA under which a central bank in need of financial support simply exchanges domestic currency for US dollars, but agrees to buy back the domestic currency with US dollars after a predetermined period. Unfortunately, the total amount committed under the ASA was a modest US$100 million (but later expanded to a total of US$200 million for the five countries) which could hardly act as an effective deterrence against currency speculators.[1]

The CMI was launched in May 2000 under which the ASEAN+3 countries (comprising the ten ASEAN countries plus Japan, China and South Korea) would expand their bilateral currency swap arrangements. A year before the launch of the CMI, Japan signed two large bilateral swap arrangements (BSAs) with its East Asian neighbors.[2] The CMI envisaged extending the network of BSAs among the Northern Asian countries (Japan, China and South Korea) and between each of the Northeast Asian countries and the ten ASEAN countries, as well as strengthening the ASEAN cooperation under the ASA.

Japan has been playing a leading role under the CMI and concluded BSAs with China, South Korea, Thailand, Malaysia and the Philippines.[3] Following the CMI, the ASEAN countries agreed in November 2001 to widen the membership of the ASA to include the remaining five ASEAN countries (Brunei, Cambodia, Lao, Myanmar and Vietnam) and enlarge the size of the swap facility from US$200 million to US$1 billion.

However, the amount of funds committed under the ASA and CMI fell short of the proposed Asian Monetary Fund (AMF) to which Japan and some other Asian countries were prepared to contribute (up to US$100 billion initially) to help out Asian currencies under stress. The AMF, which was proposed at the height of the Asian financial crisis, foundered on fears in Europe and the United States that it would undermine the authority of the International Monetary Fund (IMF) and encourage governments to defend overvalued currencies.[4]

The crisis also gave the East Asian countries a strong impetus to search for a suitable regional monitoring and surveillance mechanism that could forestall future crises. Thus far, East Asian countries have come out with three initiatives to build up their regional monitoring and surveillance capacity. These are: (1) Manila Framework Group (established in November 1997), (2) ASEAN Surveillance Process (established in October 1998), and (3) ASEAN+3 Surveillance Process (established in May 2000). Currently, the Manila Framework Group is seen as the pre-eminent forum for regional surveillance and peer pressure.[5]

Last, but not least, the crisis has jolted the thinking of many policymakers, leading some to even propose a common currency to make the region more resilient against currency speculations.[6] In December 1998, the ASEAN heads of state issued the Hanoi plan of action, which directed the ASEAN Secretariat to study the feasibility of an ASEAN currency. While a common ASEAN currency may be as far as a few decades away, regional economies could consider some form of regional monetary union to further strengthen their resilience against future currency attacks. This is because members involved in a monetary union can exert the necessary discipline on the macroeconomic policies of others and are 'obliged' to help each other to defend their currency arrangement.

To be sure, East Asian countries can, of their own accord, build strong fundamentals and adopt sound economic policies. However, there is no guarantee that these are sufficient to prevent currency attacks. Even currencies of strong economies like Hong Kong and Singapore came under selling pressures during the Asian financial crisis. East Asian countries are at liberty to cooperate with their neighbors to strengthen their capacity to ward off speculative attacks. Except for Japan, they have no influence on efforts at the international level to make them less prone to currency attacks.

In fact, two developments on the global scene have made the East Asian currencies (except the yen) particularly vulnerable to currency speculations. One is the emergence of currency blocks centered on the dollar and euro. East Asia is without any kind of regional currency union. Speculators who are no longer able to prey on currencies of the Americas and Europe can now focus their efforts on the small currencies in East Asia.

The other is the large fluctuations of the exchange rates among the three major currencies (dollar, euro and yen) which have caused a great deal of misalignments for many East Asian currencies pegged closely to the US dollar. Currently, no monetary union exists among East Asian countries except the one between Brunei and Singapore.

The particular monetary union between Brunei and Singapore is not well known, at least partly because it works so smoothly. As a monetary union can also act as a bulwark against currency attacks, it ought to be studied closely by East Asian countries now contemplating closer monetary cooperation.

11.2   BENEFITS FROM THE CURRENCY UNION BETWEEN BRUNEI AND SINGAPORE

Brunei and Singapore have a long history of monetary integration. In June 1967, Brunei, Malaysia and Singapore adopted a system of free interchangeability of their respective currencies, in order to maintain strong economic and trade ties. This tripartite arrangement allowed for the Brunei, Malaysian and Singapore dollars to be used in the three countries. Under this system, each country issued its own currency that was legal tender domestically but 'customary tender' in the other two countries. The banks in each country were obliged to accept, at par and without charge, the notes and coins of the other countries. In other words, the exchange rates of the three currencies were fixed one-to-one-to-one. The respective currency boards of the three countries, in turn, accepted the currencies of the other countries from banks and exchange it at par without charge for its own currency. In addition, they agreed to repatriate the currencies of the other countries and to receive at par the equivalent in sterling or some other agreed currency.[7] The expenses for repatriation had been borne by the currency board that issued the currency.

In May 1973, Malaysia terminated the arrangement with Singapore. Brunei decided to continue the arrangement with Singapore and to terminate the currency area with Malaysia.[8]

The monetary union between Brunei and Singapore (MUBS) allows the Brunei dollar and the Singapore dollar to be customary tender in each other's territory. It also allows the Monetary Authority of Singapore (MAS) to conduct an active exchange rate policy on behalf of both countries by managing the Singapore dollar against an undisclosed basket of currencies. Brunei operates a currency board system by fixing its exchange rate one-to-one to the Singapore dollar and by providing 100 percent backing of its currency in circulation.

The MUBS is a dual-currency system in which the national currencies of Brunei and Singapore are circulated within the two countries.[9] Although the MUBS links the two currencies to each other by one-to-one, it is not a currency union as there is no common currency like the euro. Nevertheless, it is a more cooperative and binding arrangement than a pegged system such as that between the Hong Kong dollar and the US dollar and that between the Macau pataca and the Hong Kong dollar.[10] Under the MUBS, Brunei and Singapore are more inclined to help each other over times of financial stress than would be the case if Brunei were to fix its exchange rate unilaterally to the Singapore dollar. The arrangement has both benefits and costs.

One significant benefit of the MUBS is that it has made the Brunei and Singapore dollars more stable (against all the other currencies) than would otherwise be. This is partly because Singapore (or Brunei) can have access to the foreign reserves of the other country. A country that has substantial international liquidity through a ready source of foreign currency funds is less likely to be the object of a currency attack as its credibility in defending the exchange rate is enhanced. Substantial liquidity also enables a country facing a speculative attack to defend itself better and make more orderly financial adjustments. As the Asian financial crisis has demonstrated, liquidity is the key to deter and ward off currency speculators. Strange to say, this kind of benefit has seldom been mentioned in the literature on monetary integration.

Although the MUBS does not specify under which conditions both countries will support each other in times of crises, it allows them to support indirectly each other's currency. Suppose that the Singapore dollar is under speculative pressures and Singapore needs additional international reserves to defend the exchange rate. It has two ways of obtaining Brunei's international reserves. One is simply to borrow Brunei's international reserves without any collateral. Brunei has the incentive to lend as the collapse of the Singapore dollar will drag down the Brunei dollar as well. The other is to exchange Singapore dollars for Brunei dollars under the agreement and sell the Brunei dollar for international reserves.[11] This is tantamount to collateralized credit (or a swap) facilities in which the Singapore authorities swap Singapore dollars for international reserves. Singapore's success in warding off speculative attacks of its currency in September 1985 and in avoiding the worst effects of the Asian financial crisis could have been due partly to the combined financial strength of the two countries rather than its own reserves.

Other benefits of the MUBS include the gains in economic efficiency as a result of (1) the elimination of transaction costs associated with the exchanging of the two currencies and (2) the reduction of risk arising from the uncertain future movements of the bilateral exchange rate.[12] The efficiency gain should be reflected in the size and growth of trade and investment flows between the two countries. Table 11.1 shows Brunei's exports and imports by destination. It can be seen that the MUBS has helped Singapore to retain its position as the largest supplier of goods to Brunei, accounting for some 25.6 percent of Brunei's total imports in 1997. Brunei's total exports have not been growing because it relies almost exclusively on the exports of oil and gas, which have suffered from declining prices since the early 1980s. It sells its oil and gas mainly to Japan.[13]

Table 11.1   Brunei's exports and imports by destinations

Country	Exports (B$ Million)			Imports (B$ Million)		
	1977	1987	1997	1977	1987	1997
Japan	3,061	2,473	2,108	146	194	353
USA	366	65	97	143	163	316
Singapore	160	269	264	118	326	808
Thailand	29	469	446	15	59	124
Malaysia	119	47	111	35	111	428
EC	3	7	47	146	289	565
Rest of World	262	676	900	77	208	560
Total	4,000	4,006	3,973	680	1,350	3,154

Source: Brunei Darussalam Statistical Yearbook, various issues.

The growth of capital flows between the two countries can only be partially deduced from the increase in the repatriation of the two currencies. Figure 11.1 shows that the amount of Singapore dollars repatriated from Brunei to Singapore has all along been small. In 1999, it stood at only S$5 million. In contrast, the amount of Brunei currency repatriated from Singapore to Brunei has risen steadily from a low of B$30 million to a record high of B$853 million in 1999. These figures do not include a probably much larger amount of capital flows undertaken through the banking system by way of book entries. This is confirmed by the Brunei Currency Board that 'each year commercial banks are able to move billions of dollars between the two countries without running the risk of currency rate fluctuations'.[14] The fact that Brunei uses the financial services of

Singapore more than other regional financial centers like Hong Kong is an indication of the benefits derived from the currency arrangement.[15]

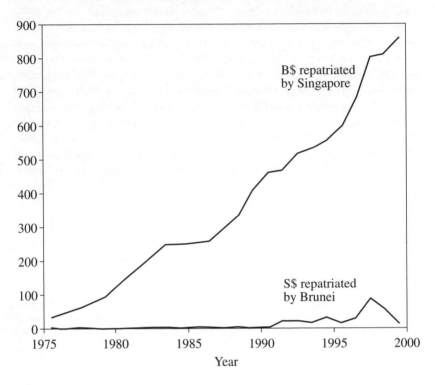

Figure 11.1   Repatriation of Brunei and Singapore currencies

Brunei has gained by linking itself with Singapore, which has acquired the credibility of maintaining a conservative monetary policy with a low inflation rate. Thus, the MUBS may be viewed as a way for Brunei to borrow Singapore's credibility in the same way that France and Italy have borrowed German credibility under the European Monetary System. This is evident from Table 11.2, which shows that the average annual inflation rates in Singapore and Brunei were fairly low during the period 1967–97, averaging 3.81 and 3.07 percent respectively. The inflation rate in Brunei had over the years converged to the level in Singapore, falling from 4.2 percent in the sub-period 1977–87 to 2.4 percent in the sub-period 1987–97.[16] Their inflation rates were highly correlated with a coefficient of 0.68 and were significant at the 5 percent level. It can be seen that two of their important neighbors, Malaysia and Thailand, had higher inflation rates. While Brunei's inflation rate was correlated with that of these two neighbors, Singapore's inflation rate was not.

However, the statistics for output growth tell a different story. Brunei's real GDP growth was a modest 1.7 percent during the period 1967–97. In contrast, Singapore's real GDP growth during the same period was a robust 8.3 percent. As expected, their output growth had a zero correlation. Although Malaysia was not a member of the MUBS, its growth rate was highly correlated with that of Singapore. This evidence suggests that one should not expect the GDP growth of union members to converge as output growth has little to do with the currency arrangement. Economic growth implies mostly improvements in the terms of trade, accumulation of factors of production, productivity increase and innovation.

Table 11.2   Correlations of output growth and inflation between Brunei and Singapore (1967–97)

	Sing.	Brunei	Malay.	Thai.	Mean (%)	S.D. (%)
Output Growth						
Singapore	1.0	–	–	–	8.33	3.26
Brunei	–0.01	1.0	–	–	1.67	8.35
Malaysia	0.55**	0.3	1.0	–	6.96	2.74
Thailand	0.33	0.19	0.35	1.0	7.09	2.77
Inflation						
Singapore	1.0	–	–	–	3.81	3.6
Brunei	0.68**	1.0	–	–	3.07	16.91
Malaysia	0.56	0.49*	1.0	–	3.93	2.74
Thailand	0.82	0.70**	0.67	1.0	5.3	4.63

Notes:
* Correlation is significant at the 0.05 level.
** Correlation is significant at the 0.01 level.

11.3   COSTS OF THE CURRENCY UNION BETWEEN SINGAPORE AND BRUNEI

The major cost of the MUBS is that in order to maintain the par rate, one or both of the countries may lose monetary autonomy. As Singapore pursues an independent exchange rate policy, it has nothing to lose from the arrangement barring serious monetary instability in Brunei. The cost to Brunei, in terms of relinquishing its right to adjust the exchange rate in the face of economic shocks, is less obvious. It will be low if the two countries have symmetric supply shocks.

This is because symmetric shocks between Brunei and Singapore reduce the need for altering relative prices between them. However, if the two countries have asymmetric shocks, then separate exchange rate and monetary policies could help stabilize national-specific (or idiosyncratic) fluctuations in economic activity.[17]

Whether shocks between the two countries are symmetrical or not depend partly on (1) the similarity of their production and trade structure, and (2) on the degree of their economic integration. When their production and trade structure is different, they are more likely to face asymmetric disturbances as specific shocks are likely to affect them differently (Kenen, 1969). The relation between economic integration and the occurrence of symmetric shocks is debatable. According to the EC Commission (1990), economic integration should lead to symmetric shocks as it encourages intra-industry trade in which countries buy and sell to each other the same category of products. This kind of trade structure leads to a situation where demand shocks will affect these countries in a similar way. Frankel and Rose (1996) reach the same conclusion, but argue instead that symmetric shocks come from the marginal propensities to import from each other as well as productivity shocks spilling over through trade. Other authors (Eichengreen, 1990; Krugman, 1991) hold the opposite view. They argue that as economic integration becomes more highly integrated, countries specialize more in production. Greater specialization will lead to occurrence of asymmetric shocks in the countries.

Although Brunei and Singapore decided to form a monetary union, it is noteworthy that their economic structures have remained vastly different. Oil and gas continue to dominate the Brunei economy as the export share of these two items constitutes over 90 percent of its total exports. Singapore, on the other hand, has a more diversified and advanced production structure. In addition, it has a world-class business and financial services sector. As their economic structures are dissimilar, there is a prima facie evidence that they are exposed to asymmetric shocks.

To verify whether their shocks are indeed asymmetrical, we estimate the correlation between movements in real GDP that can be thought of as being driven by fluctuations in aggregate demand (AD) and movements that are due to fluctuations in aggregate supply (AS). The Blanchard and Quah (1989) procedure is employed to decompose fluctuations in GDP into these two components. Underlying the procedure is an AD-AS model, which assumes that supply disturbances affect long-run output and prices, while demand disturbances only affect long-run prices. The procedure involves estimating a bivariate VAR model consisting of inflation and real GDP of Brunei and Singapore (Malaysia and Thailand are included in our estimation in order to provide a benchmark). Whether a group of countries should form a monetary union among themselves depends on how synchronized are their supply shocks rather than how synchronized are their GDP movements. For example, it is possible for Brunei and Singapore to have negatively correlated demand shocks but positively correlated supply shocks. In this case, their GDP movements are likely to be uncorrelated, but the positive correlation between their supply shocks makes them good candidates for a monetary union.

Table 11.3 reveals that both supply and demand shocks between Brunei and Singapore are not correlated. It would appear that the pattern of structural shocks does not identify these two countries as particularly well-suited for a monetary union. Our findings do not support the argument by Frankel and Rose (1996) that the fulfillment of the criteria of an optimum currency area (OCA) is endogenous since MUBS has not forced the demand shocks of Brunei and Singapore (and hence their output growth) to be positively correlated. In contrast, supply shocks were highly correlated between Malaysia and Singapore, while demand shocks were highly correlated for Malaysia, Singapore and Thailand. On this score alone, Malaysia was probably a better candidate than Brunei for forming a monetary union with Singapore. We also test whether the business cycles among Brunei, Malaysia and Singapore had become more synchronized over the years. By splitting the sample period into two sub-periods (1975–85 and 1986–96), we find that the GDP growth among Brunei, Malaysia and Singapore were more correlated in the second sub-period than in the first.[18]

As Brunei and Singapore experienced asymmetric shocks, the cost to Brunei of forming a monetary union with Singapore would, on the surface, appear to be high. However, the actual cost to Brunei is likely to be minimal as unemployment is not usually a concern to Brunei as it has a large pool of foreign workers. Unemployment can be easily eliminated through adjustment in the number of foreign workers who may be allowed to work in Brunei. In any case, the fact that the MUBS has lasted for so long without any complaint by Brunei may indicate that the benefits outweigh the cost. In fact, Brunei's Ministry of Finance provided a favorable assessment of the MUBS by stating that 'the Monetary Authority of Singapore exercises sufficient caution and such a link will not have detrimental effect on the economies of either. At the same time, this agreement is not seen as inhibiting the management of the domestic economy.'[19]

11.4   MONETARY 'CLUSTERS' FOR EAST ASIA

The idea of a large monetary union in East Asia may be conceptually appealing, but would be difficult to achieve in practical terms. The experience of the 15 members of the European Union is instructive. This group has participated in the EMS to limit exchange rate fluctuations among themselves and to establish coordinated macroeconomic polices across Western Europe. The EMS has gone

Table 11.3   Correlations of shocks between Brunei and Singapore (1967–97)

	Singapore	Brunei	Malaysia	Thailand
Supply Shocks				
Singapore	1.0	–	–	–
Brunei	–0.09	1.0	–	–
Malaysia	0.61**	0.02	1.0	–
Thailand	0.31	–0.06	0.16	1.0
Demand Shocks				
Singapore	1.0	–	–	–
Brunei	0.27	1.0	–	–
Malaysia	0.57**	0.44	1.0	–
Thailand	0.70**	0.43	0.59*	1.0

Notes:
* Correlation is significant at the 0.05 level.
** Correlation is significant at the 0.01 level.

through a number of changes since its inception in 1979, including major currency crises in 1992 and 1993, and conversion of 11 members to the euro on 1 January 1999. Perhaps the most important lesson to be learnt from the EMS is that a large monetary union with huge divergence of economic variables among members makes it susceptible to speculative attacks and put into question its sustainability. As East Asia has a much greater divergence of economic indicators than Western Europe, it should proceed with extreme caution in moving towards a monetary integration. A gradualist rather than a 'big bang' approach should enhance the sustainability of monetary cooperation efforts in East Asia.

If an Asian-wide monetary union is not practical now, the pertinent question is how Asian monetary cooperation should proceed. A two-track approach is proposed. On the broader front, East Asian countries should continue with their efforts to enlarge and strengthen their pool of credit facilities such as the currency swap arrangements and the proposed AMF. But credit facilities without any conditionality often raise the problem of 'moral hazard' as countries might be tempted to engage in dangerous practices in the expectation that they will be bailed out. Hence, there is a need for strengthening the regional monitoring and surveillance in order to reduce the moral hazard problem.

On the sub-regional front, small groups of more or less homogeneous countries may form monetary unions (or 'clusters') of their own. East Asia could easily accommodate a few small clusters. This may be easier to implement than a region-wide monetary union, given the diversity of East Asian economies. It is also more flexible as each cluster can decide on their own common exchange rate policy. Apart from the cluster involving Singapore and Brunei, Hong Kong and Macau can almost immediately form another cluster. The exchange rate of Hong Kong and Macau at HK$100 to 103 patacas is similar enough for them to pursue a similar set up to that between Singapore and Brunei.

The size of each cluster can be enlarged when a sufficient degree of harmonization and convergence has been attained. Initially, the focus should be on harmonization within each cluster. Integration between small functioning monetary unions can be subsequently considered. Once a high degree of harmonization and convergence across various monetary unions is achieved, East Asia can then consider creating an East Asian currency.

If clustering of monetary unions should be the first step in a journey of a thousand miles, then the logical question is how to determine the various clusters. One can use the correlations of supply shocks to identify the potential clusters of monetary unions in East Asia. This has been attempted by Bayoumi and Eichengreen (1994) using the procedure of Blanchard and Quah (1989). We have updated their work by using data up to 1997 and incorporated more countries (such as China, Macau and Brunei).[20] As a result, we have come out with some fascinating and intuitive results.

Our findings on the correlations of supply shocks among the East Asian countries are presented in Table 11.4.[21] The results suggest that the supply disturbances were correlated for eight small clusters of countries: (1) Japan, South Korea and Taiwan, (2) Taiwan, Hong Kong and Singapore, (3) Singapore and Malaysia, (4) Malaysia and Indonesia, (5) Thailand and Japan, (6) Thailand and Australia, (7) South Korea and Brunei, and (8) Macau and Taiwan. Interestingly, the inclusion of China in our study does not show that it belongs to the cluster comprising Japan, South Korea and Taiwan. In contrast, Bayoumi and Eichengreen (1994) find that the supply disturbances were correlated for only three clusters of countries: (1) Japan, South Korea and Taiwan, (2) Hong Kong, Singapore, Malaysia and Indonesia, and (3) Taiwan and Thailand. Similar to our findings, their study also suggests that the supply shocks of Australia were not correlated with New Zealand or with any of the other East Asian countries.[22]

Our results are suggestive rather than conclusive. This is because the symmetry of shocks is only one of the conditions for assessing whether a group of countries should form a monetary union among themselves. Even if a group of countries were confronted with symmetric shocks, they could still face different adjustment costs due to structural differences. Examining the variance decompositions (VA) offers a good way to understand the underlying structural differences among the economies. Table 11.5 gives the decomposition of the percentage change in real output at one and four-year forecasting horizons that can be explained by supply shocks and nominal shocks. The table reveals that supply shocks explain

Table 11.4   Correlations of supply shocks in East Asia (1967–97)

Nation	Japan	Korea	Taiwan	HK	Sing.	Malay.	Indo.	Phil.	Thai.	China	Aus.	NZ	Brunei	Mac
Japan	1.0	–	–	–	–	–	–	–	–	–	–	–	–	–
Korea	0.397[1]	1.0	–	–	–	–	–	–	–	–	–	–	–	–
Taiwan	0.389[1]	0.36[1]	1.0	–	–	–	–	–	–	–	–	–	–	–
HK	–0.013	0.17	0.524[2]	1.0	–	–	–	–	–	–	–	–	–	–
Sing.	–0.015	0.085	0.473[2]	0.361[1]	1.0	–	–	–	–	–	–	–	–	–
Malay.	–0.058	–0.07	0.119	0.312	0.614[2]	1.0	–	–	–	–	–	–	–	–
Indo.	0.031	–0.18	0.225	0.305	0.265	0.348[1]	1.0	–	–	–	–	–	–	–
Phil.	0.143	0.003	0.064	0.156	–0.08	–0.01	–0.027	1.0	–	–	–	–	–	–
Thai.	0.454[2]	0.295	0.3	0.15	0.308	0.161	0.252	0.016	1.0	–	–	–	–	–
China	0.254	0.105	0.141	–0.23	–0.07	–0.34	–0.133	–0.154	0.214	1.0	–	–	–	–
Aus.	0.175	0.191	0.443[2]	0.179	0.193	0.025	0.222	0.027	0.325[1]	0.248	1.0	–	–	–
NZ	–0.397	–0.24	–0.28	–0.06	0.036	0.141	0.126	–0.013	–0.38	–0.09	–0.204	1.0	–	–
Brunei	0.478[1]	0.484[1]	–0.09	–0.04	–0.09	0.02	0.045	0.2	–0.06	–0.02	–0.389	–0.206	1.0	–
Macau	–0.27	0.424	0.554[1]	0.352	0.198	–0.24	–0.14	–0.055	0.36	0.266	0.014	–0.127	–0.494	1.0

Notes:
1. Correlation is significant to the 0.05 level.
2. Correlation is significant to the 0.01 level.

Table 11.5   Variance decompositions of real output

		Percentage Change of Real Output Due to:			
		Supply Shocks		Nominal Shocks	
	Step	1	4	1	4
Japan		98.69	90.06	1.31	9.94
Korea		50.36	49.25	49.64	50.75
Taiwan		99.71	92.40	0.29	7.60
Singapore		86.75	82.83	13.25	17.17
Malaysia		53.87	54.05	46.13	45.95
Indonesia		96.31	92.33	3.69	7.67
Philippines		94.44	81.66	5.55	18.34
Thailand		96.83	95.10	3.17	4.90
China		86.94	83.31	13.06	16.69
Australia		71.42	68.40	28.58	31.60
New Zealand		86.48	86.28	13.52	13.72

the preponderance of the changes in real output in all the economies in East Asia except South Korea and Malaysia. Nominal shocks seem to be dominant in explaining output variability for South Korea and Malaysia. Although Singapore and Malaysia display symmetry in supply shocks, there are structural differences between the two countries. Japan and South Korea also face a similar situation. Structural differences between Singapore and Malaysia and between Japan and South Korea can be an impediment to the formation of monetary union by these two groups of countries.

On the basis of symmetry in macroeconomic disturbances, geographic proximity and socio-cultural compatibility, our results suggest at least three clusters of countries as plausible candidates for monetary integration: (1) Brunei, Singapore and Malaysia, (2) Japan and Korea, and (3) Taiwan and Hong Kong. These three clusters represent the Southeast Asian bloc, the Northeast Asian bloc, and the Greater China bloc respectively. Grouping Brunei, Singapore and Malaysia as one bloc, and Japan and South Korea as another, is not totally surprising as there is a great deal of trade within these two blocs. Even though Hong Kong trades substantially with China and has exhibited a positive growth correlation with the Mainland, both of these Chinese (but very different) economies have displayed asymmetric bilateral shocks. In fact, China has experienced mainly idiosyncratic shocks and its supply shocks are not correlated with any of the other East Asian economies. Hence, on the basis of the symmetry of supply shocks, a cluster consisting of Taiwan and Hong Kong seems to make economic sense but is obviously not a politically plausible option at the present moment.

In the final analysis, political factors play a crucial role in determining the process towards monetary integration. An extensive exposition of the political issues in monetary integration is beyond the scope of this chapter, but it is recognized that right now the political will for monetary integration in East Asia is practically non-existent.

11.5   LESSONS

The Asian financial crisis has demonstrated that currency crises tend to be regional, with even currencies of strong economies falling prey to regional contagion. Since currency crises impose regional costs, East Asian countries have an incentive to work together to make themselves less vulnerable to future currency attacks. Towards this end, they have banded together to protect each other by embarking on several initiatives. First, they have widened and deepened their network of bilateral currency swap arrangements. Second, they are taking another hard look at the creation of an AMF, even though the idea has been shot down by the IMF and the United States when it was first brought up in the midst of the Asian financial crisis. Third, they are rethinking the issue of appropriate exchange rate arrangements, including the creation of a pan-Asian monetary union.

An important lesson from the Asian financial crisis is that the bail-out packages provided through the IMF have been funneled out to crisis-hit countries too slowly and under stringent conditions. Without quick and substantial international liquidity (consisting of both a country's own foreign exchange reserves and foreign currency loans), a country's ability to deter and ward off speculative attacks on its currency is limited. Large and rapid disbursement of international liquidity will enable a country to prevent a currency crisis. The bilateral currency swap arrangements among Asian countries are important sources of dependable liquidity that Asian countries might have to rely on during times of crises. By standing ready like a fire brigade to quickly 'douse' currency attacks, they can act as essential supplements to the IMF lending. In addition, the mere availability of credit facilities can act as a deterrence against would-be speculators. The real concern is that these credit facilities could give rise to the problem of 'moral hazard' as countries might be tempted to engage in risky practices in the expectation of large bail-outs. Hence, regional financing facilities must be accompanied by effective regional monitoring and surveillance to reduce the moral hazard problem.

Besides creating credit facilities, East Asian countries should consider a partial form of monetary integration in view of their diverse economic, social and political background. One solution to the problem of divergence is to have a few small monetary unions (or clusters) rather than a pan-Asian monetary union. Brunei and Singapore have already formed a cluster that has been beneficial to both countries despite the fact that their supply shocks are not correlated. However, the monetary union between these two countries is a special case where the dominant factor is probably the desire by Brunei to borrow the credibility of the MAS rather the fulfillment of the OCA criteria. Other East Asian countries wishing to form such a cluster should have symmetry of supply shocks as well as a high degree of social, economic and political compatibility among themselves. Initially, the focus should be on harmonization of economic policies within each cluster. In the very long run, integration between small functioning monetary unions can be considered. In the meantime, East Asian countries should consider establishing an AMF to support the sustainability of the various clusters. The moral hazard problem inherent in the AMF will be minimized because members of a monetary union can exert the necessary discipline on the macroeconomic policies of other members.

NOTES

1. Actually, the amount that a country can borrow is very small. Under this arrangement, each country contributed US$40 million to the scheme, and is entitled to withdraw only up to twice this amount in times of need.
2. Its agreement with South Korea allows each country to swap its local currency for up to US$5 billion in cash from its counterpart. A similar agreement with Malaysia provides funds of up to US$2.5 billion.
3. The resources made available by Japan for each of the countries are: China (US$3 billion), South Korea (US$2 billion), Thailand (US$3 billion), Malaysia (US$1 billion) and the Philippines (US$3 billion).
4. China was also reported to have opposed the AMF for fear that it might lead to 'hegemony' of the yen in the region.
5. This group meets semi-annually, with the participation of 14 countries, the IMF, World Bank, Bank for International Settlements and the Asian Development Bank. The participating countries include Australia, Brunei, Canada, China, Hong Kong, Indonesia, Japan, Malaysia, New Zealand, the Philippines, Singapore, South Korea, Thailand and the United States.
6. Calls for a common currency in East Asia were made by former President Joseph Estrada of the Philippines and Mr Joseph Yam of the Hong Kong Monetary Authority. See 'HKMA Chief Calls for Creation of Asian Euro' in *The Business Times*, 6 January 1999, and Ugat (2000), p. 224.
7. In practice, the three currency boards have asked for payments to be made in their own currencies.
8. See Claassen (1992).
9. MUBS is commonly known as the Currency Interchangeability Arrangement between Brunei and Singapore. See Chan and Ngiam (1992) for a detailed account of the arrangement.
10. Hong Kong decided to peg its currency at 7.8 Hong Kong dollars to one US dollar under a currency board system in June 1983. At the same time, Macau chose to peg its currency at 103 patacas to 100 Hong Kong dollars.
11. This can work only if Brunei holds on to Singapore dollars as reserves and does not sell them off subsequently for other currencies.
12. Apart from the occasional rumors that the MUBS is to end, most people would normally regard the Brunei and Singapore currencies as highly substitutable.
13. The MUBS has not resulted in a greater flow of Brunei's oil and gas to Singapore.
14. Brunei Currency Board, *Annual Report 1990*, p. 40.
15. Some of Brunei's investments in Singapore are in the Asian dollar market. As a preliminary step, Brunei's investors may exchange the Brunei dollar for the Singapore dollar, at par and at no cost, and then convert the Singapore dollar into US dollars or other currencies.
16. See Duraman (2000), p. 142.
17. There are two characteristics of Brunei that may reduce the usefulness of an independent monetary policy. First, as a primary-producing country, it is a price-taker, which implies that its terms of trade will not vary with its exchange rate. Second, as a highly open economy, its prices and money wages are likely to respond rapidly to its exchange rate changes, leaving its competitiveness unaffected.
18. Data will be made available to readers upon request.
19. Government of Brunei Darussalam (1989).
20. See Ngiam and Yuen (2000) who have employed cluster analysis to identify the various clusters in East Asia.
21. Demand shocks are not presented or discussed, as they are unlikely to be invariant to the demand management policies and currency regimes.
22. Using the same procedure, Crosby and Otto (2000) also find that the supply shocks between Australia and New Zealand are not correlated.

REFERENCES

Bayoumi, T. and B. Eichengreen (1994), 'One Money or Many?Analyzing the Prospects for Monetary Unification in Various Parts of the World', *Princeton Studies in International Finance*, **76**.

Blanchard, O. and D. Quah (1989), 'The Dynamic Effects of Aggregate Demand and Supply Disturbances', *American Economic Review*, **79**, pp. 655–73.

Chan, K. and K.J. Ngiam (1992), 'Currency Interchangeability Arrangement between Brunei and Singapore', *Singapore Economic Review*, **37**, pp. 21–33.

Claassen, E.M. (1992), *Financial Liberalisation and Its Impact on Domestic Stabilisation Policies: The Case of Singapore and Malaysia*, Singapore: Institute of Southeast Asian Studies, and Weltwirtschaftliches Archiv, March 1992, **128**, pp. 136–67.

Crosby, M. and G. Otto (2000), 'An Australian-New Zealand Currency Union?', paper presented at the *International Conference on Financial Markets and Policies in East Asia*, 4–5 September 2000, Canberra.

Duraman, H. (2000), *A Common Currency for East Asia: Dream or Reality?*, in K. Bashar and W. Mollers (eds), Asian Institute for Development Communication, Kuala Lumpur: Brunei Darussalam.

EC Commission (1990), 'One Market, One Money', *European Economy*, **44**.

Eichengreen, B. (1990), 'Is Europe an Optimum Currency Area?', *CEPR Discussion Paper*, **478**.

Frankel, J. and A. Rose (1996), 'The Endogeneity of the Optimum Currency Area Criteria', *NBER Working Paper*, **5700**.

Government of Brunei Darussalam (1989), *Brunei Darussalam in Profile*, London, UK: Shandwick.

Kenen, P. (1969), 'The Theory of Optimum Currency Areas: An Eclectic View', in R.A. Mundell and A.K. Swoboda (eds), *Monetary Problems of the International Economy*, Chicago: University of Chicago Press, pp. 41–60.

Krugman, P. (1991), *Geography and Trade*, Cambridge, MA: MIT Press.

Ngiam, K.J. and H. Yuen (2000), 'Monetary Cooperation in Asia: A Way Forward', paper presented at the *National Economic Outlook 2001* Conference, Malaysia.

Ugat, G. (2000), 'The Philippines', in K. Bashar and W. Mollers (eds), *A Common Currency for East Asia: Dream or Reality?*, Kuala Lumpur: Asian Institute for Development Communication.

12. Costs and benefits of a common currency for the ASEAN

Srinivasa Madhur

12.1 INTRODUCTION

The 1997 Asian financial crisis has brought into sharp focus questions about appropriate exchange rate regimes for the economies in the region. In the aftermath of the crisis, with the notable exception of Malaysia, many countries in the region have now shifted toward greater flexibility in their exchange rates, although, for various reasons including the 'fear of floating', official interventions in the foreign exchange market to stabilize rates are not uncommon. While these countries are experimenting with changes in the exchange rate regimes, a lively debate is continuing on the choice of appropriate exchange rate regimes for developing countries.

Since the Asian crisis, a popular view among academic economists and policymakers is that developing countries with open capital accounts have a bipolar solution to the exchange rate dilemma they face: a free float or a hard peg. This chapter assesses the costs and benefits of a hard peg, specifically the use of a common currency or formation of a monetary union, for the Association of Southeast Asian Nations (ASEAN).

Given that the adoption of a common currency, or the formation of a currency union, was the last step in a sequence of policy initiatives toward regional economic integration in Europe that spanned more than four decades, the ASEAN may perhaps be a long way away from adopting a common currency. Yet, a debate on the adoption of a common currency by these countries is slowly emerging especially in the aftermath of the Asian crisis and after the single currency for Europe, the euro, became a reality beginning 1999.

This chapter aims to integrate and synthesize key conclusions in the literature and raise certain issues for further debate and research, rather than break new ground through fresh research. The assessment is largely organized around some of the well-known results, both theoretical and empirical, of works on optimum currency area (OCA).

The chapter is organized as follows. Section 2 presents the theoretical and empirical perspectives from the OCA literature. Section 3 examines the suitability of the ASEAN for adoption of a common currency and Section 4 assesses the key constraints on such adoption. Section 5 concludes by placing the issue in a broader global perspective.

12.2 PERSPECTIVES ON OPTIMUM CURRENCY AREA

According to the OCA literature, the key economic cost from formation of a currency union by a group of countries is the loss of national autonomy in monetary policy. Under a currency union, there is no scope for independent monetary policies by the member countries of the union. However, the cost associated with the loss of monetary independence depends upon how well the individual countries were conducting monetary policy prior to joining the currency union.

Many developing countries with open capital accounts have several constraints in the effective conduct of an independent monetary policy. This is especially so in developing countries with thin capital markets and weak central banking institutions. In general, the record of developing countries in conducting independent national monetary policies to minimize cyclical fluctuations in economic activity has been somewhat patchy. This suggests that the economic loss from giving up an independent monetary policy may not be very large for such countries. On the contrary, a currency union may, in fact, elicit commitment to greater macroeconomic stability from countries that otherwise have a mixed track record in implementing monetary policy prior to joining the currency union (Barro, 2001). It is possible that this benefit will compensate for the loss of monetary policy autonomy.

The major benefit of a common currency that has been emphasized is that it facilitates trade (in both goods and services) and investment among the countries of the union (and hence increases income growth within the region) by reducing transaction costs in cross-border business, and removing volatility in exchange rates across the union. A currency is like language (Barro, 2001). As a common language facilitates effective communication among people, a common currency could promote trade and investment among countries. In an environment of different currencies, transaction costs, including the costs of obtaining information about prices, would be higher. This would be a disincentive to trade, commerce and investment.

Moreover, under floating exchange rate regimes – the alternative to a fixed exchange rate regime – exchange rates tend to be more volatile than is warranted by the economic fundamentals of an economy (Rose, 1994; Bergsten and Henning, 1996; Williamson, 1999; Collignon, 1999; Jeanne and Rose, 2002). This is especially true of small developing economies with thin capital markets. Developing countries with large unhedged foreign currency liabilities (original sin), therefore, often 'fear to float' (Calvo and Reinhart, 2002). Monetary policies in such countries tend to be pro-cyclical rather than counter-cyclical. Belying the expectations of advocates of floating exchange rate regimes, flexible exchange rates have often become a source of shocks rather than shock absorbers. 'Market errors' and the consequent misalignments in exchange rates under floating exchange rate regimes have been substantial (Breur, 1994). Disproportionate volatility in exchange rates increases uncertainty, discourages trade, diminishes investment and reduces overall economic growth (Kenen and Rodrik, 1986; Huizinga, 1994; Corbo and Cox, 1995). It is possible to mitigate some of these adverse effects of floating exchange rates by hedging against exchange rate fluctuations. However, hedging involves non-negligible transaction costs (Adler, 1996; Friberg, 1996; Rajan, 2000). Development of perfect hedging instruments may even be difficult in practice. This may explain why in a 1992 survey of non-financial Fortune companies, while 85 percent of the respondents hedged, only 22 percent hedged fully (Rajan, 2000).

A common currency could mitigate some of these adverse effects of a floating exchange rate system. From a purely economic point of view, a set of countries should opt for a common currency if the cost of losing national autonomy in monetary policy is mitigated by the benefits of a currency union. While it is difficult to quantify these costs and benefits, the OCA literature offers some guidelines to compare them. The benefits of a currency union increase and/or the costs decrease with:

1. greater flexibility in wages and prices among the countries of the union;
2. greater mobility of factors of production (labor and capital) across countries;
3. more symmetric shocks across countries;
4. more openness among the economies within the union; and,
5. larger share of trade among the countries of the region.

A composite index of some of these determinants of the relative costs and benefits of a currency union, known as the OCA index, has been used to assess the suitability of a set of countries for adoption of a common currency. These OCA indicators should, however, be used with caution because they are not necessarily independent of the prevailing exchange rate regime (Eichengreen, 1996; Frankel and Rose, 1997; Rose, 2000; Glick and Rose, 2001; Corsetti and Pesenti, 2002). The OCA indicators, in other words, could be endogenous to the exchange rate regime. Endogeneity of the OCA indicators can arise due to a variety of reasons. Two of these deserve special mention.

First, to the extent that a common currency promotes greater trade among countries, openness and the volume of intra-union trade will be greater under a common currency than under a regime of floating exchange rates. This will make the degree of openness and the volume of intra-union trade endogenous to the exchange rate regime. Early estimates of the effect of exchange rate regimes on trade were generally small and modest at best (Kennen and Rodrik, 1986; Huizinga, 1994; Corbo and Cox, 1995). However, more recent studies find substantial positive effects of a common currency regime on trade (Rose, 2000; Glick and Rose, 2001; Rose and Wincoop, 2001; Frankel and Rose, 2002).

Second, the degree of flexibility of wages in the labor markets and the prices in the product markets are likely to be larger under a credible currency union than under a floating exchange rate regime. This is a broader application of the well-known Lucas principle that states that the very structure of an economy may be affected by changes in the policy regime. This is not to suggest that wages and prices will become perfectly flexible once exchange rates across countries are locked in, but that wage and price-setters will adapt in order to avoid increases in unemployment to levels that would provoke resistance to continued participation in the currency union (Eichengreen, 1996). Historical evidence tends to support such a market response. For example, the response of labor and product market prices to shocks was found to be faster under the gold standard than under monetary regimes characterized by greater exchange rate variability (Bayoumi and Eichengreen, 1996).

12.3   THE SUITABILITY OF THE ASEAN FOR A COMMON CURRENCY

Is the ASEAN suitable for adopting a common currency? While it is difficult to quantify the costs and benefits, applying the guidelines of the OCA literature shows there are several characteristics of the ASEAN that suggest that the benefits of a common currency may be significant relative to the costs.

In terms of the cost of giving up independent monetary policy, in practice, given the somewhat mixed track record of many of these countries in conducting monetary policy, the costs of surrendering monetary autonomy are unlikely to be large. At least some of them may perhaps be giving up something that they do not have! In fact, as a result of forming a currency union, there is a possibility that some of the countries that now have a patchy track record of inflation control and exchange rate management could benefit substantially from a monetary policy conducted by a more credible regional central bank. Such a convergence to best (or better) practices in monetary policy in the region will be a benefit, not a cost.

In terms of factor mobility, the ASEAN compares favorably with the European Union (EU) at the time of the Maastricht Treaty. The ASEAN has relatively high labor mobility as well as capital mobility (Goto and Hamada, 1994; Eichengreen and Bayoumi, 1999; Moon, Rhee and Yoon, 2000). For example, workers from Indonesia, Malaysia, Philippines and Thailand account for 10 percent of the employment in Singapore. Emigration has been as much as 2 percent of the labor force of the sending countries.

Compared to the EU, the ASEAN also ranks quite high in terms of wage and price flexibility. In fact, traditionally the countries are known for their flexibility and speed of adjustment to shocks. According to Bayoumi and Eichengreen (1994), almost all of the change in output and prices in response to a shock in East Asia takes place in about two years. By comparison, in Europe, only about half the adjustment occurs in the first two years after a shock. These results are consistent with the general impression that labor markets are more flexible in the ASEAN than in Western Europe.

Many ASEAN countries have trade-to-GDP ratios as well as trade-intensity ratios (which normalize bilateral trade by the relative share of the countries in total world trade to eliminate size effects) that are higher than in Western Europe (Goto and Hamada, 1994; Kawai and Takagi, 2000). At close to 25 percent, the share of intraregional trade in ASEAN total trade, although lower than in the EU (40 percent), is significant and rising (Bayoumi and Mauro, 1999). It is much higher than in some of the other currency unions such as the Eastern Caribbean Currency Union (about 10 percent), the Western Africa Economic and Monetary Union (about 10 percent), and the Central African Economic and Monetary Community (about 3 percent).

Although there are national differences, the symmetry in shocks among the countries in the region is comparable to the EU (Eichengreen and Bayoumi, 1999). The region-wide economic slowdown in 2001 in response to the global economic downturn is further evidence of the high degree of shock symmetry among these countries. The high degree of shock symmetry reflects both the high degree of openness (export orientation, capital flows etc.) and the similarities in the production structures among these economies.

Overall, composite OCA indices for the region, which take into account intraregional trade, wage–price flexibility, labor mobility, and shock symmetry, are similar to those for the EU (Eichengreen and Bayoumi, 1999). Using a variety of indicators drawn from the OCA literature, Eichengreen and Bayoumi conclude that from a purely economic perspective, East Asia/ASEAN is as suitable for an OCA as Europe was prior to the Maastricht Treaty.

12.4　CONSTRAINTS ON THE ADOPTION OF A COMMON CURRENCY

None of the empirical evidences presented above should make one disregard some of the key constraints on locking in the exchange rates and adopting a common currency over the long run. Sustaining a common currency may be even more difficult than adopting it. Four constraints that have generally been mentioned in discussions are worth special attention:

1. diversity in the level of economic development across countries;
2. weaknesses in the financial sectors of many countries;
3. inadequacy of region-level resource pooling mechanisms and institutions required for forming and managing a currency union, and;
4. lack of political preconditions for monetary cooperation and a common currency.

The diversity in the level of economic development among the ASEAN countries is quite large. Singapore, the richest country in the group, has a per capita income close to 300 times the per capita income of Myanmar, the poorest country in the group. Even among the ASEAN-5 (Indonesia, Malaysia, Philippines, Singapore and Thailand), the per capita income of Singapore is about 40 times the per capita income of Indonesia. This degree of diversity is higher than among the countries of the EU. It is sometimes argued that such a high degree of income differentials could make it difficult to sustain a monetary union among these countries. However, it is important to note that what is important for the adoption of a common currency among countries is that relative prices and outputs across them should have high co-movements following an economic shock, not so much that the levels of income should be more equal across them. For even if the countries in a monetary union have perfect equality of per capita incomes, if the co-movement of relative prices and outputs across countries is low, conducting a common monetary policy for the union as a whole is difficult. On the other hand, even if per capita incomes across countries in a monetary union are vastly different, but their co-movement following an economic shock is very high, conducting a common monetary policy is much less problematic. Income differentials across countries could pose a constraint to the conduct of a common monetary policy only to the extent that they reflect the dissimilarities in the production structures across countries (and hence movements in relative prices and outputs across them). However, it is important to note that some of the populous countries in the world, e.g., People's Republic of China (PRC), India, Indonesia, or United States, also exhibit large intraregional income differentials within them. Yet, each of these countries uses a single currency.

If countries with diverse sub-regional differences can adopt a common currency, why not a region with diverse countries? The answer perhaps lies in the fact that labor and capital are freely mobile within a country (although formal labor mobility across sub-regions in the PRC is constrained by official restrictions), but are not necessarily so across countries; and the budget and fiscal policy can, within limits, be used to bring about interregional resource transfers within a country, another adjustment mechanism that is often difficult to operate across countries. To manage a currency union for a group of countries with a large difference in level of development, it is, therefore, important to allow a freer flow of capital and labor across borders. This is an area that would need concerted efforts by the ASEAN governments. Member countries will have to evolve policies and mechanisms that would allow greater mobility of both capital and labor across national borders, in addition to the freer movement of goods allowed under the free trade arrangement within the region.

As for fiscal policy, it is difficult to have a large centralized budget at the union level to make resource transfers across countries. The greater mobility of factors of production should reduce the need for large fiscal transfers over the medium to long term. However, in the short run labor mobility cannot be relied upon to take care of asymmetric shocks across countries in a currency union. Country-specific fiscal policies can be used to respond to asymmetric shocks across countries within the union. However, the scope for country-specific discretionary fiscal policies within a currency union would be limited if there is a ceiling on fiscal imbalances, as is the case in the European Union under the Stability and Growth Pact.

Since, historically, fiscal irresponsibility has proven to be the Waterloo of monetary cooperation many times, it is perhaps desirable to restrict fiscal autonomy within a currency union by using mechanisms similar to the European Union's Stability and Growth Pact, but with greater flexibility at the national level. One such option could be to allow automatic fiscal stabilizers at the national levels to move the fiscal balance in a counter-cyclical fashion (worsening during economic downturns and improving during economic upturns) but within certain broad limits.

One of the lessons from some of the emerging market financial crises is that when countries with weak banking and financial sectors and heavy dependence on foreign capital peg their exchange rates, banking problems could turn into an exchange rate crisis (Eichengreen and Bayoumi, 1999). A weak banking system could, therefore, undermine an exchange rate regime such as a common currency arrangement. Historically, banking problems have not been as pervasive among the ASEAN countries as in other emerging market economies. Yet, the 1997 financial crisis in Asia has exposed the fragility of the banking systems and the financial sectors of many countries in the region.

Despite the progress in financial sector restructuring in the aftermath of the crisis, the remaining agenda of banking reforms is quite large. Significant further reforms and restructuring of the financial sectors and the banking systems will, therefore, be required among the ASEAN countries before they could adopt a common currency. There is, however, a positive side to this challenge. A currency union among these countries, accompanied by a regional integration of financial services, could enable countries with stronger banking systems to specialize in the provision of these services at the regional level. That would lead to greater harmonization of banking and financial sector practices across countries as well as raising the overall banking and financial sector standards across the region.

Inadequate mechanisms for regional reserve pooling as well as the absence of regional institutions could be another set of constraints on monetary cooperation and common currency among the East Asian countries. The reserve sharing arrangements under the Chiang Mai Initiative constitute a modest beginning in addressing this constraint. Yet, a common currency for the region would require much greater reserve pooling and sharing among the countries than is currently possible under the Chiang Mai Initiative. Europe established a whole gamut of institutions such as the European Council, European Commission and European Central Bank to manage regional resource sharing and to coordinate the monetary union. It took decades of experimentation in Europe to establish these institutions.

Given the almost total absence of institutions to support regional monetary cooperation in East Asia, developing the regional institutions to manage a common currency is likely to be a major challenge. Once again, there is a positive side to this challenge: the region can benefit from decades of European experience. It can 'leapfrog' in developing the regional reserve sharing mechanisms and the institutions, if there is enough political support for a regional currency union. That brings one to another key constraint: lack of political preconditions for a currency union in the ASEAN.

It is argued that while East Asia or the ASEAN may satisfy the economic requirements for an OCA as much as the EU does, it has not developed the political preconditions necessary for a common currency (Eichengreen and Bayoumi, 1999; Bayoumi, Eichengreen and Mauro, 2000). In Europe, the debate over monetary integration has gone hand in hand with discussions of political integration and creation of a supranational entity empowered to override sovereign national governments. At each stage of this political integration, national governments delegated a growing range of powers to the collectivity. Going by the European experience, developing political support and the institutions required for a currency union in the region, whether it is among ASEAN countries or among a broader group of countries, is likely to be a formidable challenge. One should not understate the difficulties of addressing this challenge. Yet, if the economic advantages of a regional monetary union are large, it is possible that countries may make political compromises so as to reap the economic benefits (Park, 2001). Economic interests may persuade countries to set aside political differences and forge strategically beneficial political alliances. In other words, political support may not be exogenous to the economic outcomes, just as economic outcomes may not be independent of political factors. Economic and political integration in the region may, therefore, be a joint although gradual process spanning perhaps decades.

12.5   CONCLUSION

The issue of the costs and benefits of a common currency for the ASEAN needs to be placed in a somewhat global perspective. As Barro (2001) observes, three factors are likely to encourage the initiation of currency unions across the globe in the future:

1.   the increasing number of countries in the world;
2.   globalization; and,
3.   the diminishing role of independent national monetary policies, especially for small countries.

At the end of World War II, there were 76 independent countries in the world. Today there are nearly 200. For many of the growing number of smaller countries, the costs of maintaining separate currencies and floating exchange rates are likely to be very high. For them, therefore, the net benefits from joining a monetary union (or simply using another country's currency) are likely to be significant (Barro, 2001). This could encourage the formation of an increasing number of currency unions over time.

The increased pace of globalization (including the spread of trade in goods and services and financial transactions and the heightened diffusion of technology) is also likely to encourage the formation of currency unions. In an increasingly globalizing world, there is likely to be greater synchronization of business cycles across countries, and hence the net benefits of having fewer currencies to conduct cross-border business are likely to be larger. Moreover, as the world gets more integrated, the volume of transactions involving citizens of different countries will increase. As international transactions become a larger share of total global transactions, the attractiveness of common currencies relative to a multitude of sovereign currencies is likely to increase.

The benefit that economists and central bankers attribute to national monetary policies is also diminishing. There is growing skepticism about the usefulness of independent monetary policies, especially to smaller developing economies, for counter-cyclical stabilization purposes.

All these factors have the potential to increase political support for monetary and economic integration across countries. Overall, therefore, events may become more favorable to the formation of currency unions. Should the ASEAN be part of this likely global trend? It is time to ponder this question, even if one does not foresee a conclusive answer in the immediate future. For in case the answer turns out to be 'yes', the challenges of forming an ASEAN currency union (or other regional groupings in Asia), including managing the transition phases, are likely to be formidable. The preparatory groundwork itself would involve considerable effort.

Going by international experience, the time required to complete the process is unlikely to be short either. Europe spent several decades in experimenting with regional monetary cooperation before adopting a monetary union. The task may be even more challenging for the ASEAN. But it is important not to underestimate the Southeast Asian capacity for 'time compression'. During the last few decades, time and again, these countries have turned in economic achievements at an unprecedented speed. That record of achievement earned some of them the coveted title of miracle economies.

Despite the Asian crisis, the achievement of the ASEAN Free Trade Area (AFTA) in early 2002, much in advance of the original deadline of 2008, is yet another pointer to their capacity for 'time compression'. With the launching of the AFTA, ASEAN countries have crossed an important milestone: moving closer to what some would refer to as the 'good neighbors' stage' of regional integration, in which participating countries abolish trade barriers and create a level playing field for cross-border movement of goods, services, and capital, but allow the pursuit of separate national economic agendas in other areas, especially in the areas of fiscal and monetary policies.

It is certainly a very challenging task for the ASEAN to move from the 'good neighbors' stage' to the European 'happy family stage' of regional integration, in which participating countries also share a common currency; free flow of people across borders; and common institutions, both economic and political, which are required to manage the common currency. But, as is well known, regional monetary integration, by its very nature, is a long process involving a series of small, incremental, steps over time. Viewed from this perspective, the launching of the AFTA and the regional resource sharing arrangements under the Chiang Mai Initiative may perhaps possess the potential to gradually lead to greater regional monetary cooperation. In moving the process forward, the ASEAN has the European experience to draw on, which is to its advantage.

BIBLIOGRAPHY

Adler, M. (1996), 'Exchange Rate Planning for International Trading Firms', in Y. Amihud and R. Levich (eds), *Exchange Rates and Corporate Performance*, New York: Irwin Professional Publishing.

Barro, R. (2001), *Currency Unions*, unpublished monograph, Harvard University.

Bayoumi, T. and B. Eichengreen (1994), 'One Money or Many? Analyzing the Prospects for Monetary Unification in Various Parts of the World', *Princeton Studies in International Finance*, **76**, pp. 20–30.

Bayoumi, T. and B. Eichengreen (1996), 'The Stability of the Gold Standard and the Evolution of the International Monetary System', in T. Bayoumi, B. Eichengreen and M. Taylor, (eds), *Economic Perspectives in the Gold Standard*, Cambridge: Cambridge University Press.

Bayoumi, T. and P. Mauro (1999), 'The Suitability of ASEAN for a Regional Currency Arrangement', *Working Paper*, **99** (162), Washington, DC: International Monetary Fund.

Bayoumi, T., B. Eichengreen and P. Mauro (2000), 'On Regional Monetary Arrangements for ASEAN', *Journal of the Japanese and International Economies*, **4** (June), pp. 121–48.

Benassy-Quere, A. (1999), 'Optimal Pegs for East Asian Currencies', *Journal of the Japanese and International Economies*, **13** (March), pp. 44–60.

Bergsten, C.F. and C.R. Henning (1996), *Global Economic Leadership and the Group of Seven*, Washington, DC: Institute for International Economics.

Breur, J.B. (1994), 'An Assessment of the Evidence on Purchasing Power Parity', in J. Williamson (ed.), *Estimating Equilibrium Exchange Rates*, Washington, DC: Institute for International Economics.

Calvo, G.A. and C.M. Reinhart (2002), 'Fear of Floating', *The Quarterly Journal of Economics*, **117**, pp. 379–408.

Collignon, S. (1999), 'Bloc Floating and Exchange Rate Volatility: The Causes and Consequences of Currency Blocs', in S. Collignon, J. Pisani-Ferry, and Y.C. Park (eds), *Exchange Rate Policies in Emerging Asian Countries*, London and New York: Routledge.

Corbo, V. and V. Cox (1995), 'Exchange Rate Volatility, Investment and Growth: Some New Evidence', in W. Gruben, D. Gould and C. Zarazaga (eds), *Exchange Rates, Capital Flows, and Monetary Policy in a Changing World Economy*, Boston: Kluwer Academic Press.

DeGrauwe, P. (2000), *Economics of Monetary Union*, Oxford: Oxford University Press.

Corsetti, G. and P. Pesenti (2002), 'Self-validating Optimum Currency Areas', *Working Paper*, **8783**, National Bureau of Economic Research.

Eichengreen, B. (1996), 'A More Perfect Union? The Logic of Economic Integration', *Essays in International Finance*, International Finance Section, Department of Economics, Princeton University.

Eichengreen B. and T. Bayoumi (1999), 'Is Asia an Optimum Currency Area? Can It Become One?', in S. Collignon, J. Pisani-Ferry and Y.C. Park (eds), *Exchange Rate Policies in Emerging Asian Countries*, London: Routledge.

Frankel, J. and A. Rose (1997), 'The Endogeneity of the Optimum Currency Area Criteria', in M. Blejer, J. Frenkel, L. Leiderman and A. Razin (eds), *Optimum Currency Areas: New Analytical and Policy Developments*, Washington, DC: International Monetary Fund.

Frankel, J. and A. Rose (2002), 'An Estimate of the Effect of Currency Unions on Trade and Income', *The Quarterly Journal of Economics*, **117**, pp. 437–66.

Friberg, R. (1996), 'Exchange Rate Uncertainty and the Microeconomic Benefits of EMU', *Working Paper*, **127**, The Economic Research Institute, Stockholm School of Economics.

Glick, R. and A. Rose (2001), *Does a Currency Union Affect Trade? The Time Series Evidence*, unpublished monograph.

Goto, J. and K. Hamada (1994), 'Economic Preconditions for Asian Regional Integration', in T. Ito and A. Krueger (eds), *Macroeconomic Linkage: Savings, Exchange Rates and Capital Flows*, Chicago: University of Chicago Press.

Huizinga, J. (1994), 'Exchange Rate Volatility, Uncertainty and Investment: An Empirical Investigation', in C. Leiderman and A. Razin (eds), *Capital Mobility: The Impact on Consumption, Investment and Growth*, Cambridge: Cambridge University Press.

Jeanne, O. and A. Rose (2002), 'Noise Trading and Exchange Rate Regimes', *The Quarterly Journal of Economics*, **117**, pp. 537–69.

Kawai, M. and S. Takagi (2000), 'Proposed Strategy for a Regional Exchange Rate Arrangement in Post-Crisis Asia: Analysis, Reviews and Proposal', *Policy Research Working Paper*, **2503**, Washington, DC: World Bank.

Kenen, P. and D. Rodrick (1986), 'Measuring and Analyzing the Effects of Short-Term Volatility in Real Exchange Rates', *Review of Economic Statistics*, **68** (2), pp. 311–15.

Kwan, C.H. (1998), *The Theory of Optimum Currency Areas and the Possibility of Forming a Yen Bloc in Asia*, mimeographed, Nomura Research Institute.

Moon, W.S. and Y. Rhee (1999), 'Asian Monetary Cooperation: Lessons from the European Monetary Integration', *Journal of International and Area Studies*, **6** (1 May).

Moon, W.S., Y. Rhee and D.R. Yoon (2000), 'Asian Monetary Cooperation: A Search for Regional Monetary Stability in the Post Euro and the Post Asian Crisis Era', *Economic Papers*, 3 (1), pp. 159–93.

Park, Y.C. (2001), *Beyond the Chiang Mai Initiative Rationale and Need for a Regional Monetary Arrangement in East Asia*, unpublished monograph, Department of Economics, Korea University.

Plummer, M. (2001), *Monetary Union and ASEAN*, International Conference on Trade and Monetary System in Asia-Pacific, Kobe, Japan.

Rajan, R. (2000), 'Currency Basket Regimes for Southeast Asia: The Worst System with Exception of All Others', *Policy DP*, **0028**, Adelaide, Australia: Centre for International Economics.

Rose, A. (1994), 'Are Exchange Rates Macroeconomic Phenomena?', *Federal Reserve Bank of San Francisco Economic Review*, **1**, pp. 19–30.

Rose, A. (2000), 'One Money, One Market: Estimating the Effect of Common Currencies on Trade', *Economic Policy*, **30**, pp. 7–46.

Rose, A. and E. van Wincoop (2001), 'National Money as a Barrier to International Trade: The Real Case for Currency Union', *American Economic Review*, May, pp. 386–90.

Williamson, J. (1999), 'The Case for a Common Basket Peg for East Asian Currencies', in S. Collignon, J. Pisani-Ferry, and Y.C. Park (eds), *Exchange Rate Policies in Emerging Asian Countries*, London and New York: Routledge.

Index

Adler, M. 233
AFTA 240
Aghion, P. 89
AMF, *see* Asian Monetary Fund
APEC currency area 40
Argentina 6, 7, 26, 79, 80
Arrow, Kenneth 81
ASA 215, 216
ASEAN, *see* Association of Southeast Asian Nations
ASEAN Free Trade Area (AFTA) 240
ASEAN Swap Arrangement (ASA) 215, 216
Asian crisis 9, 132–3
  components of 141
  countries that avoided the crisis 34
  exchange rate volatility 32–3, 77
  public debt 172
Asian Monetary Fund (AMF) 36, 216, 228
  proposed Japanese contribution to 15, 216
Asian Monetary Monitor 51
Association of Southeast Asian Nations (ASEAN)
  absence of regional institutions 238
  banking and financial sectors' weakness 237–8
  capital mobility 237
  consideration of currency union 240
  constraints on the adoption of common currency 236–9
  diversity in the level of economic development 236, 237
  inadequate mechanisms for regional reserve pooling 238
  intraregional trade 235
  labour mobility 235, 237

  lack of political preconditions for currency union 238–9
  shock symmetry 235
  suitability for adopting common currency 234–5
  wage and price flexibility 235
Australia
  exchange rates and interest rates 84, 85
  inflation targeting 167, 168
  percentage change of real output due to supply and nominal shocks 225, 226, 227

Bacchetta, P. 89
Banerjee, A. 89
Bank of Lithuania 49, 50
Bank of Mexico 26
Barandiaran, Edgardo 47
Barrera, Felipe 192
Barro, Robert 83, 232, 239
basket currency regime 55–8, 74, 77, 99
  implementing 76–7
  neighbouring countries 75, 76
  optimal weights 74
  width of band 74, 75
Bayoumi, T. 225, 234, 235, 237, 238
Beddies, Christian 171
Belgium–Luxembourg monetary union 36
Benassy-Quere, Agnis 74
Bergsten, C. 233
Bhagwati, J. 141
Bilson, J. 62
Blanchard, O. 222, 225
Brazil
  inflation targeting 169
  interest rates 86